# Walker

# On Walker:

"The Don Quixote of Central America."

—Horace Greeley

"A kind of revolutionary intellectual."

—Harry Truman

"Better out of the world than in it."

—*Harper's Weekly*

"That his success would have inured to the benefit of civilization, few, perhaps, in view of the present condition of Central America, will be so rash as to deny."
—W. O. Scroggs, *Filibusters and Financiers*

"Had he been successful, the Civil War might have been postponed, might never have been fought, or might have had another result."

—Lawrence Greene, *The Filibuster*

"A guy completely out of touch with reality, who thought he was acting on Christian principles but who blinded himself to the fact that he was slaughtering the people he came to regenerate. His madness is the madness of Oliver North or Elliott Abrams . . . white guys coming down to small countries thinking they can do anything."       —Alex Cox

# On "Walker":

"This story of a man whose 'true profession was hero-ism' is a triumph in half a dozen ways. It brings to life a complex character whose idealism and bravado seem alien to our time, and it places him at the center of an international intrigue shockingly familiar to us today." —Gilbert Seldes

"If this penetrates the commercial market in the United States, it is going to open some eyes and change some minds." —Sergio Ramirez, Vice President of Nicaragua

"If, both in the endeavor of its making and as a broadly entertaining spectacle, *Walker*'s metaphorical message makes a fraction of the eventual audience think more closely about what their tax dollars are paying for, then Cox's extraordinary vision of history returning will have reaped a rich dividend." —*The Village Voice*

# WALKER

## Rudy Wurlitzer

PERENNIAL LIBRARY

HARPER & ROW, PUBLISHERS, NEW YORK
Cambridge, Philadelphia, San Francisco, Washington
London, Mexico City, São Paulo, Singapore, Sydney

"The World and William Walker," on pages 63–270, is an abridgment of the book of the same name originally published in 1963 by Harper & Row, Publishers.

FIRST EDITION

Designer: Charlotte Staub

Library of Congress Cataloging-in-Publication Data

Wurlitzer, Rudolph.
   Walker.

   1. Walker, William, 1824–1860.  2. Nicaragua—History
—Filibuster War, 1855–1860.  3. Filibusters—Nicaragua—
Biography.  I. Carr, Albert H. Z.  II. Title.
F1526.27.W3W87   1987     972.85'04'0924      87-45824
ISBN 0-06-055122-4     87 88 89 90 91 HC 10 9 8 7 6 5 4 3 2 1
ISBN 0-06-096258-5 (pbk.) 87 88 89 90 91 HC 10 9 8 7 6 5 4 3 2 1

I saw Walker for the first time in San Francisco:
I remember him as if I were seeing his blond face like a tiger's;
his grey eyes, without pupils, fixed like a blind man's,
but which expanded and flared like gunpowder in combat,
and his skin faintly freckled, his paleness, his clergyman's ways,
his voice, colorless like his eyes, cold and sharp,
in a mouth without lips.
And a woman's voice was hardly softer than his:
that calm voice of his announcing death sentences . . .
thar swept so many into the jaws of death in combat.
He never drank or smoked and he wore no uniform.
Nobody was his friend.
And I don't remember ever having seen him smile.

—From *With Walker in Nicaragua*
by Ernesto Cardenal
translated by Jonathan Cohen

The U.S. Marines repeatedly landed in Nicaragua, occupying the country from 1912 to 1925 and again from 1926 to 1933. During the latter stay, the troops helped usher into power the Somoza family, which ruled Nicaragua for two generations until overthrown by the Sandinistas in 1979. Ironically, the Marines left behind something positive—baseball.

—*Los Angeles Times*

# CONTENTS

# INTRODUCTION

William Walker was born in Nashville, Tennessee, on May 8, 1824. He ruled Nicaragua from 1855 to 1857. He was executed by the Honduran authorities September 12, 1860.

William Walker's ghost is not remembered in those corridors of power where Latin American policy is now being so hotly discussed. He has been forgotten in the history books as only a loser can be, and it has been left for the movies to resurrect and identify Walker as an American "hero."

Walker's willful and righteous plunge south of the border (which led to one of this country's most theatrical demonstrations of "Manifest Destiny") will now be cheered and booed on the screen by those Latino masses he so clearly disdained and violated, even by Nicaraguan audiences in Granada and Rivas, cities he sacked and destroyed more than a hundred and thirty years ago.

## FROM ED HARRIS'S JOURNAL

*January 17, 1987*
*Granada—Main Plaza*
*The church that Walker burned down has a plaque on it. He torched the city, burning what he couldn't possess.*

*So let's think about Walker in his quarters overlooking his Immortals spread out beneath him. Walker was getting more and more carried away with the obsession of taking over the country—the continent—the world—with fifty-eight men.*

*A growing, swelling, expanding seed in his brain—to be the ruler of land and space and territory—owning property, annexing land for the U.S.—to control and use and improve.*

3

*But this seed swells to the point where it totally fills and replaces his brain and the only idea is this thought of an idea that never germinates—just swells with obsession until it destroys him and all around him.*

*March 14*

*First day of shooting . . . it feels pretty damn right. . . . Nothing else matters now except being William Walker and nailing every single moment. This man doesn't care. His love is dead and his heart is cold. He's going straight ahead until he gets stopped.*

*April 2*

*In the bus on the way to Granada . . . My thighs are getting stronger from squatting over lidless toilet bowls. . . .*

*Walker tried to take advantage of this country. He realized its backwardness. He thought the people lazy. He saw the opportunity to fill the fertile fields with wealth, to show the people they need not live in squalor, accepting their lot as peasants . . . but that through intelligence and obedience they could be masters of themselves instead of peons in the dust.*

### MANIFEST DESTINY

Our manifest destiny is to overspread the continent allotted by Providence for the free development of our yearly multiplying millions.          —John L. O'Sullivan,
                                             *The United States Magazine*
                                             *and Democratic Review,* July 1845

The policy of my administration will not be controlled by any timid forebodings of evil from expansion. Indeed, it is not to be disguised that our attitude as a nation, and our position on the globe, render the acquisition of certain possessions, not within our jurisdiction eminently important for our protection, if not, in the future, essential for the preservation of the rights of commerce in the peace of the world.          —President Franklin Pierce,
                                             inaugural speech, March 5, 1853

My investigation has shown that this evil of government domination lies, and has always lain, at the root of the Nicaraguan problem. . . . All persons of every party with whom I have talked admit the existence of this evil and its inevitable results, and all of them have expressed an earnest desire for the supervision of elections by the United States in an attempt to get rid of the evil forever.
                —Henry L. Stimson, "special representative" to
                Nicaragua under Calvin Coolidge;
                State Department release, May 6, 1927

The year 1854 marked the first of Walker's attempts at carrying the banner of "Manifest Destiny" into foreign lands. He strode forward without looking to the left or right, his confidence reflecting an incredible innocence, a belief in his own moral superiority that allowed him, without remorse or hesitation, to invade another country and declare it for himself. It was a world where, it seemed, everything was possible.

With a bunch of runaway grocers and incompetent gold prospectors, he set sail for Mexico and proclaimed both Sonora and Baja California to be the "Republic of Sonora." Unfortunately for "the Colonel," the U.S. government chose that time to enforce the Neutrality Laws against filibustering, leaving him cut off and abandoned as most of his men deserted and fled north, leaving him to barely make it to the border with only a handful of men.

### THE SONORA CAMPAIGN

The condition of the upper part of Sonora was at that time, and still is, a disgrace to the civilization of the continent. . . . Northern Sonora was, in fact, more under the dominion of the Apaches than under the laws of Mexico. . . . Any social organization, no matter how secured, is preferable to that in which individuals and families are altogether at the mercy of savages.
—William Walker,
*The War in Nicaragua*

## FROM THE SCREENPLAY

Two hundred Mexican troops, mostly irregulars, have surrounded a desperate group of American mercenaries holed up in a sheep ranch just south of the border.

The twenty mercenaries, or "William Walker and the Immortals" as they have become known to the American press, have been chased over five hundred miles from Lower California (which they tried to take for themselves), to the U.S. border, which they have not been able to reach. Wounded, exhausted, and completely frustrated, the Immortals are also, finally, without hope.

All, that is, but their leader, Colonel William Walker, who now emerges from the ranch house and walks slowly across the courtyard toward a dozen Mexican ranch hands standing under guard.

At first glance, William Walker presents a comical, even ludicrous figure. Thirty years old, small and almost emaciated, he hobbles forth on one boot, his shirt in shreds, a bizarre hat made from white beaver on top of his head. But as he begins to address the terrified Mexicans, who clearly think they are about to be executed, his entire manner changes. Suddenly he is transformed into a charismatic, spellbinding orator, his voice ringing out across the courtyard, his body quivering with belief and exhortation.

WALKER: Men of the First Independence Batallion, I will not dissemble with you. We came to Sonora with the boldest hearts and loftiest intentions. We have made her a free, sovereign, and independent state. All memories of Spanish domination are already gone. Yet our situation is not good. The reinforcements have failed to arrive. We are without food or water, trapped four hours' march from our fair country's border. Our foes surround us and are closing in. Only an Act of God can save us now.

Two raindrops fall at Walker's feet; a fierce wind begins to blow; dust whips across the rancho yard: A dust storm has arrived!

## FROM THE SCREENPLAY

At William Walker's trial in San Francisco after the fiasco of his invasion of Sonora, Mexico, Byron Cole, a newspaper editor and staunch supporter, sits next to Ellen Martin, Walker's fiancée.

On top of a page, Byron Cole has written in bold letters: THE COURAGEOUS NAPOLEONIC GRAY-EYED MAN OF DESTINY.

Taking Cole's pen, Ellen Martin crosses out COURAGEOUS and NAPOLEONIC, leaving simply: THE GRAY-EYED MAN OF DESTINY.

Back on the stand, William Walker completes his speech.

WALKER: It is the God-given right of the American people to dominate the Western Hemisphere. It is our moral duty to protect our neighbors from oppression and exploitation. It is the fate of America to "go ahead." That is her Manifest Destiny. It is with that destiny in mind that I conceived my strategy, a strategy, which, had it not been for the interference of the government, would have succeeded.

On returning to San Francisco, Walker, rather than facing public humiliation, was welcomed like a hero. Ninety percent of the population were men, and they appreciated the qualities that he stood for: blind self-serving opinions, willful and ignorant courage, implicit racism and a highly dramatic sense of decency and righteousness. In New York he was so popular they even wrote a musical about him.

## FROM THE SCREENPLAY

Walker rides his horse toward a train silhouetted in the distance. Around him, a vast expanse of empty desert. Walker dismounts as Ephraim Squier, a politician and businessman, comes running up.

SQUIER: Colonel Walker! I'm so pleased to see you. I can't tell you how happy this will make the Commodore.

They begin to walk toward the large figure of a man—Commodore Cornelius Vanderbilt—sitting in a deck chair underneath a large umbrella. Squier is somewhat awkward and out of place in a new cowboy outfit complete with Stetson and snakeskin boots.

SQUIER (*nervous*): Don't sit down until he tells you. Always address him as "Commodore." And whatever you do, don't ask him any personal questions.

They walk around and approach Vanderbilt, who looks up at them without expression. Squier makes the introductions.

SQUIER: Commodore Cornelius Vanderbilt, may I present Colonel William Walker.

VANDERBILT: Colonel of what?

WALKER: The American *Falange* in northern Mexico.

VANDERBILT: You caused quite a commotion down there.

WALKER: We had a shortage of supplies and no help from the government, otherwise we would have succeeded.

He looks down at Vanderbilt—disapproving, arrogant.

WALKER: Who's your tailor? Surely you're not entitled to wear that uniform?

Vanderbilt ignores him.

VANDERBILT: You fucked up, Walker. Next time pick on a country your own size.

WALKER: Mr. Vanderbilt, I came down on your invitation. I did not come to be insulted.

Walker starts to turn away.
    Vanderbilt smiles slightly, as if Walker's effrontery amuses him.

VANDERBILT: Come back here.

Walker turns, faces him.

VANDERBILT: Does Nicaragua mean anything to you?

WALKER: Nothing at all.

Behind them, Squier arranges a map of Nicaragua on an easel.

VANDERBILT: Nicaragua is a tiny, insignificant country somewhere to the south of here. But this worthless piece of land happens to control the overland route to the Pacific. Today there's a stage coach running across it. But tomorrow, who knows? Maybe a canal. I now control all transportation in Nicaragua. But to continue to do this I must have stability.

WALKER: What's this got to do with me?

SQUIER: Nicaragua is a divided country, in the middle of a disastrous civil war. We must absolutely make sure the right side wins.

VANDERBILT: What I want is for some man to go down there and take over. I need that country stable for my business interests and I want it done now. They tell me you're a clever man, Walker. Doctor, lawyer, surgeon, all that renaissance shit they talk about these days. Do you think you can handle the job?

WALKER: No. I do not. I plan to get married and start a newspaper.

Walker looks beyond Vanderbilt, at the horizon, where Ellen Martin now appears, like a mirage, a distant haunting dream.

SQUIER: You're wasting a golden opportunity, Mr. Walker. Very few people are offered a chance to have a country of their own.

Walker is unmoved.

VANDERBILT: Do you prize democracy, Walker? Universal suffrage? All that shit?

WALKER: More than my very life.

VANDERBILT: They need democracy in Nicaragua. Need a canal as well. I'm interested in Nicaragua, Walker, and so are you. Whether you know it now or not.

In the 1850s, he became as famous as Elvis Presley or Muhammed Ali were in their heydays. If there had been a *Time* magazine, Walker would have been on the cover as "Man of the Year." He had all the accepted virtues: he was a doctor and a lawyer, a God-saluting, mother-worshiping Protestant who was also a firm patriot and zealous defender of his country's principles. And, as a wildly popular man of action, Walker was capable of betraying his principles without blinking an eye. In Nicaragua, looking for a way to enlist the Southern states to his cause, he had no trouble contradicting his earlier statements opposing slavery.

### WALKER ON THE ADVANTAGES OF SLAVERY

The advantage of negro slavery would be two-fold; while it would furnish certain labor for the use of agriculture, it would tend to separate the races and destroy the half-castes who cause the disorder. . . . The Indian of Nicaragua, in his fidelity and docility, as well as in his capacity for labor, approaches nearly the negroes of the United States; and he would readily assume the manners and habits of the latter. In fact the manners of the Indian toward the

ruling race are now more submissive than those of the American
Negro towards his master. . . . The labor of the inferior races cannot compete with that of the white race unless you give it a white
master to direct its energies.                    —William Walker
                                                  *The War in Nicaragua*

It wasn't money or the pursuit of sex or any other earthly pleasures that motivated Walker. It was his sheer obsession with power.
Everything was sublimated to that expression. It was as if Walker
was presented with this vast, empty space with no restrictions, no
prohibitions of any kind. Literally the only boundary that was imposed on him was the Pacific Ocean. Mexico, and everything to the
south, was fair game.

The curtain was going up on the empire, and any pirate or
reprobate who could handle the frontier was encouraged to plunder
and hustle as much land as he could. Government and religion were
joined on this issue, and blessings were bestowed without discrimi-
nation. Walker was riding way out on the point, waving the flag of
freedom and destiny. He was doing what everyone else wanted to
do, only he was doing it with more verve and imagination, as well
as with a wild enthusiasm toward subjugating and destroying all
who stood in his way. Walker is still the most famous villain in
Nicaragua, not to mention all of Latin America, leaving in his wake
a malignancy of evil paternalism that has not gone away to this day.
His was a mystical vision of domination, a kind of demented crusade
of expansion for its own sake. Everything, all attachments and possessions, were reduced to the bone. Everything was sacrificed toward
imposing his will on all around him, no matter what the cost.

### ON THE DESTRUCTION OF GRANADA

As the burning went on, the excitement of the scene increased the
thirst for liquor and soldiers thought it a pity to waste so much
good wine and brandy. In spite of guards and sentries, orders and
officers, the drunkenness went on, and the town presented more
of the appearance of a wild bacchanalian revel than of a military
camp.                                             —William Walker,
                                                  *The War in Nicaragua*

### FROM THE SCREENPLAY

Inside the cathedral the pews have been stacked in one corner, the middle of
the huge vaulted room now filled with the wounded and the dead. Horses
and mules are crowded inside next to overturned wagons and empty boxes

of ammunition. Walker kneels in a side chapel, solemnly taking Mass with Father Vigil. Outside, sporadic shots can be heard as the last remnants of the Immortals fight on.

Walker mounts the pulpit, lifting his eyes toward heaven as he begins to speak.

WALKER: Unless a man believes that there is something great for him to do, he can do nothing great. A great idea springs up in a man's soul, transports him from the ignorant present and makes him feel the future in a moment. Men, we have come a long way together. We have fought together and we have died together. Now we are faced with the greatest task of all. Not just becuse we want to, but because we *must*. We fight from our natural moral superiority, at the head of the column of Progress and Democracy. We must extend our institutions to the whole of Mexico and Central America!

Seated at the organ, Mrs. Bingham starts to play *Onward Christian Soldiers,* as the wounded and dying men join in.

> He [Walker] endeavored to place before them the *moral grandeur* of the position they occupied. Alone in the world, without a friendly government to give even its sympathy, much less its aid, they had nothing to support them in the struggle with the neighbouring states save the consciousness of the justice of their cause. Maligned by those who should have befriended them, and betrayed by those they had benefited, they had to choose between basely yielding their rights and nobly dying for them. Nor did their General seek to hide from them the peril in which they stood; but from the urgency of the danger arose the greater necessity for becoming conduct. The words were few and simple, and drew little force from the manner of him who uttered them; but they had the desired effect and created a new spirit among the men. It is only by constant appeals to the loftier qualities of man that you can make him a good soldier; and all military discipline is a mere effort to make virtue constant and reliable by making it habitual.                                        —William Walker,
> *The War in Nicaragua*

Trying to rally his men, these words of patriotism are dry and sterile. Moving freely through unclaimed space—more than any achievements along the way, more than any results—was what held and impassioned Walker.

## FROM THE SCREENPLAY

Walker watches as men are pulled out of a wagon and marched over to a dingy to be rowed out to the *Vesta.*

Dr. Jones, stoned, as usual, on laudanum, observes them.

DR. JONES: Gutter trash. They wouldn't even make good cadavers.

WALKER: *(overhearing):* They *are* trash. But when Walker gets through with them, they will be immortal.

> *The New Recruits:* Worthless for military duty. A very large proportion of them were Europeans of the poorest class, mostly Germans who care more for the content of their haversacks than of their cartridge-boxes.
>
> *Crocker:* A boy in appearance, with a slight figure, and a face almost feminine in its delicacy and beauty, he had the heart of a lion. . . . To Walker he was invaluable; for they had been together in many a trying hour.
>
> *Parker French:* Had started for California in 1849, but, being engaged in some doubtful transactions in Texas, his name had ever since been suggestive of unfairness and dishonesty. . . . He was utterly unfitted for the management of the hacienda, having little knowledge of either the principles or details of public business, and not having either the modesty to be sensible of his defects or the patience to overcome them.
>
> *Norris:* The drummer of the falange, said, when asking to be excused from serving as drum-major, "in every battle scene you see a drummer-boy lying dead by the side of his drum."
>
> *Yrena:* A quick and minute observer, with all the gravity of the native race . . . fertile in resources for sending intelligence to her friends.
>
> *Byron Cole:* Thus in the bold but fruitless charge he made on San Jacinto perished Byron Cole, whose energy and perseverence had done so much toward securing the American presence in Nicaragua. It was the first opportunity he had for being under fire; and he had scarcely seen the flash of an enemy's musket before he met his fate.                    —William Walker,
> *The War in Nicaragua*

## FROM THE SCREENPLAY

Everything is chaos and confusion as William Walker and what is left of his men try to break out of their entrapment in Granada.

Suddenly a strange and deafening sound is heard. Red and green flares hurtle into the plaza. The Immortals are frozen in searchlights as a helicopter descends.

Marines deploy, encircling the plaza.

COMPANY MAN: I have instructions from the United States of America to return all American citizens to their homeland.

The Immortals frantically whip out their U.S. passports, leaping aboard the chopper.

Walker, a small, erect figure, unbowed and curiously detached, stands staring at his fleeing men, a roll of maps under his arm. The Last Man . . .

COMPANY MAN (*addressing Walker*): Your nationality, sir?

WALKER: I am William Walker, President of Nicaragua.

The Company Man shakes his head "no," and boards the chopper.

The chopper rises. Walker walks briskly into the darkness, his plans under his arm. All around, the city burns.

## FROM ED HARRIS'S JOURNAL

*April 19*

*The big Russian helicopter is sitting in the square of the Palacio Nacional in Managua before the Cathedral where we've been shooting. Blood stains on the metal gridded floor from the wounded Sandinista soldiers. They've lent us this chopper for a night to shoot the end of the picture. There are ironies and circumstances here that go deeper than the obvious. Complex and confusing and not to be sorted out at this writing . . .*

*I still feel positive and up about Walker and what he's been doing in this film. But I also feel I'll be able to let him go without a major psyche twist. We shall see. 7 weeks down here and still counting . . .*

If Walker had managed to be successful in Nicaragua (a country one-eightieth the size of the U.S.), he still would never have been satisfied, even if he had been President for life. That beast within him would never have been sated, never calmed. The fears and insecurities that insisted always on avoiding any kind of intimacy would have screamed for him to push on. It would not have mattered where as long as it was toward the margins of civilization, toward those desperate stretches of wasteland where his puritanically rigid nature could breathe.

For it was only when tramping through dangerous and alien countryside with an ignorant and unholy collection of men that Walker's odd and twisted nature seemed to be served. And his men, mostly outcasts and renegades, would have followed him anywhere, even to an unknown grave in an unknown land.

## FROM THE SCREENPLAY

Walker, his eyes sunken, his hair uncombed, stands outside the Presidential Palace in his nightshirt, pistol in hand.

In front of him, Hornsby and a squad of Immortals have captured half a dozen deserters.

WALKER (*to Hornsby*): What is the charge against these men?

HORNSBY: Desertion.

WALKER: Do you men have anything to say for yourselves?

WASHBURN: We couldn't take it no more, sir. We done our best, but it weren't good enough.

WALKER: No man can do more than his best. Perhaps it is I who have failed you. You men are free to go.

Most of the men take off, running. Washburn and Faucet remain.

WASHBURN: I cannot go, sir. I cannot leave you.

FAUCET: I see what I have attempted to do was wrong. I will stay with you to the end.

Walker's demeanor suddenly changes. Angrily he shakes his head.

WALKER: I tolerate no cowards in my command. You had your choice, now you have lost it. (*To Hornsby*) Have these men shot immediately.

Walker turns and walks away.

## FROM ED HARRIS'S JOURNAL

*April 2*

*Walker rationalizes the death of Corral: He must be executed. There is no other choice. To let him live would be to say: Stay as you are. Lie. Cheat. Don't work. Don't hold to your word.*

*Walker would say to himself: if I believed as these people do, I would buy a plot of land or give up my plot of land and squat somewhere and have a child a year until my wife collapsed and we squandered in filth forever, passing down ignorance for as long as we were allowed to.*

*April 4*

*Nicaragua continues to be a sixty-kilometer stretch of road, potholed and narrow, between Granada and Managua. . . . Staying in the present for now, work-ing and trying to be true to the obsessive spirit of Mr. William Walker.*

*April 6*

*The hidden place where these Walker surprises arise from has to be fed with some darkness, some inner searching that doesn't come from being unpenetrably calm. Peace of mind and soul does not eliminate the possibility of the search, but levels of "calm" can, often, do. 5 weeks to go and I just can't let this slip away. Walker at this point has executed Corral, assumed the Presidency, disarmed Van-derbilt, thinks he's adored by Yrena, is planning to introduce slavery as a solution, is increasingly certain of his destiny and his power. His past death-defying self-knowledge has passed into a non-conscious acceptability of his immortality and genius.*

Walker lived for those moments outside of time when he could stand in the middle of a field of battle with the dead and dying all around him and feel for a moment a certain illusion of wholeness, a vibrancy of being that was only his when he could embrace his own ultimate fear in the form of his own death and still march bravely forward, drums banging and flags flapping in the breeze. He was an ascetic, a Captain Ahab who was compelled to destroy himself, to reach beyond his capacities for a relief that could only be realized by utter failure.

## FROM THE SCREENPLAY

WALKER: Dr. Jones, when you were a little boy did you ever have a moment when you were sitting outside on the lawn and it was spring and you picked up a blade of grass or a beetle and you just watched it and it was whole and perfect and totally outside of time?

> From such facts I reach the conclusion: If Walker doesn't drink, smoke or have any devotion to Bacchus or Venus, it is clear that the only thing he desires is the sensuality of power; and for that reason a man without other passions has turned into a filibuster. Lieutenant Lewis, forgive my frankness, but I have always distrusted men who do not render some homage to vice.
> —Felix Savala, Democratic Army general in Nicaragua, to Frederick Lewis, a Walker emissary

## VANDERBILT AND WALKER

The confrontation between Cornelius Vanderbilt and Walker represents an epiphany of two American archetypes. Vanderbilt, at that time one of the richest men in the Western Hemisphere, defined power by the amount of money accrued. Uncultured and uneducated, he was the "big engine" of American free enterprise. For "the Commodore" it was full throttle ahead and fuck everyone else. Transportation was Vanderbilt's game, whereas Walker was too romantic, too much a "gray-eyed man of destiny" to bother with such crude strategies. Walker never had a chance. Vanderbilt used Walker as a front man to secure the route across the isthmus, a highway that led from the Atlantic to the Pacific where a torrent of greed was waiting to travel. The deal was: Walker was to secure the land and plant the flag. Vanderbilt would supply the ships and build the roads.

At first, theirs was a union that combined all the most potent energies of the American identity. Ambition, blind greed, ignorant religious belief, racism, and shrewdness composed the unholy alchemy. And if Walker hadn't been arrogant and frozen to his own descriptions of glory, they might have conquered all of Latin America before they were done. But Walker blew it when two of Vanderbilt's cohorts, Garrison and Morgan, tried to go behind Vanderbilt's back and make Walker a better offer. Walker, who by then had made himself President of Nicaragua, was proud enough to think he was omniscient. Without looking back, he betrayed Vanderbilt; and Vanderbilt, without looking anywhere at all, ruined Walker as quickly as if he was rubbing out a gnat landing on the back of his carnivorous hand. In one of the great lines of American history, Vanderbilt informed Garrison and Morgan:

> Gentlemen, you have cheated me. I won't sue you. The law is too slow. I'll ruin you.
>
> Yours Truly,
> Cornelius Vanderbilt

Walker's fate was sealed. Without money and supplies it was only a matter of time before his adventure came to an end.

> Reduced to our present position by the cowardice of some, the incapacity of others, and the treachery of many, the army has yet written a page of American history which it is impossible to forget or erase. From the future, if not from the present, we may expect just judgement.
> —William Walker,
> *The War in Nicaragua*

## FROM ED HARRIS'S JOURNAL

*April 19*

*M–16s being fired. Blanks. Practice. Dusty sky. Dirty air. A zillion particles of death and dry and unused earth and rotted burnt effigies of a struggle going nowhere fast. What can precisely be the result of such arrogance?*

*April 20*

*The day after Easter. We're at a beach due south of Managua. . . .*

*Solitude and quietude are such precious gifts in this noisy, constant-sound world. Time is standing still. I'm too alone and inside myself for it to move. The loneliness of this work is deep and good and so private. . . .*

*The closeness of the helicopter nearly a catastrophe. . . . I was totally crazed behind a pillar, questioning courage, thoughts of warfare and responses to battle and people shooting at me. Walker still lives, hanging on by a string from my gut to his spirit. He feels okay about what I'm doing. I've got the obsessed one's blessing.*

*May 15*

   *The last day of shooting . . .*

   *The people here are not lazy. Little boys are pushing carts, everybody is on the move in the early a.m. . . . . I ain't got it in me to wax poetic about this country and its people. They do that themselves.*

   *Looking forward to reading Moby Dick when I get home.*

# A CONVERSATION
## WITH
# ALEX COX AND
# RUDY WURLITZER

❧

Rudy Wurlitzer: It's monsoon season. Muggy and hot and we're sitting in Alex Cox's balcony overlooking the three cathedrals of Granada and the red-tiled roofs of the Italians who came in here after Walker burned the town down and reconstructed it. And it's about a hundred and thirty years from the date that Walker stood in approximately the same spot dressed in black.

Alex Cox: This little man dressed in his black preacher's suit.

RW: What do you think about Walker being this American Calvinist Puritan and choosing a place to invade that's Spanish, Indian, and south of the border, completely opposite to his temperament?

AC: It was the fashion of the times, to invade Mexico.

RW: Yeah, everyone took a crack at Mexico.

AC: It had been only two years since the United States acquired California, Utah, Arizona, Nevada, and New Mexico.

RW: So they thought that that was going to be next on the map.

AC: Yeah, as far as they were concerned, the United States was going to continue. It's like somebody said—Walker or one of those guys of the period—"America must round her territories with the sea." Which meant the United States has got to extend from Alaska to Patagonia.

RW: And that was really the pure form of Manifest Destiny; that's what they thought was going to happen.

AC: Their destiny was manifested: the Americans, people of the United States, would keep on expanding until they controlled and owned all of it.

RW: And now they're just trying to keep the Mexicans from coming across the border and overwhelming them. The frontier is over now.

AC: It was nearly over then as well, wasn't it? I mean, actually, at that time the United States had pretty much—apart from acquiring Alaska and Puerto Rico—pretty much spent itself.

RW: That was the end. But they didn't know it and they still don't know it. Or they know it but the motor still runs.

AC: The motor of control.

RW: But the sun is definitely setting, wouldn't you say? In Walker's time the sun was rising over the empire.

AC: It's interesting because, if you use the sunset as an analogy for what the United States does, it's like this incredible effort to prevent the sun from setting this sort of huge hydraulic effort to create big machines, at vast expense, to prevent the sun from setting.

RW: And that huge amount of energy draws the curtain even more, don't you think? It closes the curtain even more, just because the energy is there.

AC: Well, I don't know. The United States seems to be in a holding pattern as far as a lot of things are concerned. I mean the United States and the Soviet Union are both really afraid of nationalist insurgent movements in the countries they control. Like in Russia with Afghanistan and the United States in Central America. They're really afraid of the People—whatever "the People" are—or just of people who are not the chosen representatives of the U.S.A. and of Russia getting ahold of the power. And they are actually in a holding pattern, I mean there hasn't been a successful revolution in El Salvador yet.

RW: That's true. Or Honduras—

AC: Which it looked like there would be eight years ago when the Nicaraguan revolution succeeded; it seemed like El Salvador was just about to go next. And the United States, by pouring in a huge amount of money and just giving them limitless military aid and by setting up this sort of puppet Democrat, Duarte, they've managed to create a holding pattern. It's interesting when you talk to people down here, they talk about the Zonas Bajo Control—the "under control" zones in El Salvador

—and what they mean are the zones that are in the hands of the rebels and the other two thirds are in the hands of the United States and it has been that way for about five years. Neither one is gaining ground. Except that once the United States ever blinked or faulted, El Salvador would instantly be gone.

RW: You think that will happen?

AC: I do think so. I mean, I'm optimistic to the extent that I think what happened in Nicaragua will happen in El Salvador as well. There's just too much repression, too much fascism in El Salvador, too many people are sick of it. I know that it's a different country and the situation is different in every country. I don't ever expect there'll be a revolution in Mexico, but I think there will be in El Salvador. . . .

RW: Don't you think that deep down they're afraid that there'll be a revolution in Mexico, and that they subscribe to the domino theory?

AC: I'm sure that's the rationale, but fascism just creates its own rationales, domino theories and everything. It's like George Orwell said: imagine the future as being like a jackboot stamping on a human face forever. And that's really how the United States and the Soviet Union and Britain in its colonial past and its treatment of the Irish behave: the colonial powers just stamp on people's faces endlessly and create rationales for it.

RW: Right, right.

AC: An interesting thing is, do they really believe it? Do they really believe that because of the revolution in Nicaragua that there'll be a revolution in Mexico and then there'll be Russian troops occupying Wisconsin? Does anybody really believe that or do they just say that?

RW: Last night you were talking about the whole thing, about how the right—the fascists and the conservatives—didn't have any real true ideals. And I said that I thought that in some demented way they did have ideals—that they do believe, in fact, in their own righteous descriptions, in their language and rhetoric.

AC: I think you're right, actually. Because look at Walker—he had the most tremendous principles. He was in favor of women's suffrage and freeing of the slaves and if he started spouting all this stuff about the rights of women and stuff today he'd be on the Moral Majority's hit list.

RW: He'd be on the crest of the liberal wave.

AC: To the left of Cuomo. The left of Gary Hart. But I mean it's interesting the change that Walker went through. It's inexplicable really.

RW: That's always confused me about Walker and I've thought about that a lot. You can rationalize his reversal in terms of the strategies of power and what he had to do to reverse the situation, but it doesn't really play. I mean, it still doesn't really explain his adopting slavery.

AC: No, it doesn't.

RW: Because he didn't have to do it.

AC: No.

RW: He didn't have to come to that.

AC: He didn't have to execute Corral either. He didn't have to alienate his supporters in Nicaragua. He didn't have to betray Vanderbilt. In a sense Walker had very good principles and very bad judgments. He began with all these good liberal beliefs, but he just—

RW: He betrayed each and every one of them.

AC: And it's interesting that he says in his book at one point, talking about Parker French, he just starts going on about Parker French and bitching about him and at the same time he made Parker French the Commissary of War to keep him out of trouble. Parker French had started for California in 1849 but, being engaged in some doubtful transactions in Texas, his name had ever since been suggestive of unfairness and dishonesty. And so Walker bitches about Parker French and what a bad guy he was. And yet Walker made Parker French his ambassador to the United States.

RW: And he was never cynical about it, was he? It was always total belief.

AC: Yeah! But he would go on bad-mouthing these guys and yet they were in his employ: he chose them and he put them in positions of authority and then he bitched about them. And

said what doubtful reputations they had and what bad characters they were. I mean, his book is very interesting in the sense
that in 300 pages and several years of a man's life, Walker *never*
made a mistake.

RW: *No,* he never did. He never erred.

AC: Even though Parker French was a bad hat and he sent him to
Washington; you know Parker French was a scoundrel.

RW: Do you think that Reagan says that about a few of his people?

AC: That they're soundrels—

RW: Yeah, they're scoundrels. North and Abrams and people like
that.

AC: I don't know if Reagan's in touch enough to even know who
those guys are.

RW: To even have that kind of strong opinion about them.

AC: I think we shouldn't name anybody that's involved in Reagan's
policies.

RW: It just brings it all down to a kind of a topicality.

AC: It gives them a little high, I think, that when X—a prime
asshole in the State Department and an architect of Reagan's
foreign policy—when he sees his name in print he gets a little
buzz out of it. I think we have to deny these guys the buzz.
The worms that work for Reagan and the worms that will come
after Reagan to continue the fascism—they're just gray little
men. They're not like Walker, because Walker in the end
would never have pled the Fifth.

RW: No, he wouldn't have. No way.

AC: —you know—Ha, Ha, Ha. I admire Walker in a lot of ways.

RW: I do too.

AC: It's very funny because I started the film hating him and
thinking he was like a murderous little clerk, and then just
through—

RW: His sheer audacity—his amazing adventure.

AC: And then watching Ed Harris be Walker and realizing that the
man that never drinks and smokes and swears and gambles—

well, that's his public persona. But why does anybody believe that's true? Why do the historians believe that's true?

RW: Because *he* says so in *his* book. No one ever heard from the women and the scumblies and the Immortals—no one got their stories.

AC: Various guys wrote books, actually, and poems. But they're all outsiders. They're all guys who say, "Oh, I saw the Colonel on the parade ground today and you know he looked at me."

RW: It's interesting that in Latin America Walker is one of the most famous people in their entire history. And in the United States nobody knows who he is. He's never mentioned in American history books. And from 1855 to 1857 he was one of the most famous men in the U.S. Today, he would be on the cover of *Time*. But we completely overlook him because he lost. He was a loser and so his name was stricken from the record books.

AC: I read an interview with Fassbinder. He never knew about the Nazis until he got to university. They don't teach the years 1935 to 1945 in Germany.

RW: It's just a blank.

AC: You have to go to the university to learn about Nazism. I suppose all nations, all cultures do this. So if you have bad experiences—

RW: You repress them.

AC: A bad romance or a bad car crash, you just try to put it out of your mind.

RW: Or you bully somebody. You put the heel of your boot on somebody's face. One of the other refrains that we've remarked on a few times is the parallel between Walker's relationship with Vanderbilt and the film company's relationship with the studio. The whole power, the adventure, the invasion of a film company coming down here and strip mining images and ripping them off and carrying them back as loot and booty to show on the screens of an affluent, decadent society. That's an ancient, ancient tradition. Very Roman.

AC: It's true, and we are part of that.

RW: We are pirates. We are just as much pirates—cultural pirates —as Walker was in fact; you know, a mercenary and a real pirate. We're mercenaries too, and we have the same kind of dialogue in some sense with the powers that be. There's that ancient quarrel and dialogue with the money source and the strategies of power and how you extract the money for your adventure and then try to come back and not get ripped off by the money people who own you and who control the final product. How you deal with the illusion of that is quite complicated.

AC: The whole expedition is kind of a parallel with Walker's adventure.

RW: And the irony also is that initially the Liberal party in Nicaragua invited Walker down to help them as, indeed, the Sandinistas encouraged our film. For their own ends, of course. And they might live to regret it. Who knows what they will finally think?

AC: I think it'll be okay but it's . . .

RW: One goes by other laws at the same time. So your initial intentions are nearly always qualified if not betrayed.

AC: . . . it's interesting that the script ended originally with that scene with Walker in Miami, Florida.

RW: That's right, that was an important scene.

AC: Yeah! Attending like a 500-dollar-a-plate dinner for the contras and making a speech—the speech that he now makes in the cathedral instead. And that was dropped. Really it was Ed's idea to drop it because he said, "Look, man, Walker's not like that. Walker's not a low little asshole from the State Department that would sulk around."

RW: I mean he's Napoleonic in a way: he was not a small man.

AC: Walker wouldn't just slink away. Walker would go down with all his engines on fire. He would say to the people that came to rescue him, I am William Walker, President of Nicaragua. And these CIA guys say: "We're only authorized to take Americans with us, Mr. Walker. What's your nationality again?" And he says, *"President of Nicaragua!"*

RW: And that's another amazing thing about Walker, that he would actually come back. Two years later he would get a bunch of scumblies together. Totally hopeless guys you know, completely fucked up, totally outmanned in conditions completely unfavorable. He would land in another country, Honduras, and try to do it again.

AC: He tried to march across Honduras into Nicaragua through the jungle and do it again. It's interesting because in the sense of Walker as a contra, there's an interesting parallel with a variety of those guys, the way that the United States kind of winked at Walker's expedition when he left.

RW: They were actually very much in favor of it, but they couldn't acknowledge it publicly because of their situation with the English and all of that.

AC: When Sheriff Purdy comes to stop Walker from sailing, it's because Walker hasn't paid for his sails and the shopkeeper's got a lien on the boat. Then Byron Cole comes out with all these papers and says, "Look here, I have a letter from Jefferson Davis, Secretary of War"—they're given every assistance. The government's turned as many blind eyes as it can to the mission which is totally illegal and against American law because everybody wants Walker to succeed. They even do musical plays and songs about Walker.

RW: Right. He was a great American hero.

AC: He was more famous than the President.

RW: He probably was, for a year or two, the most famous guy in the country. He epitomized in some way the American Dream.

AC: The way Americans like to see themselves.

RW: Always being totally independent, with complete integrity, with God on their side, always controlling their moral destinies.

AC: Viewing other races as little more than animals, really. Savages, like the Mexicans and others.

RW: Walker the Calvinist with his Anglo-Saxon arrogance. This Puritan fundamentalist going against the decadent Catholics and ignorant Indians.

AC: Walker the regenerator.

RW: Regenerating a culture that's already decadent and fallen apart and lost; so that gives him permission to rebuild. You can't imagine him going against the French or the English that way.

I mean, it would never happen. Even a French colony that had fallen apart in the Caribbean. There's the inherent opinion of the Anglo-Saxon fundamentalists feeling racially superior to the Spanish Catholic Indians.

AC: Well, it's interesting because Walker who started off so anti-slavery—

RW: That's what I'm trying to get into, the slavery thing. Why was it so easy for him to make that turn?

AC: Yeah, what did he think? When he writes all this stuff—there's a whole chapter about slavery—about the superiority of the white race, you know, which is just what the State Department thinks as well about the people south of the border.

RW: It's American history, it's south of the border and west of the border all the way to Japan and Vietnam and Korea and on and on so that the Japanese and Vietnamese are just another Indian tribe.

AC: Just savages performing strange rites.

RW: You can drop the bomb on them . . .

AC: Yeah, yeah, it's okay—kill 'em all.

RW: . . . you can do that and Walker would have done that; he could have done that. You feel that because of his incredible brutality.

AC: Oh, if he'd had an atom bomb, he would have set it off—

RW: Dropped it on Nicaragua—

AC: In Granada.

RW: He did, after all, burn Granada to the ground.

AC: He destroyed the city. Interesting as well that Nicaragua was also the first place where an air force bombed a civilian population. It was the U.S. Air Force and it was in Nicaragua in the 1920's.

RW: The Marines did it to Sandino, trying to get him out of the mountains.

AC: And they just bombed all these villages. Just like Guernica, going after the civilian population from the air with bombs. The first aerial bombardment of civilians in history.

RW: How do you feel about the Sandinistas and their obvious inclinations toward the film?

AC: We were very well received. We made a film in Nicaragua that
we couldn't have made anywhere else. Especially in Granada
and the countryside, you've got these incredible visuals for free.
But also because the entire wardrobe department was set up
here by Pam Tate and almost all the costumes were made here
by people who earned around two dollars a week.

RW: And it gave to the people participating in the film, sort of a
moral sense of participation. That they were working for some
cause that wasn't just your usual sort of movie venture.

AC: That is definitely true even though we're probably kidding ourselves about the essential nobility of our efforts—I mean, we
were just a bunch of pigs, you know.

RW: We were just pigs playing boys' games.

AC: (laughing) Yeah. A bunch of pigs playing cowboys and
Indians.

RW: But that rhetoric made it possible to have the adventure, to
finish the adventure.

AC: But in actual fact, even though we are by Nicaraguan standards
a bunch of pigs that eat too much food and have too much
luxury, by American standards everybody did live a comparatively humble existence here.

RW: They certainly did. From movie standards, they totally did.

AC: There were no trailers, no honey wagons, no toilets.

RW: And all with pretty good will.

AC: The feeling among the actors was the best, in my limited experience of any film.

RW: Mine too, by far. Very little whining and complaining.

AC: Yeah. I mean everybody whines and complains. Rene Auberjonois said that and he has been in a lot of films; he said that
he has never enjoyed a film so much.

RW: And it certainly made me think even more about what a luxury
it is to be able to make a film that's involved in something; that
has a higher metaphor or a more interesting and complicated
metaphor than just the film itself—that touches on an event or
a situation, however topical. In a sense, the Nicaraguan dia-

logue with the United States increased one's energy pulling one through that more or less profane morass of filmmaking where it's—

AC: It's totally decadent.

RW: Totally decadent and the worst form of capitalism—all greed and ego. But one had little moments of relief, however illusory or deluded, that gave one a kind of courage.

AC: I don't think it is deluded, actually. I mean we made the film because we wanted to contribute in some way to the dialogue about Nicaragua.

RW: And I really believe that, because the intentions were in a relative sense pure, that that made it possible to do the film. Because, if they weren't, this film never would have been able to have been made here. It never would have happened. I'm sure of that, aren't you?

AC: Yes. But also the good thing is the fact that when you're working for no money, it means you have nothing to lose.

RW: It gives you courage.

AC: Because it's very unlikely that I would get fired during the making of the film because they would have to *pay* somebody to replace me. They'd have to close down—then have to *hire* someone to take over and there's no one else who's going to edit the film as fast as this or as obsessively or make everybody else work 15-hour days—because nobody else has got so much passion for it. That's one thing I can't understand about your pal Sam [Peckinpah], how he could let the editing of *Pat Garrett and Billy the Kid* get away from him.

RW: Well, Sam had a compulsion to battle and struggle with authority. It was part of his complicated nature. He was finally somewhat adolescent about his relationship to power.

AC: I understand that role.

RW: And, in a sense, he had to let himself be defeated. In terms of *Pat Garrett,* there were many, many ways he could have avoided that confrontation with Jim Aubrey, who was the head of MGM at that time. He could have edited the film all the way through but it seemed like there was something in him that wanted the film to be taken away. It's complicated, it's not just black and white, there are lots of grays, but Sam had those tendencies. I think he needed to come up short. A failure of intimacy, perhaps.

AC: He was like Walker, then.

RW: Very much like Walker. I thought a lot about Sam in terms of the similarities between the two. Probably the most similar character to Walker who I thought of while we were doing it, you know? And Sam had to have those kinds of adventures and he had to ultimately be betrayed by that paternalistic authority that he could not finally find an equality with. He was totally equal if not superior to everyone he was dealing with and completely charming and could get them to do anything he wanted. I felt he had to feel their authority and be defeated and betrayed by them and he was hooked on that rage.

AC: Before he was directing films he felt that way?

RW: Oh, I'm sure. His father was an old Western judge, you know, from Peckinpah Mountain in California. This really tough old bird. I mean, without really knowing his psychological history, it was totally apparent his whole sense of bravery and machismo and equality and friendship between men was all based on finding relief and transcendence from authority and some sort of equality, the way his films all kind of end the same, with male camaraderie and buddies riding off over the cliff together.

AC: That's exactly it. Yeah, riding over the cliff together!

RW: But it's over the cliff. It's not up to the top of the mountain for the big view. Very much like Walker. Even though Walker was finally a man completely alone.

AC: He wasn't interested in friends.

RW: No, he had no friends.

AC: But it's interesting because Walker's kind of like the meanest film director you could ever meet, and everybody, especially the actors, really want to please him. And all the actors in Walker's drama just want to do good, so much so that they'll *die* for Walker. All they want is for Walker to say, "Well done, Mr. Hornsby. Well done, Mr. Washburn"—and Hornsby's heart would just swell with pride and he would do anything.

RW: He would walk into a hail of bullets.

AC: They all would. They would all die for Walker and all they wanted was to feel that in some way he appreciated them.

RW: And in some way that got into the flavor of the film with the Immortals and their energy. I felt that very strongly, you know.

AC: It is funny because, in a sense, leading a mad endeavor off into a foreign country—even though the part of Nicaragua we're in is not dangerous at all, I mean, the greatest danger here is to be hit by a car in the road—but it still seems like a dangerous adventure when you're in Malibu.

RW: All the letters from the States say don't forget to duck—I mean, I was much more shocked and depressed going from here to New York. The psychological warfare and the suffering in New York is much worse, much more out of reality than here.

AC: Oh yeah, yeah, yeah. I've seen much more suffering there.

RW: And almost everyone in the film remarked on that—the transition from Nicaragua back to the States. And finally the dialogue that one has here is not so much with Nicaragua, though one thinks about Nicaragua a lot, but it's with one's own country and what the nature of that reality is. I think a lot of people really became, in a primitive sense, somewhat changed or historically educated a little bit, wouldn't you say? I, for one, feel very much changed.

AC: I was really changed by my trip. Most of all the first time I came. I went back and just felt absolutely empowered. I went back and I felt like man, you know, I can single-handedly persuade everybody in Britain not to vote for Margaret Thatcher or something like that. It's not right for me to feel bummed out and defeated about politics and about the way the world is because here are some guys in a bar—soldiers, teenage soldiers—who have been wounded fighting in the war against American-financed mercenaries and these guys are saying, of course you can come down here and make a film if you want. What are you talking about, no money? Just get some—

RW: —and get on with it.

AC: Yeah! You're from the United States, you can do anything!

RW: Which is true in a way. But we're also stuck in our fun.

AC: We're stuck in our own little thing. I feel especially sorry for people in the film business—Britain or U.S.A. or anywhere—who have a lot of possessions and responsibilities.

RW: It's the biggest curse of the film business . . .

AC: The biggest curse.

RW: . . . because it's all the desire realms that are constantly being quested for and obsessed over.

AC: Guys that earn like a hundred grand or two hundred grand a year.

RW: And it's a complete curse, because you can't go beneath it or over it or around it.

AC: You've got a mortgage, you've got a home, a couple of cars, you've got a family or a wife or a divorce or something.

RW: But that's the ancient dilemma, isn't it?

AC: It is, it's not just a dilemma of the film industry by any means.

RW: Without being pretentious, it's sort of the dichotomy of the spiritual and the worldly. Being careful of the word spiritual, but you know what I mean.

AC: It's funny because you're a kind of spiritual guy!

RW: Well, who knows? But you are spiritual more than you realize. You're a mad monk, an ascetic. In the best sense of the word I feel that, because you strip the sizzle from the steak, you cut everything down to the bone and you operate with the maximum kind of freedom that you yourself can handle and be responsible for. That's a spiritual definition. I'm not talking about religious . . .

AC: No, I know what you mean.

RW: . . . I'm talking about the sense of being able to be effective and function in a way that doesn't betray your own sense of your own self, what you want to do, in that sense.

AC: I don't really have a sense of myself, it exists purely to service the film. I mean, if this film wasn't happening, there would have to be another film happening. I have to go on making films because I don't really have a definition of myself other than through that process. This is really pretentious to say because I haven't always been a film director, but I kind of always wanted to be. Like Washburn always thought he was Walker's brother.

RW: Right.

AC: You know, when I was a little kid I always kind of thought I was a film director; when this film is over then I'll go live somewhere else where another film is happening. Until I get married and have kids or something, it'll always be like that. Because there's nothing else that really matters.

RW: What's going to happen to the Nicaraguan film industry? When we came down and did this film, they hadn't thought that much about what a film industry is or what they could get from it or whether it could work or whether they could in fact attract people from other countries. And, as soon as they started to think about it, all these tendencies started to occur: more money, more possibilities, more ambition. So they have become more capitalistic in the venture. Isn't that what has happened?

AC: It's very interesting because you come down to Nicaragua and it is an impressive place. There's a lot of poverty, but it's not as bad as other places in Central America or even the U.S.A.

RW: As we said, the poverty's much worse in New York City than anywhere in Nicaragua and psychologically the suffering is more intense.

AC: I don't sense the same desperation even though they're at war. There are a lot of good things about Nicaragua. If I lived in Latin America, I wouldn't want to live anywhere but here because with modest means, even though there are shortages, I know that the government isn't going to come and murder me in the middle of the night or torture me. You can't bribe the police here, you know.

RW: You hear these stories about the Sandinistas becoming more totalitarian and more crystalized in their bureaucracy.

AC: I'm sure the bureaucracy's a real nightmare.

RW: Yeah, it's got to be. You know it's got to be, but still at the same time you don't feel this blanket of fear or paranoia that you feel in El Salvador or Honduras.

AC: You don't see murdered people lying in the road. You don't see beheaded corpses or the kind of stuff you see in El Salvador.

RW: And you don't get afraid when you see a policeman.

AC: It's the only country in the whole world where I'm not afraid of the police. I'm afraid of the police in Britain and L.A., but I'm not afraid of them here. Then again, they're all fourteen years old so. . . . But it's funny, because Nicaragua's not like Cuba. When they took over the country they didn't nationalize all the American oil industry; they didn't take over all the private corporations. They left the private sector. I mean, they nationalized 20 percent of the private sector; something like that. The rest of it was left in the hands of the people who owned it. Any rich person who stayed in Nicaragua and didn't flee to Miami after the revolution was allowed to keep his gold.

RW: That brings us to In Cine, the Nicaraguan film commission, which is now going through some changes.

AC: In Cine is there to promote a national film industry and also to get foreign films in here and supply them with assistance. And it did that spectacularly well with *Walker*. I mean, they haven't been as successful in terms of a national film industry because it hasn't really opened up. They haven't really made a search for Nicaraguan directors and there's not a lot of money so the thing is, if you're a rich guy you can be a film director, and if you're not you can't. In that sense it's very like the U.S.A. You know, it's not a meritocracy. A lot of things about Nicaragua aren't a meritocracy. They want to keep the Chammoro family in the country; they don't want the Chammoros all to leave for Miami because they are the most influential family in the country, so they reward them with some little jobs and some little benefits. And in the same way, the Minister of Tourism goes to the government and says: "Look here, you put me in charge of the film industry and I'll bring in lots of foreign movies and we'll get dollars, we'll get hard currency." And so Ramirez, the Vice President, says: "Yeah, okay, the film industry's all yours." But what they forget is that the people who come to Nicaragua to make films are people who come here through a genuine sense of commitment even though they're no doubt opportunists as well. I mean, we're all opportunists, everybody that comes here is an opportunist of some kind, I think, unless they're like a saint. It's interesting because nothing's as pure as you think it's going to be. There are capitalists here; there are people who would get on really well with the moguls of Hollywood because they're not interested in films *at all*.

RW: Yeah, there are a lot of people here who are not particularly in favor of the Sandinistas; but there is nobody here who is in favor of the contras, who even entertains the possibility of the contras. There's a dialogue that people have with the Sandinistas here about mistakes they think they've made or the good and the bad and, you know, because they're like every other government, they've made their mistakes.

AC: I definitely don't think many people support the contras, that's for sure. Because the contras, in seven years or something, haven't been able to take a single town or even a village. They murder people. They torture people. They rape women. I mean, popular guys don't do that kind of thing. I'll tell you something else: even though people read repeatedly in all the English-language newspapers about how support for the Sandinistas is waning and the Sandinistas themselves worry about it, I also know that whenever we get a new batch of Sandino T-shirts—ironically from London because they get printed in really bright colors, they look really good—they're snapped up like that. I've never seen anybody refuse an FSLN T-shirt. But admittedly, those are the people who worked on the movie, and they're kind of gung-ho, you know.

RW: That's a special thing.

AC: Here in Granada especially I think a lot of people don't support the Sandinistas.

RW: Yeah, well, Granada is an old conservative city. They don't support them, but they don't support the contras. They don't want the contras to move into town. But what do you think will happen, getting back to El In Cine—which is a subject that fascinates me—which way do you think they can go? Because it sort of parallels certain other directions of the country.

AC: Lorenzo [the producer] had a conversation with the mayor of Granada, and the mayor said some interesting stuff to him, including the fact that, as far as he was concerned, he didn't give a fuck if they ever made a penny, if they ever made any money. Nicaragua, as far as he was concerned, could be poor forever, because in their poverty there was a certain strength and a certain purity that they would lose in a sort of an undignified rush to become like Costa Rica.

RW: I think simply put, that's really what most people who worked on the film felt. In the poverty here they found a certain reality and dignity.

AC: And also there are only three million people here and the whole country has six elevators or something; I mean, it's like the most insignificant country in the world. Except in terms of its example as a country that refused to bow down.

RW: Right.

AC: Because they've always been rebellious. They're a rebellious, arbitrary bunch of bastards and they'll just give you all kinds of shit, and I got a lot of shit from various people for not being sufficiently respectful or whatever, and I respect that! I respect what an arbitrary bunch they are and that they won't do what you say.

RW: And they've always had this sort of geographical dilemma because they are this little strip of land that connects the Atlantic to the Pacific and the whole thing about the canal has always been here since Walker's day and will be here forever, really. I mean they've been overrun by pirates many many times.

AC: Granada was burned down twice before Walker burned it down.

RW: Wasn't it seven times altogether?

AC: Really? That many? Maybe.

RW: And then in this century the Marines came in and took over repeatedly.

AC: But if you're just in Granada, it's a funny place. If you go to a place like León or Masaya, they're really battle damaged because they fought big, big battles there, and a lot of shooting went on before the National Guard surrendered. Granada was the last city to fall. When the Sandinistas get here ready for a big fight, white flags go up everywhere and everybody surrenders because they don't want to have a fight here.

RW: They'd been down that road before.

AC: Yeah! And when Walker marched into Granada—

RW: Everybody was wearing red flowers in their lapels.

AC: In Rivas they get involved in a bloody battle, but when they get to Granada it's white flags. Oh oh, don't spoil the town.

RW: That's right. The oldest town in North America.

AC: They do say that, don't they?

RW: Yeah, it is the oldest colonial town in North America, which it probably is. But you feel that, just in terms of the historical line of it all, it's going to go on and on and on, isn't it? That the relationship to the States is never going to be resolved. Do you feel that?

AC: I do, because no matter how much they try to ape the States with baseball and with Michael Jackson T-shirts . . . and with capitalism and stuff—because they *are* capitalists. They love capitalism—

RW: Yeah, they love it, they love it.

AC: You now, they want to make dollars, man. They would rather try to make a few bucks off some international coproductions than make "film art." It seems. I don't know if that's really true because I think there's a lot of people here who would like to make film art.

RW: But at this point in time.

AC: They haven't got the access to the material. The material's still in the hands of the rich guys. But it's funny. I suppose it will always be like that, the United States will go on and on prodding and shoving at Nicaragua.

RW: They will, and they'll always have this attitude that they have to control Nicaragua's external destiny because of where it is geographically. Don't you think a lot of it just comes back to their relationship to where Nicaragua is?

AC: I suppose. Oh, do you think that they really have some type of contingency plan to dig a canal across the isthmus? Yeah, they do.

RW: Of course they do. They have a contingency plan for everything.

AC: Yeah, for bombing London, they have a plan for bombing London to deprive the Soviets of a major asset. It's funny because making this film makes me think about how short the human life is.

RW: How impermanent it all is?

AC: How nothing much will have changed by the time of my death. Maybe El Salvador will be free of American domination.

RW: For a while—you know, for a few minutes.

AC: Yeah . . . well, maybe forever.

RW: Yeah, maybe.

AC: That's the good thing, I don't think Nicaragua will *ever* be dominated by the U.S.A. again. Because the government has handed out machine guns. They've handed out like 200,000 machine guns. And that's a lot of pissed-off guys, a lot of pissed-off fourteen-year-old kids who are ready to kill; who are ready to kill the *gringo,* man—and that's something, you know.

RW: What do you think will happen if the inflation gets worse and worse and worse and the economy is just, as it is now, almost on it knees?

AC: Just the same as in every Latin American country.

RW: People just keep going on, just surviving.

AC: People just keep on and the government will do something. But I don't think Nicaragua is in hock to the world bank the way certain other countries are. Because they can't get loans; because when the loans are gone then you're in hock. You know, better to live poor but free.

RW: That's what we were saying, it's the only way to make films.

AC: Only way to make films, too. It really is. Only way to make *good* films. Because otherwise you just go the way of *Dune* or something.

RW: Yeah, I know. I know that largeness is a real metaphor for the United States and Nicaragua, too, isn't it? And what one worries about in In Cine is that they equate making films with how big or large everything is.

AC: Yeah, well, that's more the government and the Minister of Tourism that think of the bucks, because the guys at In Cine, especially Carlos Alvarez, he's a real filmmaker. He gets things done and he loved the film, and all he wanted to do was make the film well, and he didn't want to rip us off. So we came here and made a very cheap film. We made a film that we couldn't have made anywhere else in the world.

RW: But what one hopes is that they understand why it was able to be made for the price it was.

AC: You see, I don't think that they do. I don't think that the people in Tourism or the government understand that Ed Harris and Rene Auberjonois are down here working for peanuts. And that all the guys from the Mexican union are sleeping five to a room. And that this isn't the way we normally make films.

RW: If this had been made in the normal way, it would have been a fifteen- to twenty-million-dollar film, don't you think so?

AC: Yeah, I think so.

RW: I mean, that's being very realistic.

AC: It would have been about that. Everybody made tremendous sacrifices. Not only the actors but also the rank-and-file grips and electricians from Mexico.

RW: And the extras.

AC: All the *gringo* extras, some of them who stuck through all nine weeks on five-dollars-a-day wages and that was the *GRINGO* wages, you know, five dollars a day to be an Immortal. They did it because they believed in the project and that's the thing that the Nicaraguans perhaps don't know about: that most films aren't made with this sort of idealism.

RW: Right, right.

AC: They're made by just a bunch of guys who want to make a lot of money and do drugs in their trailer and don't care about the film, don't love the film with a passion. But it's just a job. Just a boring job, and that's their mistake, because you see they're not going to get a twenty-million-dollar coproduction down here because the guys on the twenty-million-dollar coproduction expect trailers and honey wagons.

RW: Yeah, they'll go to Cancun, they'll go where the five-star hotels are and the cable television and the toilets. The Nicaraguans don't have an infrastructure for sprawling, hideous, multi-million-dollar coproductions.

AC: They only have an infrastructure for films of good will where everybody's making sacrifices.

RW: So unless they understand that, they're going to be in trouble.

AC: Well, there are people who want to come here and make films, like Pontecorvo wants to come here and make a movie. There's always somebody coming along saying he wants to make the Sandino story. Every year a new guy turns up who says he's got money from Spanish television to make the Sandino story, and—

RW: They have to make it possible to make it here, not in Spain.

AC: Because the thing is that the prestige that accrues to Nicaragua is immense. While we were here, we got thrown out of the Hotel Intercontinental in Managua and had to move everybody to Granada because there was a parliamentary convention and it was like the biggest number they'd ever had here. They invited this parliamentary convention from somewhere in the world to come and have its meeting here. And so it took place at an enormous financial deficit to the Nicaraguans, because they made a bit of money off *Walker*—not a lot, but they made a little bit. They just wasted a ton of money on the parliamentary convention and they didn't get an *inch* of media coverage about it. Simply nobody heard about it and it was all done as a propaganda exercise to demonstrate the maturity of Nicaragua and the fact that Nicaragua is a proper country that hosts these events. Whereas we brought them *hundreds* of column inches of mostly favorable press.

RW: In the Western press.

AC: That's very beneficial when people open up *Variety* or *The Hollywood Reporter* and there's Richard Masur talking about Nicaragua.

RW: Right.

AC: And you know, reading that, the U.S.A. should wise up and stop supporting the contras and people should go down to Nicaragua and see it for themselves.

RW: It was like NBC—

AC: They got a lot of good media out of this. NBC. Ted Koppel and all that. And they will in the future, too, if they host similar films of goodwill.

RW: Right.

AC: But they mustn't view it as a way of making big amounts of dollars because they don't have the infrastructure to support those kinds of greed films. Big slurpy budgets.

RW: Yeah.

AC: The good thing about *Walker* is that it has made me think about history.

RW: Me too. I think I've learned more about history in this film than anything else I've ever done. I mean, we're on this balcony and you see a hundred and thirty years in front of you: the currents and cycles of history, how history is really not linear, and that it comes around with its own laws. In terms of the *Walker* situation, the dialogue that provoked us is one that has come and gone in Nicaraguan—in Latin American—history, really, for over four hundred *years*. And you feel that dialogue's not going to stop; it's going to go on and on and on.

AC: And we're just a tiny part. A human life is just a short thing and you witness just a few events.

RW: I think most people on the film felt very grateful to be in he middle of an event and to witness it. It doesn't happen very often.

AC: There was a time when I would leave Nicaragua and wonder if I would be able to fly back. Or if the country would be undergoing aerial bombardment by the U.S.A.

RW: It's an irrational feeling, but I felt that just coming down here this time. I felt a certain resistance and there is this, this barrier, this envelope, that you have to go through. Sometimes. Not all the time. Sometimes it's very easy to come down. Sometimes it isn't.

AC: Oh, I never mind coming down. No, I always like to go somewhere; the act of going somewhere is always exciting.

RW: But I mean in terms of the situation in Nicaragua?

AC: I would just worry that when I would leave that the country wouldn't really be here in any recognizable shape—

RW: That you wouldn't be able to come back.

AC: That I wouldn't be able to come back because there'd be a full-fledged war going on and Sandino Airport would have been bombed and . . .

RW: Yeah, I felt that too.

AC: . . . there'd be no airliners and the people I knew would be dead. That all these Nicaraguan people that I know—

RW: Would be dead.

AC: Would be dead in this war that America had started.

RW: And also that you didn't really know what the reality was down here because of the press as you perceive it in the West, as you get your information about Nicaragua. . . . From being here you realize that it's totally not real; it's fabricated and manipulated so that it builds a certain level of misinformation and anxiety about what you're coming into because you're not getting any true information about it.

AC: I met the bureau chief of the *New York Times* here. He did an article on the film. His skin is so pale that you can see the veins through it.

RW: Right. I saw him.

AC: I bet he never goes out*side*. You know? (laughing) and if he never goes outside, how can you know about a country? How can you learn anything if you don't go outside? You spend all your time in an air-conditioned room.

RW: And yet he, in some ways, in his lame way, gives out more information than almost all the others. I mean, the level of information that comes, for instance, from the other papers we read here, the *Miami Herald* or the *Chicago Tribune* or whatever.

AC: I think they're all as bad. I haven't found a good newspaper. I mean the *LA Times* is supposed to be a quality paper, but I think it's worse than the *Herald*.

RW: It's worse because it's more pretentious. It has more cultural power. So I learned a lot about the media for this film. About what the media is and the effects of the media. Stuff that you know intellectually but you sort of experience in a different way. Don't you feel that?

AC: I did feel that. It's just interesting to learn—just to read, say, an article by an American journalist that's supposedly about making the movie. And just to realize that the guy is making it up.

RW: Right.

AC: That he's just making up interviews with people and pretending he's talked to people and you talk to someone and you find it's not true.

RW: And that's 98 percent of the time.

AC: Yeah, yeah. And you know whenever they don't give the guy's name, whenever they say "a Western diplomat" or "a stuntman said," they never talked to anybody. They made it up and that's so funny. Because I talked to both the stuntmen: "Have you talked to this guy?" "No. I never talked to him." "No I never met him. Which one is he?" And it's like, they make it up and it's so funny to realize that journalists—that they're just hacks, they're worse than—worse than even *you!*

RW: No, they're not *that* bad.

AC: I'm afraid so, Rudy. But I'll tell you something funny. Something that is good and it is sort of like imbued by the spirit of Nicaragua, the possibility of change and the possibility of taking control of events and doing the impossible. Because getting this film on—

RW: This was impossible.

AC: Going to make a film in an enemy country of the U.S.A. in the middle of a war . . .

RW: With an embargo.

AC: . . . with an embargo and getting American money to do it with—

RW: It's impossible.

AC: And getting all these actors down here and making a film with no toilets and having them work fifteen-hour days and—

RW: And doing a fifteen-million-dollar film for five.

AC: Doing a fifteen-million-dollar film for five; and this is just two guys bullshitting, this is just you and me talking.

RW: Yeah. Right. It's amazing.

AC: And it *happened*. It really happened. It's the most amazing thing.

RW: Yeah, because if you had gone in to any studio or any of the usual traditional money sources at the wrong time and said that's what you were going to do, you would never have gotten a call back. Right?

AC: Well, no.

RW: So you just started the process. You just got committed to the process and you just went ahead.

AC: This process happened and—Oh, we're going to shoot it in Mexico with a little bit of Nicaragua; and then we're going to shoot it half-and-half in Nicaragua, and by the end—

RW: It was all in Nicaragua.

AC: And by the end, the executive producer catches on to the fact that it's cheaper to shoot in Nicaragua and turns around and goes "Well, I mean, you should shoot it all in Nicaragua."

RW: Right.

AC: Because it saves the cost of a move you know, and it goes through full circle.

RW: But it had to be step by step. If the timing was wrong, forget it. If you'd said that one step before, he'd never have gone for it.

AC: Also, some of these guys with a lot of money and even some of those guys at Universal, they're kind of liberal. Take the guy from the bond company, he's a—

RW: Yeah, a lefty.

AC: They're liberals. Not lefties as such, but they're kind of liberals, you know, and they don't think that murdering is right.

RW: I guess you could call them limo liberals, but they're still . . .

AC: I think all liberals are limo liberals.

AC: It's part of their—

RW: Part of their brochure.

AC: I didn't know that being a liberal was actually an abusive term until I came to the States, because in Britain, I mean there's the Liberal party, which is sort of not very successful but relatively reputable. But in America for the radical left, it's usually meant as a term of disdain, and right-wingers use it as a synonym for commie. But it is good, it demonstrates that there are still sentiments in the U.S.A., that not everybody is a fascist yuppie. Look at the Screen Actors Guild. Even as Ed Asner gets fired from his television show for speaking his mind, he's the president of the Screen Actors Guild because the actors think, This is the guy to represent us.

RW: Right.

AC: So maybe in Hollywood something will happen; maybe more films. I mean you've been asked to make another film, to write another script about Nicaragua.

RW: Yeah, that's true.

AC: A film that deals with contemporary problems on what the CIA is doing and what the contras do and how they're all tied to the drug trade.

RW: And maybe if this film has some sort of success on some level, it'll open the door toward yet another film.

AC: Yeah, another film can be made about an interesting theme, an interesting little-known American antihero. But it is funny about Walker because I've got to just learn more about the gray areas—I think in making the film I learned a lot more about the gray—there's not so much stuff that's absolutely black and white. I started off with this opinion of Walker and now, as much as I detest everything he stands for politically, there's a part of me that's drawn to his sheer audacity and madness. It's a hard thing to explain to the Nicaraguans.

RW: Most people in the film thought they followed you like the Colonel.

AC: Yeah!

RW: And so you were following the Colonel and they were following you.

AC: And it's just like the Colonel says it, so it must be. And he's so mad! All this walking into barrages of bullets and stuff. He seems to seek his own death and be denied it constantly. And Ed Harris and I would have these conversations where Ed would say "Well, what does Walker want?" And I'd go "Well, he seeks his own death but is denied it," and Ed would say, "Well, tell me something else!"

RW: Give me something more!

AC: "I mean, what can I do with that? You know, tell me something *else,*" and I just didn't understand much more about him than that. But I did by the end of it. He's such an idiosyncratic guy. He's such a crazy mad man, but possessed with such energy and such conviction—totally demented and totally wrong. And yet there's something about the real Walker. Maybe it's not the real . . .

RW: So what's the seduction? Is it that somebody has that total commitment to his own beliefs? Or that he has no doubts? That's a tremendously seductive thing; that's a *real* pull.

AC: Most people are looking for something to give their lives meaning, they're looking for something to follow, they're looking for a bunch of beliefs.

RW: Authority, they're looking for authority.

AC: And Walker was that. I mean a film is sort of a play-acting thing because you bow to someone's orders for six weeks and then you can go home—

RW: Then you can tell him to go fuck himself.

AC: Yeah, go fuck off, man, we're not making the film now. And so there's sort of a play variant to Walker, playing around.

RW: Was this the first film you ever made with an historical character?

AC: No, Sid Vicious.

RW: That's true. There was Sid.

AC: And the other thing, it was the same thing about Sid. I mean I think the real Sid was probably a lot more horrible than Sid in the film. Because Sid in the film—I really admired Sid.

RW: I did, too. He had tremendous courage.

AC: Yeah. And Nancy.

RW: Nancy, too. They lived on that edge and they were able to sustain it . . .

AC: Yeah, highly admirable characters.

RW: . . . facing total adversity. Sid's a lot like Walker. I mean, a totally mad adventure that's doomed to failure but he kept his chin up all the way through it.

AC: Well, not *just* like Walker. I mean, there are many differences, but essentially they were both leaders of outlaw bands—you know, outlaw communities.

RW: You're finding your subject: alienated outlaw bands.

AC: That's what everything I've ever done has been about—outlaw communities. Yours is too—

RW: Yeah. Alienated outlaws, looking for a leader.

AC: That's right. Because those guys in *Billy the Kid,* they're lost when Billy goes away.

RW: Yeah, they're fucked.

AC: They don't know what do to. They're in a daze . . .

RW: They don't know. They're not going to follow Garrett, that's for sure, because he has sold out.

AC: . . . and they just stay waiting—and he comes back and they're still there waiting for a leader. Punks are outlaw communities and Pat Garrett and Billy the Kid and Walker's Immortals—pirates, a whole bunch of pirates.

RW: They're pirates, and making a movie is sort of an act of piracy, too.

AC: Well, it's like you said, you're storming in and stealing images and storming out again. And that's why I'm glad we stayed here to do the editing for many reasons. It's much easier to work here because there are no distractions at all. You know, the phone isn't always ringing.

RW: Did you have any fears about doing it down here in terms of being subjective—too subjective? Not being in another sort of mix that would enable you to see the film a little bit differently. By being here you're sort of stuck with your own point of view.

AC: Yeah, but we're only taking it as far as the first screenable version of the film and then we're taking it to the States.

RW: So then you can go back and you still have a long process to go in terms of making changes.

AC: And there's still plenty of time for changes afterwards.

RW: Because people come in and certain things that we would react to they might not, not that that necessarily calls for a change but . . .

AC: Yeah, but I was happy for another reason as far as just the concentration that was available, but also just to stay. You know, we finished shooting and the Nicaraguans would come up and say "So when are you leaving?" I'm not leaving. And that was just good to be able to say, you're not entirely a filibuster. You're not storming out as soon as it's over.

RW: Do you think you'll come back after the film?

AC: Oh, yeah.

RW: Will you show the film down here?

AC: Definitely. I'd like to make another film down here if we can; if the capitalists don't rip us off too much, I'd love to make another movie down here. Especially because the people who we worked with, the Nicaraguans we worked with on this film, will be even better when we come back because there will have been other films as well.

RW: They've been trained. And you'll leave some stuff here for them, too.

AC: Oh, they've got about a thousand peasant and townspeople costumes from the 1850s and some rubber rifles—

RW: And a lot of memories.

AC: And a film. We'll bring them back a print of the film and that's when it'll pay off. It's hard to see the benefit of the film—for a long time afterwards all people see of a film is the discomfort and the havoc that gets caused and the fact that nobody got rich—Buncha *gringos* came and played cowboys and Indians. But I think that when they see the film—hopefully—they will like it because they love all things American, even though Uncle Billy Walker is this terrible man who did these terrible things.

RW: And they'll cheer when he gets killed.

AC: They'll cheer when he's dead, and they'll cheer him when he's alive. The film doesn't actually treat him respectfully. It shows the sort of down and dirty side of Uncle Billy, too. And, I hope they like it.

RW: It will be interesting what they think about the anachronisms —the helicopter coming in and all.

AC: You know, we were looking at that shot with Anderson and the two guys—with that bottle of Coke and a package of Marlboros—and I was just sitting on the flatbed looking at that and thinking, "This is too much, come on, out it goes." And in came Lester the taxi driver, the black guy who speaks English. He comes in and he goes, "What?" And he stares at this thing and I go, "Hector, do you think I should cut this out?" And he goes, "No way, that's really funny, man." But it's like supposedly the Nicaraguans are not very sophisticated, right? We're the ones that aren't very sophisticated, because the Nicaraguans can see.

RW: They're innocent in terms of film. They're open, they don't . . .

AC: But no, they're not.

RW: No?

AC: They see movies all the time. The movies are super popular here. I went to see *Ride the High Country*.

RW: How was it?

AC: It was—well, the print was pink and about fifteen minutes of scratches but—

RW: It had some good moments.

AC: It's a good film.

RW: Joel McCrea.

AC: Yeah. It has good acting in it. Peckinpah's films have very good acting.

RW: He was great with actors. Because his own relationship with authority inspired actors, because he was very authoritative with actors. He was a hero to them. And they were a little afraid of him. So they—

AC: They tried for him—

RW: They tried hard and they believed it more because there was something in him that believed it more. Same with you, Al.

AC: Well, I think that's very nice of you to say. I don't know if . . .

RW: It's true. People really get wildly enthusiastic.

AC: I don't know if it was the same with Peckinpah, because I don't know what his thing was, but it just seems like the best thing.

If you cast the actors, the best thing is to have confidence in them and—

RW: And let them go. I agree. I feel that way about not holding onto a script and about being able to go with the changes, which is really one of the secrets of films: not holding to your own definitions. Or your own descriptions. In the sense that this script and this film changed a lot. All of which was great. As long as it comes like it did with John Diehl, from the inside, and it's not just a bunch of actors playing for the dailies, self-congratulating themselves.

AC: I got in there! There's me! You have to tell about the cats, too, in the book. That we had cats specially made and stuffed.

RW: What we should do is get a photograph of you with the cats.

AC: Because we had this scene where we just thought, We'll have Walker go completely crazy at this point.

RW: I thought it was in, I'm very upset that it . . .

AC: No, it was this special scene where Yrena is trying to persuade him not to execute Corral and he just won't stop playing with these cats, these two stuffed cats in little tricornered hats with dueling swords and he's just going at it with the cats, clash, clash, clash. He won't listen to her. I talked to Ed about this and I said, "So you're going to do the thing with the cats, Ed?" And he'd say, "Yeah, I'll go for it."

RW: Why not? Why not?

AC: And he comes in to do the scene and he sees the cats there on the desk in front of him. And he says "God, I think we can do without the cats." He didn't feel genuinely that Uncle Billy Walker, as mad as he was, would have those cats! Because his insanity was always more—always more—grounded.

RW: But he sang "Silver Threads Among the Gold" in the middle of a battle.

AC: Oh yes, he sang "Silver Threads Among the Gold" without a question. I mean he did put in some very very funny stuff, always playing it very straight and always at the expense of Walker. Just making him—

RW: So fallible.

AC: So fallible and foolish and idiosyncratic, but always within that austere preacherly manner; never just doing something for the wackiness of it. Because that's really what the cats mean.

RW: Just like Uncle Sam—defending one's external appearance at all costs.

AC: But if Walker played with the cats, he wouldn't do it in public.

RW: No, he wouldn't, he would do it in the sanctity of his rooms, his inner sanctum.

AC: Or like the most improved player, Billy O'Leary, in the role of Walker's younger brother.

RW: Yeah, he really invented that part. It was an act of inspiration.

AC: Norvell is the interesting brother because Norvell's the dissolute, and James is, in the script, the dull, good kid . . .

RW: The wimpy young kid—the hero worshipper.

AC: . . . who is only there to die—and get some sympathy. And Billy just turns him into this frightening mirror image of his brother in every way. He even looks like Walker. Billy got sick and he lost about twenty pounds, thirty pounds of weight, and his face was so thin. He would say to Pam Tate, "Do you think I can have a suit of clothes just like William Walker's?" And she goes, "No problem." You know—only have seventeen other costumes to make for tomorrow—and he just created this character. He made James Walker the potential successor to Walker's empire, the guy who's going to take over and control it.

RW: He's going to continue the lineage.

AC: The dominators. Of course, none of it is really historical. We played fast and loose with history but—

RW: Well, in the big view it's historically true.

AC: The story is really—it's pretty faithful.

RW: The whole thing about making this kind of historical film with the anachronisms is sort of wonderful for me because it broke that old literal time convention and it would be hard for me to go back and make a purely historical film.

AC: Everything is different now. Let's talk about what you said about patriotism, about these Congressional hearings that are going on. You made a comment that they don't proceed from the basis that what went on in Nicaragua is criminally wrong.

RW: No, it's a defense of the patriotic gesture, defense of patriotism. It's a slap on the wrist for them, that's all. The boys exceeded their boundaries, they got a little bit carried away. And they have to be scolded and maybe one or two of them will be relieved of their jobs. But nothing's going to change.

AC: Because the idea is—

RW: It's very similar to Walker's day. When Walker made his transgressions in Nicaragua, he got a mere slap on the wrist. And tremendous publicity, great hero, the same as North and all.

AC: And it's very funny because I was reading about one of those guys, that scammed all this money off of the arms deal with Iran to finance the contras, and it was in the *Miami Herald,* and it said some call him a saint and a patriot; others call him a wily con man, and . . . how about raving asshole? Or fucking murderer? How about you know—

RW: Degenerate scum.

AC: Degenerate swine! I mean never mind the choice between con man and saint. How about Nazi or genocide artist? But it's so funny, it seems like going down and really, really fucking with people in foreign countries is what America is supposed to be doing.

RW: That's the old Manifest Destiny.

AC: Yeah, the cops of the world. Whose song is that about the Cops of the World?

RW: Whose is it?

AC: (*singing*) "We're the cops of the world, boys, we're the cops of the world. After we've murdered your sons, chum, have a stick of our gum." I—my friend Varnum used to sing that. Maybe he wrote it. . . .

Rudy, you said that we must never forget our sense of outrage. Because we've been sitting here talking about the Sandinistas and are they good government or bad government, do they commit human-rights abuses ever, and asking all those other questions that people ask you when you've been to Nicaragua. They say, "Well, is it true that such and such happens," and "Why did they close down that newspaper," and—

RW: It's not our business.

AC: It's not our business.

RW: And that's the whole point. We don't have the right to interpret Nicaragua for Nicaraguans. We don't have that right.

AC: Even about In Cine and what's right and what's wrong about their film policy—it's not our business.

RW: It's not our business with left governments, right governments, any governments, you know? And we must defend our right to be innocent that way. Our fight not to be sophisticated. We must defend our right not to join that language, to be innocent and to refuse that dialogue.

AC: The funny thing is, we're sitting here and we've been calmly talking for ninety minutes or so about all kinds of stuff including American foreign policy, and the fact is that we're coming from the wrong place because American foreign policy is outrageous. It's criminal genocide. It has been condemned in the world court.

RW: And it's not really a foreign policy.

AC: No—there is no policy at all.

RW: No, there is no policy. It's a national-security paranoia act.

AC: But it doesn't even make security. It just makes enemies and bereavements and tears apart families and murders children. Rapes women. It's like we came, we started this process, we started this film because we were angry . . .

RW: Right.

AC: . . . because we were angry about what the United States was doing in Latin America and we felt we had to find a voice.

RW: And I think that we were afraid to lose our anger. So we looked for a cause that would increase our anger rather than diminish it. Because in that anger, in the core, in the central part of anger is something that approaches the truth. Don't you think?

AC: Yeah, I do.

RW: So that we need that anger because we're all asleep, we're all completely asleep. Snoring in ignorance . . . and everyone that came down to work on this film, one way or the other, was sedated. And I think that when they left after the film was over they were a little less sedated.

AC: They were wakened a lot.

RW: They were wakened a lot. And just that act alone made it worth it. It made an event that sort of transcended the film in a way. For me, anyway.

AC: The whole process of coming down here and bringing media attention to the place, getting other journalists down here, getting movie journalists down here—

RW: And initiating a dialogue, we initiated a dialogue about a dilemma.

AC: Yeah, but we didn't do it in a "Well, yes, it might be interesting to get a dialogue going here" way. We did it because—

RW: We did it out of a sense of play—

AC: Because that's how we get paid to play. We came and played here, not in Acapulco, because we were pissed off. Because something was wrong. And also because I personally was challenged by these guys to come and do something, not just to be a fucking wishy-washy liberal.

RW: Right, say how that happened, Al. You were in this bar—

AC: I was in this bar in León. I was on one of those tours that you can go on, that you go to the collective farm and you go to the women's cooperative and stuff and we went to this bar and drank, because we were bored with seeing the good works. And I was down there with Peter McCarthy, who is a film producer from L.A., and we met these two guys who were soldiers who had been wounded in the war against the contras. One of them had lost an eye. One of them had been shot in the stomach. And they had been invalided out of the army and were waiting to go to medical school. That was their story. And we were asked "So what do you do?" "Oh, we're film producers from L.A." And these guys, one of them said "Well, why don't you come down here and make a film?" And we started making all these excuses like "Oh, well, it's very expensive to make a film"—treating these guys like they were simple or something.

You know: it's very expensive, mucho dollars needed to make a film, we're not rich men. And these guys, they looked at us like we were stupid.

RW: Like you were assholes.

AC: Like we were assholes because we were from the United States, land of money and, you know, if we couldn't get it together— two white guys—if we couldn't get it together to raise a few bucks and come down here and make a film, what good were we? We were just a pair of assholes.

RW: Yeah, with no money at all they made a whole revolution.

AC: Yeah! Because with no money they made a revolution. And they were pissed off. At our complacency.

RW: They were indignant.

AC: And the only way I could get off the hook after that was by coming down here and making a film because I was challenged by these guys to make a change. To stop being a guy that lived in L.A. and was going to make his next three films in L.A. and just come down here where it's more difficult, where it's not so easy, and make a film. But we must always proceed in thinking about Nicaragua and talking about it, not from this complacent sense that yes, well, there are human-rights abuses on one side and on the other, and the Sandinistas, yes, there are problems with the Sandinistas because, as you said, it's not our business. We're not Nicaraguans. I don't have a vote here.

RW: Right. Right. It's their dialogue and we're messing with their internal process. And we've crystalized their evolution. We're trying to stop it, we're trying to create a sense of stasis in the internal workings of their government.

AC: Yeah.

RW: And it's wrong. It's morally wrong. And it's indecent and it's dangerous because it's, it's not just Nicaragua—we start to do that and it spreads, it's like a cancer that spreads everywhere.

AC: Like "we know best."

RW: It's a terrifying arrogance. Really an ignorant unconscious arrogant gesture that's lethal, that kills people. And ultimately, it's going to kill us. It's not just that we're wiping out these other appendages to our culture.

AC: Because we lose our souls if we stand by and watch it happen, if we don't stay angry and stay on the case. At the end of this film, it's not enough to say—like a certain famous cinematographer said to me when he decided that he didn't want to shoot this movie: "I've already done my charity work this year," You *never* can do enough charity work, man. You've just got to go and do some more charity work. It might not be for Nicaragua. Because there's other stuff to be mad about as well, there's other stuff that's a big problem that needs dealing with, and the people that have a voice, like writers and filmmakers have a *duty* to speak out about what bugs them and what angers them.

RW: Where the itch is.

AC: *Yeah!* Because it *is* possible—as the Nicaraguans demonstrated —it is possible to affect major changes in even the most ossified and crystalized social structure, that you can shake it up and make some changes.

RW: Right. I don't think people, certainly not people in the States, realize what forty years of Somoza was like, they have no idea.

AC: They have no idea what it's like to live in a fascist country. Where a death squad might come and take you, where your children aren't safe at school.

RW: They have no idea what it's like to lose, to be invaded. The United States has never been invaded. Not one foreign soldier has set foot on United States soil.

AC: That's a very good point, and you should get that researcher, that Walker guy, to find out how many times Nicaragua has been invaded by the U.S. Marines.

RW: I think it's five, but I'm not sure. Very important point. And of course, initially, Vanderbilt invaded Nicaragua economically. There are all kinds of different levels of invasion.

AC: And your guy Morgan. Vanderbilt and Morgan knew where we were going, and down in Nicaragua, they made money off the *dead.*

RW: And that whole thing, that amazing thing about Somoza in the hospital selling the blood of the poor; totally undernourished Nicaraguans starving, coming to the hospital—the Casa de Vampires.

AC: Come to give a pint of blood—

RW: To sell their blood, that Somoza quadrupled the profit on to sell to the United States Blood Bank.

AC: Yeah, well, I'll tell you something else that I haven't really been able to spend too much time thinking about, but it's been in the Mexico City newspapers quite a lot, including the Mexico City *News,* which is an English-language paper. I don't know if its been in the American papers at all, but in various countries in Central America, specifically Honduras—also I think in El Salvador—there is a trade in the organs of living children—

RW: Of young, living children.

AC: They remove eyes and kidneys from living children and send them to the United States. For transplants. That's like something out of Dachau!

RW: That's a real transgression. That really profanes something completely essential, that's worse than the slave trade.

AC: It's like science fiction. That's unbelievably horrifying and that's going on now. There's a trade in the body parts of living infants, flowing into the United States. At the same time as they bitch about the Mexicans who want to come and pick grapes.

RW: And there's no information about that in the States.

AC: But for a while, I was in Mexico at a time when it was quite big news in all the Mexican papers, but yet with all our wonderful freedom of information, why isn't *Newsweek* interested in that? Why isn't *Time* interested in that?

RW: I don't know, because it would be an amazing headline. I would like to know why. Why do you think?

AC: Somebody says no—

RW: That's the way it happens?

AC: I do think so. I also think it's a mindset: the reporters, dull and turgid reporters. Being a journalist is a highly paid occupation now.

RW: You have to protect your job. You have something to lose.

AC: Whereas when a journalist was a really sleazy guy with a trench coat and no money at all . . .

RW: And a lot of anger.

AC: . . . a guy with a lot of anger, and he would stay on that like a terrier. But they leave all that stuff to Alexander Cockburn.

RW: That's right.

AC: And Marc Cooper, there are so few crusading radical angry journalists—

RW: And they're just published in these little magazines that only the people who already know what they're talking about already read.

AC: I know! I know! But you've just got to stay angry and keep fighting even though maybe you don't win. But you won't know if you win or not because the battle will continue after your demise.

RW: It's not anything so vulgar as actually winning or losing in that sense. It's a bigger thing. An engagement of your being in something more important than yourself. To not do it diminishes you in some way. Once you know that, you suffer your paralysis in a terrible way.

AC: Once you know it.

RW: And it's a hard responsibility, but it gives you far more than it takes from you. I mean, this Nicaraguan thing has given people so much more than anyone ever gave—they gave us so much more than we gave them, you know.

AC: Well, what *did* we do? We taught someone how to be a prop master or something like that.

RW: Yeah, we gave them nothing. They gave us so much.

AC: We are very fortunate to be blessed with this experience and this knowledge. Even though it's also a curse. Because once you are blessed with that knowledge, you can't really go back and work for John Landis.

RW: Turn a trick, it's hard to turn a trick—

AC: It's hard to go back to Hollywood and be a hooker now because its like we're working for a higher cause, working for a higher power than some.

RW: That's true, it's hard to work for the lowest common denominator.

AC:  And that's a funny thing because in Hollywood they think the lowest common denominator is the audience, but actually it's *them!* It's the hacks in Hollywood who are the LCD. Because the people aren't as stupid as they are. A lot of people went to see *Easy Rider* and *Midnight Cowboy.* They were very sophisticated and very popular films. And the reason that films as good as that aren't made anymore is not the fault of the movie-going public. It's the fault of the people who—

RW:  It's the corporate sensibility.

AC:  Yeah, the money.

RW:  It's the computer that makes the decisions.

AC:  There's a computer now that supposedly Paramount and De Laurentis and various others have that lists actors and who they appeal to. And like the best actor you can possibly have in a film is Arnold Schwarzenegger because he appeals to—

RW:  All the kids and across the board—

AC:  All the kids. Yeah.

RW:  And the computer, for sure, would never have allowed us to make this film.

AC:  Oh, God, Lord, no.

RW:  Would never have put you and me together to make this film.

AC:  Oh what a horrible combination, what a pointless combination.

RW:  Never, never work.

AC:  You know, cultist fans of road movies—all fifteen of them.

RW:  Yeah, yeah.

AC:  And the computer said Ed Harris is like an actor who appeals to—what?

RW:  To mature audiences.

AC:  Mature audiences! And cineastes, you know.

RW:  The kiss of death.

AC:  *(laughing)* So it would be marvelous, it would be marvelous if kids went to see this film. And dug it.

RW:  And shouted and screamed, yeah.

AC: Shout and scream and come out going, "Uncle Billy!" you know, and "Fuck you," and whatever they come out thinking, because the computer would blow a gasket.

RW: It would. It would be great to fuck the computer up just for a second.

AC: Just surprise that computer. But that's another story. Then the next battle is to make a film without a completion bond.

RW: That's right.

AC: But there are more important battles than that. I was stupid, really. I think I lost track of what was important at that time worrying about that. I should have made a nice phone call and smoothed it all over.

RW: No, I think it was more complicated than that. I think you needed that battle. Don't you? I mean, didn't you sort of need that war in a way? To propel you onwards?

AC: To understand Walker better. To understand why you turn against your benefactor and—

RW: You sort of needed that edge in a way, to convince yourself you were at war on some level? It was about anger. I mean, it was a way to give yourself permission to feel, to be angry and not to be too necessarily careful or considerate about who it was directed toward, which I think is good. I think that's important. Not to be too polite.

AC: Yeah, I'll tell you something this time, though. This might not be interesting for the book, but I think I was actually better behaved on this film than I've ever been.

RW: With the rank and file—you were quite well-mannered.

AC: Yeah, because I have a tendency when I'm upset with someone, and because they're a powerful person and they're not there and I can't vent my anger at them, I just get mad at somebody else, tell off some poor guy who doesn't really deserve to be shouted at.

RW: Right, right, right.

AC: And I think I didn't really do that, and so that was good for me in terms of learning to behave better.

RW: But the fight helped the film in a strange way. I don't think it hurt the film.

AC: It created a sense of controversy. Also threw down the gauntlet.

RW: You initiated a dichotomy of Us versus Them, you know, which was sort of good to feel.

AC: When all that stuff was happening and the bond was cancelled and it looked like the film was going to get shut down, it was funny to have to explain that to the actors on their way to work in the bus, that "Well, you know, I'm sorry you haven't been paid yet. It looks like you may never get paid now because, you know . . ." and that kind of stuff because it did create—

RW: A bond.

AC: It was like we were all—

RW: Another bond!

AC: Yeah a different bond.

RW: Did you have the feeling that they would have gone on even if they weren't paid? The actors?

AC: Yeah, most of them (laughing).

RW: They were too far gone.

AC: Most of them.

RW: They didn't know how to get out.

AC: I think maybe the stunt guys on principle would have gone home if they didn't get paid, but I may even do them a disservice.

RW: Yeah.

AC: It only takes a few guys to be so stupid as to stick around for no money. Like in the last week, there was a whole bunch of guys who were terminated because they weren't in the script. And I kinda said, well you know, if you were here. . . . So Eddy Pansullo and Louie Contraris came up to me—they're pretty strong-minded guys, you know—and they came up and said, "Well, Al, see ya, too bad we're not in the courtroom." Well I said, "If you were around, even though you wouldn't get paid—"

RW: "You could find your way in."

AC: And Eddy and Louie were sleeping in some little room in Granada that was the size of a postage stamp for a week.

RW: No fan or nothing. Like the black hole of Calcutta.

AC: And no money and no per diems. Just because they wanted to be in the film some more. They didn't want to leave until it was over. And that's not something that money can buy. You can never *buy* that kind of love. No matter how much money you have. You can never ever buy that kind of commitment or affection, because that's something that's like . . . it's respect.

RW: It's a spontaneous offering. It's not a preconceived or conceptual thing. It just happens. It's either there or it's not.

AC: And it did, because all those guys—Fred Neumann, Dick Rude, Joe Strummer, Ed Pansullo, David Chung, Louie Contreras—they all got terminated a week early and they all stayed. For nothing. For a hovel.

RW: For a hovel.

AC: For a hovel and some beans.

RW: In Nicaragua.

# THE WORLD
## AND
# WILLIAM WALKER

Albert Z. Carr

A great idea springs up in a man's soul; it agitates his whole being, transports him from the ignorant present and makes him feel the future in a moment. . . . Why should such a revelation be made to him . . . if not that he should carry it into practice?
—William Walker

# THE
# GALAHAD COMPLEX

In Nashville, Tennessee, where Walker was born and raised, every literate and prosperous home had in its bookcase, alongside the Bible, Webster's Dictionary, and Marshall's *Life of George Washington,* half a dozen books by Sir Walter Scott. "The Sir Walter disease," as Mark Twain called it, was then rampant throughout the South. In the 1830s and 1840s everyone read pirated editions of *The Lady of the Lake, Ivanhoe, Marmion, The Talisman, Quentin Durward,* and the rest. *Ivanhoe* especially, according to Mark Twain, set the South "in love with dreams and phantoms." But popularizations of Malory's Arthurian legends also had a great vogue, and the chastity and dedication of Galahad were as much admired as the strength and nobility of Ivanhoe. It was a period that gave to its favorite books a devotion approaching reverence, with the result that the dreams of a generation of Southerners were shaped by medieval romance.

The yearning for the ancient glories of chivalry was more than a literary passion. Almost certainly, young people of Walker's day and place turned to Scott and the *Morte d'Arthur* out of psychological need, as a response to social conditions then prevalent. Contrary to a popular impression, the puritanical austerity of life in most parts of the South was more extreme than in the North, and this was especially true of inland communities, such as Nashville, where the Protestant sects vied with each other in repressing the normal impulses of youth. Millions of youngsters like Walker had the virtues of male "purity" drilled into them by countless preachments from adolescence on, and were brought up believing that the sexual impulse, outside of the marriage bed, was the prompting of the devil. In this strict moral environment, anything that evoked the romantic mood was bound to reach deeply into the lives of the young. They wanted to idealize the relations between the sexes so as to be better able to resist the natural temptations of sensual pleasure and conform to the mores of the community. Many a Southern youth, compelled to remain virginal too long, filled his mind with all the high and impossible traditions of chivalry and learned to make a virtue of abstention.

## II

During Walker's childhood an ailing mother was his special care. In a memoir of the time, a friend of the Walkers' wrote, "I used often to go to see his mother and always found him entertaining her in some way." The chief form of sickroom entertainment was a reading from a favorite book. Many an afternoon, while his mother lay back on her pillows, Walker, reading in his soft Tennessee voice, must have evoked and been carried away by the mood of chivalry, in which any damsel in distress had a claim on the true knight, in which no honorable chevalier permitted a woman to be wronged if he could help her, in which one willingly gave up one's life for a friend, in which the feat of derring-do had the greater fame if the odds against one seemed hopeless. These were attitudes that stayed with him all his life.

During his heyday as a conquerer, when he was leading an army of hardened soldiers of fortune to whom the looting of conquered cities and the raping of women seemed altogether reasonable, he many times risked his popularity by imposing unheard-of standards of personal restraint on his men. "On entering a town," wrote the poet Joaquin Miller, who served under him in Nicaragua, "he as a rule issued a proclamation making death the penalty for insulting a woman, for theft, or for entering a church save as a Christian should." Drunkenness among soldiers on duty was more heavily punished than in the United States Army. When his own brother, Captain Norvell Walker, got drunk on the eve of a battle, Walker publicly reduced him to the ranks; and at the most desperate point of his military fortunes he was capable of warning his men that he intended "to see properly punished, socially as well as legally, the intemperance which is calculated to bring the army into contempt and disgrace." He himself did not need to drink. For him danger was wine enough; it made him glow.

His youth in Nashville was painfully good. In sophisticated New

Orleans, where the lively Creole tradition was strong, glossy young bloods kept mistresses, bedded slave girls, seduced coquettes, and slept with widows, but in the Walkers' circle in Nashville even talk of such libertinism was unthinkable. There were, of course, Nashville men who made concubines of their female slaves, but they were not likely to be found among the Disciples of Christ, the stern sect to which the family adhered. In such an environment the only chance for the sexual education of an adolescent boy was seduction by some bold and amorous girl, and what girl would bother with a lad who was short, slight, towheaded, freckle-faced, shy, bookish, and oversensitive?

Doubtless before he reached manhood he had some kind of sexual experience—he lived for a year as a medical student in Paris. But if his friends took him once to a brothel, he would have been repelled by the experience. There was nothing in his background to prepare him for frank nudity, bawdy talk, and casual sex. One can imagine him, after his first hopeless encounter with a laughing Parisian prostitute, flinging his cloak around him, stalking out into the night, and pacing the cobbled streets of the Left Bank, indignant, disturbed, unwilling to admit his frustration even to himself, determined more than ever to maintain his knightly ideals.

Then, in New Orleans, he met Ellen Galt Martin* and found the beauty, the virginity, and the affliction. She was a year younger than himself, twenty-three, desirable, intelligent—but a deaf-mute. The sight of beauty cut off from all the sounds of life must have called forth every protective impulse in Walker, made him wish to hold his shield before Ellen and by his personal force keep her safe from the hurtful world. He fell deeply in love.

The only extant picture of Ellen, a stylized painting, suggests a considerable charm: a high forehead, searching dark eyes, a heart-shaped, piquant face, firmly molded features, and a delicate sensuality of figure, so far as petticoats and pantalettes permit judgment. There is an alert look about her that accords with other testimony to the effect that she was exceptionally well-read and deeply interested in the questions of the day. After an attack of scarlet fever at the age of five had robbed her of both voice and hearing, her parents sent her to a school near Philadelphia which specialized in the teaching of handicapped children. On her return to New Orleans she

---

* Her name erroneously appears as Helen Martin in most of the Walker literature. New Orleans *Times-Picayune*, Sept. 26, 1937.

revealed a spirited quality of mind that enabled her to share in the social life of the Martins, who were a well-to-do and prominent family. Ellen, says a family account, "Used to go to balls and parties, carrying a tiny pad and pencil which she used to exchange lively repartee with many beaux."

In 1848, when Walker met her, her brothers had married and left home, and she was living with her widowed mother, Clarinda Glasgow Martin, in a large house fashionably situated. Among their aquaintance was a young lawyer and man about town, Edmund Randolph, who coming as he did of the noted Virginia family (his grandfather had been George Washington's Attorney General) had entrée everywhere; and Randolph, who had become Walker's closest friend, brought him to the Martins' home. The result might have been predicted. Ellen responded to his love. No doubt they could read each other's feelings in eyes and expressions, in shy embraces, but their frustration at their inability to communicate in speech must have been overwhelming. A book on the manual sign language for the deaf and dumb had been published not long before and Walker spent long hours practicing its spectral routines, until he could read Ellen's patient fingers and gesticulate his way letter by letter through brief replies. It was a courtship charged with tenderness, urgency, and intense concentration.

Randolph was able to give Mrs. Martin the necessary assurances as to Walker's background and respectabilty, but beyond this, Ellen would have learned from her mother the striking facts about him that all New Orleans knew: that before he was twenty he was a physician with a degree from the University of Pennsylvania Medical College; that for two years he had traveled in Europe, pursuing his studies in Paris, Edinburgh, and Heidelberg; that he had put aside medicine in order to study law in New Orleans, and had practiced briefly and brieflessly as Edmund Randolph's partner; and that he had just given up the law to become an editor of the city's youngest newspaper, the *Crescent*. But she needed answers to a thousand questions, too many to be conveyed by sign language. Many a night Walker must have sat at his desk and dashed off, with ink and quill, the long letters that she craved. The written word came naturally to him—he was always fluent on paper, laconic in speech.

# III

The stern spirit of Calvin and Knox was strong in the Walker home. The Disciples of Christ maintained that a primitive and stark simplicity of ownership and a literal adherence to the Bible was the only route to godliness. Religious conviction may account for the fact that James Walker would not own slaves. Too canny a businessman to let himself be called an abolitionist in a Southern community, he yet made it a point to employ as servants free Negroes to whom he paid wages—a practice not uncommon to the border states, where the example of Washington and Jefferson in freeing their slaves had not been ignored. The economic condition of the free Negro was generally little better and sometimes worse than that of the slave, but for Negroes freedom was nevertheless the only word of hope. William was brought up in a home with a nonconformist attitude toward slavery, and without firsthand experience of slave owning.

James Walker was not an unkind man, but he was a pietistic and austere father. The relationship between him and his eldest son evidently followed a classical pattern of authority and rebellion. In his early years, William was a difficult child and a reluctant schoolboy—avid for learning, but impatient of discipline. One guesses that the pride, the silence, and the tenacity that characterized him in later years were conditioned in him early by the bullying of larger boys—and most boys of his age were larger than he. From the very beginning his chief weapon in life must have been his fighting spirit. There is a certain type of small boy who is an insoluble problem to the lads of superior muscle who knock him down. They cannot make him stop coming at them; they can never have an easy moment until they make peace with him. Walker the man created the impression of having been such a boy.

His father similarly gave way before him. When he was twelve, and James Walker pressed him to study for the ministry, William successfully resisted. His stubbornness must have shocked the older Walker, while for William the triumph of this, his first rebellion, opened a whole new vista of possibilities in life. Later, when he determined to leave Nashville, he had his way again. Perhaps his father was glad to get the rebel out of the house.

William's first choice of a career was strongly influenced by his intense feeling for his mother. He was one of those boys who wish that they had been immaculately conceived. Mary Walker was a quiet woman, and during his school years William saw her stoically endure persistent pain which her physician was unable to diagnose or to ease. He was seized by a boy's dream of returning home as a master physician and effecting her cure; and the same dream may well have been the spur that thereafter speeded him through his schooling. Before he was ten he turned a psychological corner and became an exceptional student; he entered the University of Nashville at twelve and graduated at fourteen, *summa cum laude.* This was, of course, less prodigious a feat than it would have been at Harvard or Yale. Nevertheless, to qualify for admission at the University of Nashville, Walker had to be fluent in Latin through Caesar's *Commentaries* and Cicero's *Orations,* and in Greek through the New Testament; while the compulsory courses at the university included algebra, geometry, trigonometry, and calculus; surveying, navigation, and astronomy; chemistry, mineralogy, and geology; logic, experimental philosophy, and natural history; Greek and Latin classics, rhetoric and belles-lettres; history, political economy, international and constitutional law; composition, criticism, and oratory.

Religion was strongly stressed, with classes in theology and "moral training." Walker's class of twenty prayed twice every day in chapel, attended church on Sundays, and rose to hear a long benediction before every meal in the dining hall. But the puritanical spirit showed itself even more in that which was banned. The light indulgences known to college students elsewhere—balls, horseraces, cockfights, theaters—and such luxuries as dogs, horses, carriages, and servants—were strictly forbidden at Nashville. Even the study of music was permitted only as a special dispensation. It seems that Walker was allowed to practice fencing under a private master; the longing to handle a sword had been in him since childhood, and he had a wiry physique well suited to the art.

After his graduation, some months spent in reading medical books in the office of the family's physician, Dr. Thomas Jennings, confirmed his desire to pursue a career in medicine. He had no difficulty in entering the Medical College of the University of Pennsylvania, at Philadephia, and in 1843 he graduated with his degree in medicine. He was then nineteen years old—certainly one of the youngest qualified physicians in the country.

The subject of his doctoral essay was "The Iris," and there is some reason to believe that Walker at this period became interested in mesmerism. His extraordinary eyes, "which burned with a cold gray fire," and to which some later attributed hypnotic power, were

enough in themselves to attract him to a study of what was then
called "mesmeric phenomena." The possible pain-relieving power of
hypnosis was much debated among medical students, at a time when
no effective anesthetic for use in surgery was yet available.

Although a career was waiting for him in Nashville, he showed
no interest in pursuing it. His heart was set on further study, this
time in Europe. Edinburgh, the Mecca of aspiring American medi-
cos, seemed the obvious choice among foreign universities, and
James Walker's family was in Scotland, but William elected to go to
Paris. The faculty of the Sorbonne may have been of less importance
in his decision than the appeal of France for romantic spirits.


## I V


The disillusionment that led Walker to give up medicine began in
the hospitals of Paris. Medicine, no less than business and government, had become hopelessly reactionary. Of all Frenchmen, a wry
wit said, physicians shrugged best. Except in those hospitals which
served the wealthy, facilities were medieval, sanitation negligible,
and methods ruthless. Infant mortality was far higher than in London; epidemics of contagious disease within hospitals were frequent;
and human suffering under the surgeon's scalpel was beyond description. The conditions observed by Walker at nineteen made a
mockery of his Hippocratic ideals; and the mood of the city, for all
its surface gaiety, must have been equally trying for a young puritan
who did not patronize brothels, drink, or gamble. The chief values
of Paris for him lay in his exposure to French literature. Victor Hugo
became one of his idols. His political ideas especially leaped ahead.
But Parisian *politesse* also left its mark on him; his manners took on
a formality and a subtlety which many Americans considered "sis-
sified," and which, in his filibustering* days, startled those who,
meeting him for the first time, expected to find a roughhewn swash-
buckler.

After a long, rough, transatlantic crossing he returned to Nashville, where he was received with all the admiration that a widely
traveled young man with university degrees evoked in those days.
"The most accomplished surgeon that ever visited the city," he was
called. But there was bitter irony in his situation, for he found his

* "Filibuster"—from the Dutch *vrijbuiter*, freebooter.

mother not very far from death, wasted away, gray before her time, in pain most of her waking hours from "rheumatism" and "neuralgia"; and he could not pretend to know, any more than the family physician, how she should be treated.

The profession of medicine now seemed futile to him. He made a brief attempt to practice, but without zest. Although he never lost his interest in medical theory or his respect for dedicated physicians, he quickly realized that the dispensing of calomel, the administering of purges, and the obstetrics which filled the doctor's daily round were not for him. That he was tossing aside the fruit of years of study and a large financial investment, and bitterly disappointing his father, made no difference.

He was determined not to remain in Nashville. Of all the cities in the United States, New Orleans attracted him most, with its Creole glamor, its international flavor, and its metropolitan culture. Nowhere else in the South could there be found in one city theaters, opera, publishers, literary clubs, a variety of newspapers, and a famous cuisine. And it was easy to find a reason for going there. Having long since rejected the ministry, and having no inclination, or so it seemed, for military life, he was left with only one "gentlemanly" profession still open to him, the law. He would study law, and in New Orleans; the superiority of the Code Napoléon, as established in Louisiana, was a favorite conviction of romantic young Southerners.

His father's assistance, if it was forthcoming at all, was on a meager scale, for William as a law student in New Orleans had very little money. Two years of reading for the bar saw him qualified for practice. He was then twenty-three years old, and although hardly gregarious, had formed a wide and useful acquaintance. Edmund Randolph, a few years his senior, and who was Clerk of the United States Circuit Court, was closest to him. In type they were sharply different. Randolph was a cheerful blade, with a pretty quadroon mistress in a house on Rampart Street and a proper collection of gambling debts and bar bills. He evidently saw in Walker qualities needed to complement his own, for at his urging they opened a law office, as partners. But the firm did not prosper. Randolph was more interested in the pursuit of pleasure than in his practice, and although Walker was a fluent and effective speaker when he chose, he tended to be silent and enigmatic with strangers. His style could not have been inviting to potential clients; he dressed without regard to fashion, and made an unimpressive appearance. Standing only five feet, five inches, weighing less that 120 pounds, he seemed even younger than his years. If one did not observe his eyes, his face gave no special indication of latent force. A high unwrinkled brow under lank, light-brown hair; a long straight nose; a wide mouth, not unfriendly, but with a hint of the satirical in the quirked corners; an angular jaw—all this was familiar American physiognomy. Only the heavy-lidded eyes suggested the possibilities within him. Gray, brilliant, luminous, they seemed to penetrate the skulls of the men he talked to; they quickened the interest of friends, arrested strangers, and threw antagonists off balance.

It would not have taken him long to discover that practitioners in the courts of New Orleans had to have as thick a skin as did physicians in the hospitals of Paris. A tight cabal of politicians controlled the municipal government, rigged the elections, hand-picked the judges, packed the juries, ran the police force, had keys to the jails, and made mockery of the Code Napoléon. New Orleans' men of wealth came to terms with the political bosses in the usual financial way, but there was little justice and less mercy for the citizen without money who came up against the civic authority. As for serious municipal administration, it was conspicuous by its absence. No money was forthcoming for sanitary improvements, the draining of marshes, construction of sewers, repairs of the levees, paving of muddy streets, and the regular garbage collections needed to protect the city against recurrent epidemics. Gambling and vice flourished, however. Brothels, protected by the police, openly distributed handbills advertising their "virgins just in from the country" and "filles de joie trained in Paris."

Randolph, with his realistic outlook, was able to play the game, but Walker could no more accommodate himself to the chicanery of the city's courts than he could have patronized Madame Fifi's Select Cabaret. He had no real interest in the ordinary run of legal business. It was only the drama of the courtroom that attracted him.

The excuse that he needed to throw aside his new profession came early in 1848, when he was approached by two experienced newspapermen, A. H. Hayes and J. C. McClure, who had just resigned from the staff of the conservative New Orleans Delta. They were planning to publish a paper of their own, to be called the Crescent, and they were looking for a man to edit news from abroad and write on foreign affairs. Walker, with his European experience, his several languages, his classical education, and his medical and legal training, struck them as hopeful for their purpose. He could not have hesitated long before accepting. A newspaper would give him needed opportunity for self-expression, enemies to tilt against, and above all the chance to make his reputation. Time was moving fast. Educated young men in those days liked to quote Schiller's *Don Carlos*: "Twenty-four years old and still nothing accomplished for immortality!" Napoleon, Pitt, and Bolívar were not long dead, and their gigantic careers had already been in movement at twenty-four.

For an additional spur to his new enterprise, there was his need for Ellen. Marriage was their hope; but that would have to wait until Walker could offer a suitable home and reasonable prospects. It was essential for him to prove himself a man of substance, one to whom Mrs. Martin need have no fear of confiding her daughter. The offer from the *Crescent* came at a propitious time. Although his first pieces, signed with his initial, W, were contributed experimentally, he was soon a full-time member of the paper's small staff. By March 1848, he had given up his uncliented law office to become a journalist, with a small income but large aspirations.

# FAR TO THE LEFT

Eighteen-forty-eight was a great year for American newspapers. Sensation followed sensation. It seemed that year as if the entire human species felt a spontaneous urge to burst its bonds. The revolutionary furor first revealed itself in Paris, where in three days of street fighting republican insurgents toppled King Louis Philippe from his throne. From France the contagion spread swiftly eastward. The King of Prussia, his hair standing on end as he heard rumors of a new and frightening creed called Communism, felt compelled to grant a constitution to appease the grim crowds of Berlin. In Vienna, the Hapsburg emperor was saved only when Cossack cavalry sent by the Czar of Russia came to his aid; but even the feared Russians could not prevent Hungary, led by Kossuth, from achieving independence, or the Balkans from blazing in rebellion, while the entire north of Italy shook off the Austrian yoke. Spain held its breath as Spanish exiles from a bloody rule established bases in France from which to launch a civil war against the Bourbon monarchy. Starving men in Ireland vented their panic and grief in riots against the British government as they counted one fifth of all the Irish, a million and a half people, dead or emigrated in three years of potato blight and famine. Even in dispirited Asia men were challenging established authority. The anti-imperial rebellion called Taiping, or Great Peace, began to make itself felt in China. Hardly a month passed in India without action by British troops to punish states and tribes foolhardy enough to contest the might of Queen Victoria.

All this passionate turmoil would soon subside. France would return to Napoleonism, kings and dictators everywhere would continue to reign. But while the year ran its course, anything seemed possible. The managing editor of the New York *Herald,* Charles A.

Dana, reported from France, "I find that . . . socialism has gained
very greatly. A shrewd observer, who is not a socialist, remarked to
me the other day that the ultimate triumph of the new ideas was
certain. The future will show whether he was a true prophet."

Of the great powers of Europe one alone escaped the revolutionary tremor—England. A few daring spirits went so far as to advocate the abolition of child labor and the shortening of the factory
workweek from eighty to seventy-two hours, and workers assembled under the Chartist banner tried to demonstrate in the streets.
But the British as a whole, although they wept over the plight of
Oliver Twist and Little Nell, were at the same time so charmed and
stimulated by recent triumphs of British arms, diplomacy, and commerce that Monday's protests were drowned in Tuesday's cheers.
India was yielding undreamed-of riches. American rivalry in trade,
while energetic, was by no means alarming. The Atlantic stood between the Yankee factories and the European market; while the Cape
of Good Hope route to the Orient gave England a long advantage in
distance and time over American vessels compelled to go around
Cape Horn. Gold poured into London from all quarters, including
the United States, where British manufacturers had a huge market.
In so congenial a situation, the mood of England's governing class
was benign.

As for the United States, its people could hardly have cared less
about the fall of kings and the overturn of governments abroad—
except to agree, in general, that it served them right. Great events
close to home that year were exalting the American state of mind.
The surrender of the Mexican army under Santa Anna had enabled
President Polk's administration to wrest nearly half of Mexico's territory from her, on pretexts so thin that some leading Americans—
Daniel Webster and Henry Clay among them—were apologetic. But
many on the contrary berated the President as a "Slow-Polk" for his
failure to make all of Mexico forthwith a territory of the United
States. At any rate, what was done was done; and then came the
breathtaking news of vast deposits of gold in California, making
every American a millionaire in his dreams, and setting off a burst
of speculative enthusiasm on Wall Street. At the same time, American industrial genius was displaying its power on all sides. In
Chicago, Cyrus McCormick had begun to manufacture his revolutionary reaper. In Philadelphia, Richard Hoe's steam-powered rotary
press was turning out newspapers four times faster than had ever
been possible before. Samuel Morse's electric telegraph now ran the
length of the American coast from Boston to New Orleans.

Especially there were the railroads. With the aid of British capital, tracks were being laid from New England to the Mississippi,
from the Great Lakes to the Ohio. Asa Whitney that year appeared
before Congress to urge the building of a transcontinental line. President Polk made a treaty with the South American country of New
Granada (Colombia) for the construction of a railroad across the
Isthmus of Panama, to transport passengers between the Atlantic
and Pacific oceans. The steam locomotive was hope, it was wealth,
it was the future. Monied men were buying railroad stocks, and
every child aspired to be an engineer—except those who longed to
be captain of a China clipper or pilot of a Mississippi steamboat.

Such a year of good news, military, mineral, and industrial, the
American people had never before experienced. The country was on
the move, growing, surging, rushing. But as 1848 drew to its close,
beneath the shimmering surface of events was a current of deep
concern. Unemployment was high, wages were low, and crime was
mounting in the cities. Bitter old John C. Calhoun of South Carolina
was saying that the slavery question "must be brought to a final
decision," and that if the government attempted to prevent the
spread of slavery to the West the question of Southern adherence to
the Union might soon be vital. He went so far as privately to threaten
the President of the United States with immediate secession. Horace
Greeley in the New York *Tribune* ominously demanded, "Men and
Brethren, how shall this great question be decided?" Yet there were
men both North and South who still looked for gradual emancipation of slaves, to be achieved by nonviolent means.

## II

With so much excitement to be had for a penny, newspaper circulation soared and advertising revenue multiplied. All over the country papers sprang up, and educated young men turned to journalism
in increasing numbers as they recognized in the press a shortcut to
influence, fame, and wealth. In New York the *Herald* alone had a
circulation of almost 17,000 daily, and the *Tribune* not much less.
Never before had the press exerted so much power. Columns of
telegraphed news made it possible for the first time to shape the
opinions of the American people quickly on a national scale.

Of all the infant newspapers of the year none had a better beginning than the *Crescent*. New Orleans was the metropolis of the
South, the heart of the all-important cotton trade, the chief port for

southbound shipping, and the focal point for news from Mexico. The *Crescent* set out to offer its readers something more than they could find in the well-established *Picayune* or *Delta*—a broad and less specifically Southern view of the world. Here, for those able to read between the lines, was a daring hint of something less than enthusiasm for the institution of slavery. The *Crescent,* added a front-page editorial, "would discuss the great questions of State and National policy with impartiality and freedom"—or in other words, they would not necessarily support the prevailing Southern view of states' rights, among which the alleged right of secession was uppermost in men's minds. The generally lucid style of the *Crescent's* editorials stood in contrast to the murky and adjectival rhetoric then favored by many journalists in the South. Walker's contributions especially were distinguished by a certain intensity of feeling, indignation or enthusiasm. He respected facts—a trait instilled in him by his medical and legal training—but the main quality of his writing was its heat. At the same time, according to reporters who worked for him, he was a dependable and effective editor. One of them later described him as "very silent and very kind, with the look of a man bent upon a hard course of study, and a book always in his hand."

Almost from the first, the paper throve surprisingly, for its opinions were stimulating, its news coverage professional, its format creditable, and its writing superior. One of the *Crescent's* successful novelties was a first-page feature called "Sketches of the Sidewalks and Levees, with Glimpses into the New Orleans Bar (Rooms)." The author was a young journeyman printer—Walt Whitman—who had adventured to New Orleans from the North, and was entranced by the city. Although he earned his living in the *Crescent's* pressroom, the abundance in him flowed constantly into reportage. He saw the colorful life around him with a poet's fresh and loving eye—the sensual excitement of the streets, the gay cries of the street vendors, the strong Negro women in their blue dresses and bright turbans, the beautiful quadroon girls paraded and guarded by watchful mothers, the half-starved grisettes of the seamstress shops, the elegant French restaurants with their noble wines, the drunken squalor of the rivermen's bars, the cotton, slave, and horse markets in and around the grand Hotel St. Louis, the love of Napoleonic glory, the streets named after Bonaparte's victories. All this he caught with a lightly satirical pen.

Where Walker was preoccupied with large political issues, Whitman explored the troubled soul of the city, perceiving that its polite society of a few thousand people of means and education was merely a gloss over the broad, bawdy, and orgiastic life which teemed below. In no other large city in America—it was then third in rank after New York and Philadelphia, with a population, white and black, of 125,000—did the ordinary citizen spend so much time in the pursuit of pleasure, in the forms of women, cards, alcohol, prize fighting, cockfighting, and well-cooked food. Throughout its history, under Spanish, French, and American rule, New Orleans had always been a wide-open town. Perhaps its extreme sensual indulgence grew in part out of its acute sense of the chanciness of life. More than in most metropolises, to live in New Orleans was to live with peril—peril from Mississippi floods—peril from almost annual epidemics of cholera, the plague, and most dreaded of all, the yellow fever—peril from hooligans and thieves swarming in the dark streets at night—peril from brawling backwoodsmen and roistering boatmen on their drunken sprees—peril from venereal diseases that spread from scores of thriving brothels—economic peril from the violent movements of cotton and sugar prices—psychic peril from the corrupting effects of Negro slavery on the young of both races.

As for the 60,000 Negroes of the city, of whom all but a few were slaves, their characteristic broad placatory smiles meant only that they had learned to live with their terrors and resentments. The great torchlit slave dances held to the beating of drums in Congo Square, and watched by Whites as an entertainment—where glistening black bodies shuffled, swayed, and pranced—and where the rhythms of jazz are said to have had their origin in American culture—these provided not merely recreation but more important, a way for the young Negro to work off in uninhibited physical movement his week's accumulation of frustration and hostility. Even the seemingly gay little "Gombo" songs and sayings in French dialect that the Negroes made up almost daily, and sang in the streets, often had an undertone of bitterness and served as a kind of running social commentary. One was nothing more than a little musical sigh: "I don't die. I don't get well." The plight of the pretty quadroon girls was caught in a sardonic little song: "Ah, clever one, we know you— you're colored—there isn't any soap white enough to let you pass."

## III

It was the *Crescent's* loss and poetry's gain when Whitman's wanderlust, or it may have been the fact that he had drawn advances on his salary beyond hope of repayment, prompted him, in the summer of

1848, to make his farewells and catch a northbound riverboat. His departure left Walker as the only writer of outstanding ability on the newspaper. Almost certainly it was through his pen that the *Crescent* greeted the European revolutions.

As for national politics in the United States, the *Crescent* refused to be either Whig or Democratic. It pronounced itself "neither pleased nor grieved" on the election of that high military personage and intellectual nonentity, General Zachary Taylor, to the Presidency. But there was unmistakable heat and sincerity in its frequent outbursts of indignation at social injustice.

Walker unquestionably stood far to the Left, even among the advanced liberals of the time. The vein of compassion which revealed itself in his love for Ellen Martin carried also a strong flow of democratic principles. He began to wear a black, wide-brimmed Kossuth hat, named after the Hungarian revolutionary, who had become an idol of American democrats. It is perhaps a legitimate surmise that Ellen shared his dangerous idealism, and encouraged his bold thrusts in the *Crescent*. She must have been pleased when the newspaper one day risked the mockery of New Orleans' male population by advocating "the rights of women" to suffrage and property, and praised the example of a legislative measure which had then been introduced for these purposes in the French Chamber of Deputies. The *Crescent* even declared its willingness "to lay ourselves open to the accusation of radicalism, jacobinism, agrarianism and . . . other hard names." It jeered at "well-fed and well-clad propriety" for refusing to admit "that the poor man has rights which it is his duty to assert by all the means in his power—by reason or by force."

The *Crescent's* views on slavery were less overt than on other issues, for to exist in New Orleans it had to escape the deadly label of "abolitionist," but the knowledgeable reader could feel no doubt as to its stand.

On only one main issue of the day did the *Crescent* stand with prevailing Southern opinion. It believed that Cuba should be part of the United States. Said one editorial, early in 1848, "Cuba *must* be independent of Spain, and as an ultimate consequence, a member of our union." But as to the means of acquisition, the *Crescent* differed with the Southern view. Most leaders of the South were unwilling to entrust the island's future to any federal administration dominated by Northern politicians. Either Cuba would become a slave state, under Southern influence, or it was better left to its Spanish owners. The solution, as seen in New Orleans, was a Cuban revolution under leadership sympathetic to the Southern position. To foment such a revolution was a major objective of Southern expansionists, and a filibustering military expedition recruited in the South and financed by private gentlemen was their chosen means.

The *Crescent* would have none of this. As always where slavery was concerned, its position was against expansion. Ostensibly the *Crescent* based its stand on the need to maintain the integrity of the Neutrality Laws, established thirty years earlier, which forbade unauthorized American military intervention in the affairs of friendly nations. This argument could not, however, disguise from readers the newspaper's lack of enthusiasm for Negro slavery.

Late in 1848, word came that Congress was debating a measure to abolish the slave trade in the District of Columbia, and that the Southern members, led by Senator Calhoun, had threatened to walk out in a body and dissolve the Union if the bill were passed. Popular sentiment in New Orleans was strongly in their favor. Alone among the city's papers, the *Crescent* urged caution. "Being friends of peace and good order, and devotedly attached to our Union, we thought it our duty to say a word in behalf of its preservation." This was almost a slap in the face to those in the South, and they were many, who regarded the Mason-Dixon line as the northern boundary of their country, except perhaps on the Fourth of July and Washington's birthday. Angry editors of newspapers in South Carolina and Mississippi openly branded the *Crescent* "a Yankee paper," a reputation that it never thereafter was able to shake off.


# I V


The extent to which Walker influenced the total editorial policy of the *Crescent* must be conjectural, but to judge by the internal evidence of content and style, his individual mark was all over it. A series of studies of French philosophers, including Pascal, Montesquieu, and Chateaubriand is probably attributable to his influence. His advanced intellectual interests were a source of pride to the newspaper. When, in October 1848, he was invited to Nashville to deliver the commencement address at his university, choosing as his subject "The Unity of Art," the *Crescent* reported the event with satisfaction, and quoted from the Nashville press to make the point that "Mr. W. acquitted himself with great ability in composition and delivery."

This address,* reprinted by the University but long lost from sight, throws a revealing light on Walker at the age of twenty-four. "Were I called upon to state succinctly the object of University education," he begins, "I should say that it is the cultivation of art. . . ."

Of all the arts, it was heroic poetry that touched him most deeply. He saw Shakespeare and Milton as the poets of heroism, Byron as the hero of poetry. Byron's life he considered to have been lived artistically—"although he died young, yet was he old in fame and deeds." Life itself was an art form. It was only through the pursuit of the art of living that man, "half worm and half angel," could rise above the primeval. Man's artistic self found an outlet even in war—"the strongest and fiercest expression of patriotism" —and the artist in life must strive to achieve the "perfect and radiant countenance" of courage.

Walker's entire subsequent career may in some sense be regarded as an expression of these ideas. They gave the directional thrust to his life's trajectory. He had already begun to formulate the principles of heroic conduct by which he tried to live; from the ideal of Galahad to the ideal of Byron was a natural evolution for him. In his time, for a young man to strive for a life of Byronic grandeur was not considered absurd. The striving was its own justification.

Late in December, 1848, one of the *Crescent's* editors, and not improbably Walker, set himself to the composition of an article, such as newspapers have immemorially presented to their readers, appraising the significance of the year. "The year which has just completed its course . . . is crowded with events which will cause it to stand out in such bold relief that posterity will look back on it as the beginning of a new era." Europe was convulsed by revolutionary and democratic agitation. The United States stood as victor in war and proud possessor of vast new territories. Incalculable possibilities for the country had been opened up by the gold of California. The dream of riches was causing thousands of starry-eyed Americans to leave their homes and journey westward. In New Orleans the mood of excitement was caught in a local witticism: "Last year it was yellow fever, this year it's gold fever." The entire front page of the *Crescent* that New Year's Day was given over to descriptions of California and a map of the mining regions.

* Library of the Tennessee State Archives, Nashville.

But the editorial concluded on a sobering note. A severe epidemic of cholera had broken out in New Orleans. "In the midst of these golden dreams . . . the cup of happiness is dashed from our lips. The returning pestilence has invaded our land, carrying . . . misery to many a heart." Over a thousand deaths had already been reported. Many New Orleans families were fleeing northward. Walker must have worried deeply about Ellen and her mother, who remained in the city. "Thus ends the Old Year, and begins the New with the souls of men flamed with the desire for gain and the Asiatic plague recommencing its deadly and terrible march."

# "LET IT COME"

❦

It was while he edited the *Crescent* that Walker took the specific political position on which he based his subsequent career. Like the majority of Americans in his time, he believed ardently in the nation's "Manifest Destiny" to establish its institutions and its power throughout the Western Hemisphere. He felt, as did many of America's political leaders, that the best chance for preventing the nation from tearing itself apart over the slavery issue was to rally the people in a common cause, with a moral justification. That cause, that justification, as he saw it, lay in the Monroe Doctrine. In 1849, the country learned that England had been almost contemptuously flouting the Doctrine by its actions in Central America. The London *Times* openly boasted that almost half of the isthmus was in British hands.

The point of contention that arrested Walker lay in a broad strip of land along the Atlantic coast of Nicaragua, a territory known as Mosquitia, or Mosquito. Belatedly, the United States had awakened to its strategic importance. Europe, however, had long believed that Nicaragua was one of the main keys to the world empire of the future. More than a hundred years earlier, in 1740, a French scientist, La Condamine, had said as much before the Academy of Sciences in Paris and had proposed the construction of a canal in Nicaragua to connect the Atlantic and Pacific oceans. His paper came to the attention of the British Foreign Office; and while the French were still considering the matter, England sent warships to Nicaragua, then a possession of declining Spain, and hoisted her flag on the swampy east shore. The primitive Mosquito Indians offered no opposition. Always careful, the British then justified their action in diplomatic terms. A document was solemnly produced to show that in 1720 the "King" of the Mosquitos had voluntarily put his territory under the protection of the governor of Jamaica.

Spain protested; England shrugged; and so the matter stood for a century. But when the Central American states shook off Spanish rule, and under Bolívar's inspiration formed a Federation, Nicaragua felt emboldened to ask by what right the British governed in part of her territory. England's representatives in Central América decided that the old Jamaican authority would no longer serve. Accordingly they dressed a descendant of one of the former Mosquito kings in the uniform of a British major, formally crowned him King Robert Charles Frederick of the "Mosquito Shore and Nation," surrounded him with a court of "noble lords," and solemnly asserted his sovereign powers.

Here arose an unforeseen development; King Robert took his role seriously, and since he was fond of whisky and bright clothing, began to give away large tracts of his country to Yankee traders, in return for liquor and gay cotton prints. The British intervened, spirited the King away, and imprisoned him for the rest of his life, but not before he had signed (with an "x") a document appointing an Englishman as his regent, "in recognition of all the favors heaped upon him and his people by the English." Thereafter the country was ostensibly governed by a native Council of State, who provided a diplomatic screen for the British officers in the background.

All this was part of a larger British plan—to get rid of the Central American Federation, which, being democratic in tendency, was already under heavy pressure from the large Nicaraguan landholders of Spanish descent. Its destruction took some years, but in 1838 the Federation fell apart in a welter of civil war and confusion. This was the moment England had been awaiting. First she seized the east coast of Guatemala, known as Belize, and which she thereafter called British Honduras; next, she took possession of Cape Honduras, which lay just to the north of Mosquito; and finally she pushed the Mosquito protectorate southward. For it had now become clear that the best canal route across Nicaragua would utilize the San Juan River, close to the boundary of Costa Rica. A drowsy little town of grass-thatched huts, San Juan del Norte, lying at the mouth of the river, had taken on strategic importance. There, one day, appeared a party of armed Englishmen. Raising the Mosquito flag (which had a small Union Jack in its corner) they formally claimed San Juan in the name of the Mosquito King, and ordered the Nicaraguan customs officer of the port to leave. When he refused, he was forcibly taken off in a boat and abandoned miles away on an uninhabited shore. The Mosquito Kingdom was thereafter alleged to run to the southern limit of Nicaragua, and even beyond into Costa Rica. San Juan del Norte was renamed with the brisk English syllables of Greytown.

## II

England, with her eternal vigilance for weeds in her diplomatic garden, knew that the issue was far from dead. With the outbreak of the Mexican War in 1846, talk of a transisthmian canal mounted. Nicaragua protested that there had never been, and still was not, a Kingdom of Mosquito; and in a mood of recklessness, sent troops into Greytown, who took prisoner every Englishman they could find. The British reply was the arrival of a naval squadron on January 1, 1848, and the landing of a strong force of marines, who quickly recaptured Greytown, reasserted England's authority "in the name of Mosquito Indians," and marched inland toward Lake Nicaragua. This development shook the Nicaraguan government into hasty appeasement. A parley was held, a treaty was drafted, Nicaragua apologized and recognized the existence of Mosquito, if not British authority there.

James Buchanan was then Secretary of State, and his response to the British action was altogether in character. In a letter to the American minister to Nicaragua, he said, "The object of Great Britain in these seizures is . . . to obtain control of the route for a railroad and canal between the Atlantic and Pacific oceans," but he warned that "the government of the United States is not as yet determined what course it will take." During the ensuing year Washington made no progress toward a decision, and when the Taylor administration took office in 1849, the country's sense of frustration in the Greytown issue had grown into a major issue. Was England to be allowed to tear up the Monroe Doctrine? The question was asked repeatedly in the Senate, while many newspapers warned President Taylor that the nation would not tolerate supine timidity in the face of British aggression. Among them was the New Orleans *Crescent,* with Walker as editor of foreign news.

# III

Walker did not as yet know—only a few people in Washington then knew—just why the United States after so long had begun to challenge the presence of the British in Mosquito. The fact was that his life was becoming intertwined with great forces of which he was not even aware. The springboard from which he was to leap to fame was being secretly shaped and set by men occupied with vast affairs—peace or war, millions made or lost—in London, Washington, New York.

The central figure in the Nicaraguan situation was a man who in type, conditioning, outlook, and purpose stood so far apart from Walker that they might almost have belonged to different species. Cornelius Vanderbilt was tall, strong boned, physically powerful, loud and blunt of speech, domineering. In his middle fifties, although white-haired, he was still a man spectacularly virile, who had produced thirteen children, all of whom he bent ruthlessly to his will; whose wife, having once been confined by him in an institution for the insane, lived in mortal fear of his temper; and whose mistresses were open secrets in the gossip of New York City. But his ruling passion was money. He was the economic man personified—practical, realistic, impatient of theory and philosophical speculation, contemptuous of legalism and sometimes of the law—a man who believed that the one test of sound business was the size of the profit, and who regarded wealth and power as interchangeable terms. "What do I care about the Law?" he is quoted as saying. "Hain't I got the power?" Far more than Walker he was the true type of the freebooter, ferocious in attack, merciless in conquest.

In 1849, Vanderbilt had as yet acquired no more than five or six millions—in itself a reasonable success for the poor boy who at the age of sixteen had gone into business as a ferryman—to which he added steadily through the profitable operation of a large fleet of steamboats on the Hudson River and Long Island Sound. It was from this business that he took his favorite title, "Commodore."

One of his mortifications just then was that a former competitor on the Hudson River, a man of almost equal aggressiveness and sagacity, George Law, had stolen a march on him. Founding the United States Mail Steamship Company, Law had prevailed on the government in Washington to grant him a subsidy of $290,000, for which he agreed to provide steamships to carry California mail between New York and Panama. A similar grant had been made to a San Francisco ship owner, who was providing comparable service between Panama and San Francisco. What irked Vanderbilt, however, was not the governmental bounty these men received, so much as their luck. Their contracts with the government had scarcely been signed when California's golden news arrived. From that moment, with the gold fever raging on the east coast, the passenger service from New York to San Francisco became a bonanza. It was estimated that each trip of a Law steamship from New York to its Panama port netted a profit of over $100,000, and in 1849 the line made the run thirty times. Even the hardships of the overland crossing of Panama, by oxcart, mule, or foot, with ever-present danger of brigands, sunstroke, fever, and snakes, did not deter many "forty-niners" who knew that by this route they might be in California five months sooner than if they went overland. To add to Law's windfall, work had been begun on a railroad across Panama, in which he had an interest, and which would still further increase the popularity of his steamship line.

Hearing of Law's triumph with huge Atlantic steamships, while he himself owned nothing more than riverboats, Vanderbilt asked himself the inevitable question: how could he, a late-comer, overtake his rival? He began to study maps of Central America, and they disclosed to him a possibility that seized his imagination. Panama, obviously, was the narrowest part of the Central American isthmus, but did that make it the best point for transit? Why not instead use Nicaragua, which would take 500 miles off the route to California? Let the Panama Railroad be built; it would require six or seven years to complete the track over the mountains that ran down the center of the isthmus there. And the railroad would soon become obsolete, if there were a canal through Nicaragua which would enable passengers, freight, and mail to go from ocean to ocean without having to be disembarked. Although on the map Nicaragua at its narrowest point looked three times as wide as Panama, it actually seemed to offer the better route for a canal, for Lake Nicaragua permitted unimpeded ship travel for nearly half the distance, and use could be made of the San Juan River, which flowed from the lake to the Atlantic. Construction of a canal east of the lake, he estimated, would be comparatively easy, requiring few locks. Only in the strip between the lake and the Pacific would there be difficulties, and this was a mere eleven miles.

The plan took shape: he would form a company to build the

canal, and while it was in the building, he would create a line of
steamships from New York to Nicaragua, and another from Nicaragua to San Francisco, with an overland transit of passengers between; he would not only collect mail subsidies, but by offering
passengers the shortest route to California, he would scuttle George
Law's scheme and make millions.

## IV

Vanderbilt realized that before anything could be done, England
would have to be persuaded into cooperation. If she remained adamant, it might require nothing less than a war to bring her to reason.
Early in 1849, one of his associates went to Washington to explore
the matter with the new Taylor administration. Suddenly the capital
buzzed with talk of Mosquito, the sanctity of the Monroe Doctrine,
and the comparative strength of British and American arms.

It was a report of debate on Nicaragua in the United States Senate
that caught Walker's attention. "If the war must come," he wrote
enthusiastically in the *Crescent* "then let it come!" Gone now were
all pacifistic inclinations. "America will be found fighting where she
has always been morally—at the head of the column of Progress and
Democracy." He did not use the phrase "Alliance for Progress" but
something similar was in his mind.

# THE ANGRY MAN

◦◦◦◦◦◦◦

The death of Ellen Martin was a turning point in Walker's life.

A fever, followed by pneumonia—described by the attending physician as "congestion"—and all at once she was gone. The loss must have been the more shocking since by that time, April, 1849, the cholera epidemic had almost run its course, and she had appeared to be safe. Moreover he had just then begun to achieve the success which might have made their marriage possible. Only a few weeks earlier, his name had appeared on the *Crescent's* masthead as one of the publishers.

A Nicaraguan writer who investigated his years in New Orleans declares, "Walker, who held in his heart the love of two women only, his mother and Ellen, returned from the cemetery a spirit shattered; and sick with loneliness, threw to the winds all that he had. So ended the first phase of his life." This judgment has a somewhat operatic sound, but all the available evidence supports it. The extent to which he was shaken can be read between the lines of the *Crescent's* editorial page. For several weeks the characteristic Walker articles were missing from the paper, which in his absence almost ceased to comment on foreign affairs and the slavery issue. When he began to write again, his editorials sounded a new note of stridency and bitterness.

It was almost as if Walker was obsessed by a wild and joyless purpose to destroy the *Crescent's* circulation, and as if he had infected his associates with his rage. Gauntlets were thrown down right and left. A sharp attack on the municipal government for making no effort to arrest men known to have committed murder was followed by a sudden slashing indictment of the powerful *Picayune* and the *Delta,* because they had failed to condemn graft in the state

90

capital. When these formerly courageous rivals replied in kind, they evoked a snarl of outrage against "a petty clique, to whom the *Crescent* is an object of jealousy and hate." This was journalism in a very different tone from that of a year earlier. And the mood of anger alternated with Hugoesque and mystical flights of the pen, which heralded the emergence of the new Walker. "Unless a man believes that there is something great for him to do, he can do nothing great. Hence so many of the captains and reformers of the world have relied on fate and the stars. A great idea springs up in a man's soul; it agitates his whole being, transports him from the ignorant present and makes him feel the future in a moment. It is natural for a man so possessed to conceive that he is a special agent for working out into practice the thought that has been revealed to him. . . . Why should such a revelation be made to him, why should he be enabled to perceive what is hidden to others—if not that he should carry it into practice?"

What was the revelation? With Ellen gone, he had begun to dream of himself at the head of that "column of Progress and Democracy" of which he had written, riding in the name of America's Manifest Destiny, diverting the passions of the nation from civil commotion to the uplifting of peoples from whom the benefits of civilization were being withheld by European imperialists. He felt an evangelical mission in which the highest ideals of the America of his time were fused—the spreading of democracy—the enhancement of the national power—the uplifting of downtrodden peoples—the prevention of fratricidal war.

## II

For a controversial journalist, the South then held special hazards. Offended readers brandishing horsewhips were a recurrent spectacle in newspaper offices, and in spite of laws against duelling, challenges from rival editors were to be expected whenever they regarded themselves as insulted—a frequent phenomenon, since their thresholds of tolerance were low. Nevertheless, Walker had come through the year 1848 unscathed, unchallenged, and uncompromised in conviction. Perhaps the boyish look of him turned away wrath.

The change that came over him with Ellen's death expressed itself in a sudden urge to personal as well as journalistic violence. Soon afterward he fought a duel with an editor named Kennedy, the cause unknown. Neither man was wounded. The duelists, says the account, "met with pistols at twelve paces, exchanged shots, and retired, satisfied." There was also a contemporary story to the effect that an anonymous New Orleans journalist had challenged a man who insulted him to "a duel with the cholera"—that is, exposure to the disease by nursing its victims. This has the sound of a Walkerism. Later in the year, he is known to have administered a severe flogging to the editor of the Spanish newspaper, La Patria, for printed remarks that he considered offensive.

It was a stormy time for the Crescent. In the summer of 1849, the Cuban issue boiled to a crisis, when the Spanish consul in New Orleans was accused of complicity in the kidnapping of an American citizen. The abducted man was a Cuban revolutionary named Garcia-Rey, who had taken out naturalization papers. His story was that a ship's captain, one McConnel, had brought him against his will to Havana, where he was held incommunicado and subjected to beatings until diplomatic representations by American officials effected his release. On learning of the charge, the Spanish Government recalled its consul, but McConnel was arrested and brought to trial. For his defense he retained J. C. Larue, one of the Crescent's proprietors and a noted attorney.

Southern expansionist leaders promptly took up his case as their own. Here at last, so it seemed to them, was a "legitimate" reason for the immediate invasion and seizure of Cuba. Their philosophy was crisply summed up by General John A. Quitman, one of the ardent proponents of the plan. "Our destiny is intertwined with that of Cuba. If slave institutions perish there, they will perish here. Thus interested, we must act. Our government, already distracted with the slavery question, cannot or will not act. We must do it as individuals."

The time seemed especially right for the purpose, because a suitable man to lead an expedition against Cuba was then available. There had recently come to the United States a famous fighter for Cuban independence, General Narciso Lopez, a Venezuelan by birth, who had just met with Calhoun and had received secret encouragement from the fountainhead of Southern wisdom. A group of New Orleans extremists proposed to Lopez that he raise a small army in their city, transport it to Cuba, rally the Cubans to his revolutionary banner, drive out the Spanish governors, set up his own administration in Havana (retaining the institution of slavery), and then apply for the admission of the island to the American Union.

Recruitment was no problem. New Orleans was crowded with veterans returned from Mexico, restless, roving fire-eaters as ardent for adventure as their descendants would be for security a century later. For them, the conquest of the Caribbean appeared a natural and proper sequel to the Mexican campaign. Money was available. Although Lopez was careful to keep in the background, his agents printed bonds on the Cuban treasury, to be redeemed at par as soon as Cuba should become independent; these were offered at a few cents on the dollar, and were snapped up by speculators. Management of the enterprise was in the hands of the so-called Cuban junta, which, according to the New York *Sun,* included some of the South's most distinguished men.

The only problem was publicity, or rather, its avoidance. During the summer of 1849, shipping for the expedition was secretly assembled at an obscure island in the Gulf of Mexico, just off the delta. It was imperative that federal authorities in New Orleans remain unaware of the rendezvous, or at least look the other way, until Lopez and his troops were on the seas, and beyond the danger of interception by the United States Navy. Otherwise the Taylor administration would feel compelled to invoke the Neutrality Laws against the expedition.

The *Crescent* had thrown itself into the Rey case (as the newspapers called it) partly no doubt because of Larue's active role as lawyer for the defense, but also out of conviction. It reaffirmed its stand against violation of the Neutrality Laws, and by implication against the expansion of slavery. Long editorials appeared denying the right of American citizens to retaliate for the alleged kidnaping by intervening in Cuban affairs. But the paper was inviting more punishment than it could return. In opposing the Lopez scheme it stood alone among the journals of New Orleans. The owners of the *Delta* were intimately connected with the Cuban junta, and the *Picayune* was of the same persuasion. Theirs was the popular side, and they made the most of the advantage. Daily they blasted at the *Crescent,* until the sheer weight of their invective caused the city to respond, and the *Crescent's* circulation and advertising fell away.

Desperately, the *Crescent* fired its last remaining shot. In August 1849, it published an article which made it impossible for Washington to ignore any longer the fact of the Lopez expedition. Under the heading "The Mysterious Expedition and the Laws," it described "mysterious gatherings designed for the invasion of the island of Cuba," and gave the exact location of the ships and encampments. Under such prodding, the Federal Marshals in New Orleans, with whatever reluctance, were compelled to act in support of the Neutrality Laws. Washington was notified, and United States Navy gunboats were ordered to prevent the Lopez expedition from sailing.

The intervention of the Navy was a victory, but a Pyrrhic victory for the *Crescent*. Torrents of abuse poured on its editors from all sides. They had, it was said, betrayed the South; they had befriended the Yankee abolitionists. Against attacks so virulent and sustained, the paper was defenseless. Hayes, the chief owner, had no illusions as to the outcome. To stay in business would have meant the putting up of more money and probably the fighting of more duels. Late in 1849 he suspended publication, and subsequently sold the name and the presses.

# III

Now New Orleans no longer had any hold on Walker; he was loveless, jobless, and even friendless, for Edmund Randolph had succumbed to the spell of the Golden Fleece and had gone to California. In the autumn, Walker followed. All that is known of this passage in his life is that in June of 1850 he appeared in San Francisco, sunburned and weather-beaten, an unimpressive figure in dusty old clothes and a broad-brimmed black hat, and almost penniless.

# THE
# HIGHER DIPLOMACY

Late in 1849, Cornelius Vanderbilt initiated the enterprise for control of which, a few years later, he would contend with the President of Nicaragua, Walker. A company with a resounding name—the American Atlantic and Pacific Canal Company—was incorporated, and Vanderbilt was careful to include in its management a lawyer, Joseph L. White, who had intimate ties with the country's leading politicians. White journeyed to Washington, and wheels began to turn.

A new minister to Nicaragua, George Squier, was appointed, Secretary of State John M. Clayton gave him a letter of instructions, the nub of which lay in a single sentence: "We are willing to enter into a treaty stipulation with the government of Nicaragua, that both governments shall forever protect and defend the proprietors who may succeed in cutting the canal and opening the water communication between the two oceans for our commerce." The "proprietors" whom Clayton had in mind were Vanderbilt and his associates. Soon Squier wrote that "Vanderbilt and Company has made a proposition to the Nicaraguan government which, if I am correctly informed of its details, is most extravagant."

The "extravagant" offer consisted of a promise to pay $10,000 on signing of a suitable contract; $10,000 a year thereafter until completion of the canal; $200,000 of stock in the enterprise; and 20 per cent of the net profits of the canal. It was enough. The Nicaraguan Congress ratified a contract with Vanderbilt, and in the autumn of 1849, Squier was able to write to Clayton: "I have the satisfaction of informing the department that I have succeeded in accomplishing the objects of my mission to this republic. The commissioner of the 'American Atlantic and Pacific Canal Company' has concluded his contract."

## II

England's chief agent in Central America, Frederick Chatfield, had observed the activities of Squier and Vanderbilt's agents with misgivings. Letters from him to Lord Palmerston in London warned that the Yankees were seriously negotiating with Nicaragua for a canal route. The possibility was obvious that the United States, by invoking the Monroe Doctrine, might encourage Nicaragua to seize Greytown, to assure an Atlantic entry for the canal. Whether or not war resulted, England would be at a disadvantage; her claim to Greytown was undeniably weak, and the place was impossible to defend against assault from the interior.

Palmerston, who was known for his bold diplomacy, responded pugnaciously. England's first need, he decided, was to preempt the Pacific end of the proposed canal route. His eye was on an island known as Tigre, owned by Honduras. Occupying a dominant position in one of the world's great natural harbors, the Gulf of Fonseca, it could give England more obstructive power on the west coast of Central America than could any other single spot. What he wanted now was a diplomatic excuse to justify occupation of this island. The specialists of the Foreign Office obliged him. With just such a purpose in mind, they had been nursing an ancient claim against Honduras for alleged mistreatment of some of Her Majesty's subjects by Honduran officials. Orders went to Chatfield, and simultaneously the British admiralty was instructed to move strong squadrons of warships to both sides of the isthmus.*

Chatfield wasted no time. Hastening to Truxillo, the chief Atlantic port of Honduras, he demanded immediate settlement of England's claim. When the Hondurans denied the validity of the claim, Chatfield called their attention to the British battleships which were by then standing off Truxillo, with their guns trained on the town.

The American minister in Nicaragua, Squier, was a man of ability and resource. Sensing England's intention, he rushed to Truxillo with the draft of a treaty under which the United States offered to pay Honduras generously for Tigre Island and for permission to fortify certain mainland stations on the Gulf of Fonseca. As between the free-spending eagle and the threatening lion in these circum-

* R. W. Van Alystyne, "The Central American Policy of Lord Palmerston," *Hispanic-American Historical Review,* Vol. XVI, pp. 352–7.

stances there was little choice, and the Hondurans hastily signed the Squier treaty.

The frustration of the British was expressed by the naval squadron which, just before sailing from Truxillo harbor, fired a single indignant cannon ball at the town. Chatfield, however, had only begun to fight. Riding westward across Honduras, to the Pacific, he met with the admiral in command of the British fleet which was by then anchored in the Gulf of Fonseca, and authorized him to seize Tigre Island "for debt" in the name of the Crown, to hoist the British flag, and put down a garrison. This the admiral did on October 16, 1849.

The shadow of war was now dark over Central America, but still Squier did not hesitate to assume responsibility. A terse note went to Chatfield, stating that England had unlawfully taken possession of land belonging to the United States and must evacuate Tigre immediately. When Chatfield, with the diplomatic equivalent of a sneer, refused, Squier issued nothing less than an ultimatum, requiring the British to withdraw from Tigre within six days. Otherwise, he said, their occupation of the island would be regarded by the United States as an act of aggression, and dealt with accordingly. But the British stayed where they were, and with the Union Jack still flying over Tigre, Chatfield reported the situation to London, Squier to Washington.

This was the situation when Vanderbilt prodded Clayton to take a positive stand on the Nicaraguan question. Specifically the financier wanted to know what the British would say to his contract with Nicaragua. The problem confronting Clayton was thus two-pronged. On the one hand he wanted to prevent a war if he could. At the same time he felt the obligation to advance the cause of an American-controlled canal in Nicaragua. The best hope, as the Secretary saw it, lay in the time-honored diplomatic technique—a club in the right hand and a gift in the left. If England were plainly confronted with the danger of war, and at the same time were offered a chance to share in the Nicaragua canal, she might just possibly consent to a peaceful compromise.

### III

The United States government, on behalf of Vanderbilt, now sought to entice England with an offer of shares in a nonexistent canal, or to coerce her by the threat of war into giving up the strategic position.

Peace or war, then? England's trade with the Orient, vital to her prosperity, was already feeling the competition of the Yankee merchant marine. Let the Americans open a passage for cargo through the Central American isthmus and they would gain a significant advantage of distance and time in reaching the profitable markets of China, Southeast Asia, and the East Indies. The British government would not tolerate the building of a Nicaraguan canal unless England herself could control the route. It was for this reason, more than any other, that the British had held so tenaciously to the swamps of Mosquito for over a century. To share such a canal with others would be to give away one of the chief assets of the Empire, the strategic scheme of trade routes dominated by English guns. The Cape of Good Hope was British; so were the Falkland Islands that lay on the route to Cape Horn; and if there was to be another way for ships to Asia, it would have to be under the flag of England.

In Palmerston's view, Vanderbilt's proposal that England share in ownership of his canal company was naïve. Did the Yankee actually expect to get the benefit of British capital for a project which, in the final test, was bound to be more beneficial to the United States than to any other country?

It was only the Nicaraguan route across the isthmus that concerned Palmerston. The possibility that the United States would seek to dig its canal in Panama struck him as remote. Surveys made for the Royal Geographic Society left no doubt that, with the construction techniques then in use, the Cordilleran range in Panama presented insuperable obstacles to a canal; and he himself had flatly said as much to Parliament. As he saw the situation, Nicaragua was worth a war.

Not that Palmerston wanted war. On the contrary, he was only too aware of its perils. The United States was now a far more formidable nation than it had been in 1812. Moreover, some of England's largest financial houses, notably the Rothschilds and the Barings, had large and profitable investments in American railroads, and were eager to see the peace preserved. There was much to be said for finding a peaceful solution of the Central American problem. If diplomacy could serve to avoid war while keeping Greytown and Tigre under England's control, let the diplomats by all means have their chance.

What if England were to strike a conciliatory pose, perhaps sending a new minister plenipotentiary to Washington specifically for the purpose of negotiating with Clayton—and without giving up anything, yet keep the peace? It would be a master stroke, and it would take a master of diplomacy to bring it off. And Palmerston knew the very man to whom such a mission might be entrusted.

## I V

On December 24, 1849, Sir Henry Lytton Bulwer, in full dress uniform, presented his credentials as Envoy Extraordinary and Ambassador Plenipotentiary to President Taylor—a glittering Christmas present from Great Britain to the United States. Almost at once Secretary Clayton and the ambassador went to work on the draft of a treaty covering the problem of the Central American canal, setting the stage on which Walker was triumphantly to leap five years later. Every advantage in the contest went to Bulwer. Clayton's disadvantage was inherent in the situation, in the fact that he was emotionally involved with the Nicaraguan canal project. His interest was more than political, more than a matter of commitment to Vanderbilt and White. The canal had long been a favorite dream. To go down in history as the man who made the canal possible was his ambition. He was eager—always a defect in diplomacy.

Six weeks later a draft of the treaty was complete. Its essence was the agreement of the two powers that neither would seek exclusive control of any canal built through Nicaragua, and a declaration that neither would "assume or exercise dominion" over any part of Central America. As Bulwer saw the issue, it hinged on the meaning of the word "dominion." The treaty, he wrote, with his tongue unmistakably in his cheek, left England "protecting" Mosquito, "but forbade the protection to be used for the purposes of dominion." Where did the one end and the other begin? On this matter of definition, the treaty was silent. What then had Britain conceded? Nothing.

The United States, however, had conceded a good deal. At one point in their negotiation, Clayton conveyed to Bulwer that it would be comparatively easy to bring all Central America into the American Union.

Bulwer was well aware that, as matters then stood, the North was unwilling to let the Central American republics, any more than Cuba, join the United States under the domination of the South, while Southerners wanted them on no other terms. It was also ob-

vious that Clayton wished to avoid a war for the isthmus, such as
would almost certainly result if the United States were to force the
issue at once. Immediate annexation was therefore out of the question. On the other hand, if the Americans bided their time until
England became involved in difficulties with Russia, they might well
be able to establish hegemony over the isthmus without war; and in
such an inviting situation, North and South might work out an
accommodation in the matter. Unquestionably, Clayton's threat had
some basis in reality; so that, in agreeing not to seek dominion in
Central America, the United States was yielding up a useful counter
in the game.

Even better, from England's standpoint, was the treaty's provi-
sion that the United States could not proceed with a Nicaraguan
canal without British assent and participation. Bulwer did, however,
make a friendly gesture in the direction of Vanderbilt. The compromise was a clause giving a "priority of claim" to any company that
already had a contract for the construction of the canal, and that had
"made preparations and expended time, money and trouble on the
faith of such contract." The name of the "gentleman of great weight"
never appeared in the correspondence.

Bulwer had fulfilled his mission. He had negotiated a treaty
which, while committing the United States, left England uncommit-
ted; and so he told Clayton graciously that "Her Majesty's Government would freely undertake to obtain the consent of Mosquito" for
the canal. By March 1850, both sides were ready to proceed with
ratification.

V

As soon as Clayton showed the draft approved by Bulwer and himself to members of the Senate Foreign Relations Committee, he was
sharply challenged. Was England, said the senators, to retain Mosquito? If so, ratification by the Senate was unthinkable. Knowing
that England could not be persuaded to abandon her protectorate in
Mosquito, Clayton was in a quandary. At last, however, a possible
way out occurred to him. When he next saw Bulwer, he had with
him the draft of a new clause to the effect that neither nation would
"make use of protectorates or alliances for the purposes of . . . occupying, fortifying or colonizing . . . any part of Central America."
Clayton reasoned that if England agreed to this clause, she would be

virtually abjuring the use of force in Central America; and if she abjured the use of force, was that not for practical purposes equivalent to eventual withdrawal from Central America? And would not the Senate be willing on these grounds to ratify the treaty?

Bulwer, of course, understood perfectly well what was in the Secretary's mind. Reading the proposed clause, it struck him as having little practical significance in the light of other sections of the treaty. The loopholes in the document as drafted were large enough to permit a British fleet to pass through them if necessary—and if the new clause would serve to assure ratification of the treaty, he would not reject it. But neither was he willing to accept it out of hand. His agreement had to be made to look like the large concession that Clayton wanted to report to the Senate. Assuming an air of injured innocence, the ambassador gently reproved Clayton for inconstancy. But when the Secretary, in considerable distress of mind, threatened to jettison the treaty, Bulwer appeared to capitulate. "It is no use our trying to get around each other," he wrote to Clayton, "and it is in neither of our characters. . . . I now agree to all you have asked."

Clayton was elated. Popular opinion, as reflected in the press, was sharply divided. Some papers praised the treaty as a masterpiece of high-minded statesmanship, by means of which war with Britain had been averted. Others saw it as a repudiation of the Monroe Doctrine. The New York *Herald* went so far as to assail Clayton as "weak" and "ignorant," and alleged openly that the treaty had been "concocted" by Joseph White for the Vanderbilt interests. The senators, responding perhaps less to the Secretary's eloquence than to Joseph White's lobbying, rushed the treaty to a vote, and ratified it.

This was the moment for Bulwer to play the winning trump concealed in his hand. It took the form of a short note simply stating that he did not "understand the engagements of the convention to apply to Her Majesty's settlement at Honduras or its dependencies." As Clayton read, the icy touch of reality must have shocked him. The treaty did indeed say that the British would not occupy, fortify, or colonize any part of Central America. But what was Central America? It was merely a loose geographic term, like the Orient, or the Levant. Did it comprise all of the isthmus or only the five independent republics? Nowhere in the treaty was it defined. Not that Clayton had ever seriously hoped to bring British Honduras, a long-established Crown colony, under the restrictions of the treaty. If England chose to regard this possession as distinct from "Central

America," the United States could hardly object. But the real menace of Bulwer's note came in the word "dependencies." Why was it now for the first time introduced into the dialogue? Here was a distinct implication that England had decided to make her other Central American holdings dependencies of British Honduras, and in this way remove them also from "Central America" and free them from the restrictions of the treaty. If Mosquito were to become such a dependency it could be occupied and fortified as England chose, without technical violation of the treaty. Moreover, since the boundaries of Mosquito were largely undefined, as were, indeed, those of the five republics, there would be nothing to prevent "the King of the Mosquitos" from claiming still more Central American territory as part of his ancestral lands, as had been done in the past.

Clayton could envisage the storm that would be stirred up in Congress and the press if the suspicion arose that the treaty had accomplished no more than this. The resulting anger and ridicule might prevent the promulgation of the treaty, destroy the prestige of the administration, put an end to all hope for the canal, injure the investors who had bought stock in Vanderbilt's new companies, and conceivably lead to war. On the other hand, the Secretary could not afford to ignore Bulwer's note. An evasive tactic was his only solution. Writing to the Chairman of the Senate Foreign Relations Committee, he asked for that gentleman's personal concurrence in the view that the treaty was not intended to apply to British Honduras; but he carefully omitted any mention of "dependencies." In this way he succeeded in extracting from the innocent senator agreement that "the Senate perfectly understood that the treaty did not include British Honduras."

Clayton had in effect agreed to an amendment of the treaty without consulting the Senate. His painful awareness of his predicament found expression in a memorandum that he wrote and secretly deposited in the vault of the Department of State, together with Bulwer's decisive letter. "The written declaration from Sir Henry Lytton Bulwer was received by me . . . I wrote him . . . carefully declining to affirm or deny the British title [to their Central American possessions]. The consent of the Senate to the declaration was not required and the treaty was ratified as it stood."

The British view of the transaction was as clear and unambiguous as that of the Americans was hazy and obscure. The London *Times* called it "a contest in the use of terms," and had no doubt as to the victor. As soon as the signed treaty was in Palmerston's hands, he ordered a warship to Greytown, where marines were landed to perform yet another flag-raising ceremony, and to reassert once more the authority of "the Mosquito King." It was as well to remind all concerned that England had given up nothing.

In this way, "the convention between the United States of America and Her British Majesty for facilitating and protecting the construction of a ship canal between the Atlantic and Pacific oceans" became law. Its immediate effect was to prevent America from asserting her power at a point of high strategic importance to her interests. The nation now had no way in which to control the situation in Nicaragua except by privately organized military expeditions. The moment that the treaty was signed, Walker's spectacular adventure became possible.

# THE MAN
# OF PRINCIPLE

❦

**W**alker's first action on arriving in San Francisco was to seek out his old friend Edmund Randolph, who had by that time put down roots in the community; and through him he met John Nugent, the proprietor and editor of the youngest of the city's dozen newspapers, the *Herald.* Nugent gladly put him to work. The little paper was thriving, for every San Franciscan was avid for news. Like its bouncing competitors, the *Herald* charged twelve cents per copy, filled much more than half of its four pages with advertising, and published a "steamer edition," at one dollar per copy, for passengers on outgoing ships. Its chief problem was the shortage of newsprint, which had to be imported from the east, and which cost twenty times its price in New York. San Francisco's publishers had to accept what supplies they could get, however cheap, coarse, or discolored, and when ships failed to arrive on time, desperate printers would turn out editions on grey paper used to wrap Chinese tea, or on legal foolscap.

The *Herald*'s deficiencies of appearance, however, were more than offset by its vitality. It had a definite and usually liberal opinion about everything. It was for free trade and right of divorce in unhappy marriages. It strongly opposed the introduction of slavery into California. It believed that the slavery issue in the Union as a whole could be settled without secession and civil war if extremists on both sides could be held in check. It resented the American ambassador to England who, in an address in London, boasted that "We Americans are of the Anglo-Saxon race, reared in the Protestant faith." The *Herald* exploded into satire. "Wonderful! What geniuses we must be! Only think of it—to be of the Anglo-Saxon race!" What of the Celts and the French? What of the Catholics and the Jews? Were they not also Americans?

Two months after the Clayton-Bulwer treaty was signed, news of it reached San Francisco and was published in the *Herald,* as in other newspapers. Taken at face value, it seemed a hopeful development, and editorial comment was favorable. But international diplomacy meant little to the San Franciscans of 1850. The great topic of the day was crime in their own midst. Wars and treaties were nothing by comparison. Even gold strikes had become secondary. Gangs of robbers and murderers, many of them from Australia's convict colonies, nightly roamed the city and made it a hell for the law-abiding. No respectable man, whatever arms he carried, could safely walk the street after dark. There was no room in the newspapers to deal with more than a few of the sensational murders, assaults, and burglaries that were committed every day. Most of the city's bars and taverns provided women as a sideline and, thus baited with liquor and lechery, served as traps for the unwary. As the Herald reported: "These ruffian resorts are the hot beds of drunkenness and the scenes of unnumbered crimes. Unsuspecting sailors and miners . . . are filled with liquor—drugged if necessary—until . . . they fall an easy victim . . . Many robberies are committed which are not brought to light through shame on the part of the victim."

It could not be said that law enforcement had broken down, for it had never got started. In a few months of 1850 over one hundred murders were committed, without the execution of a single criminal. Worse: three times that year the city was devastated by fires which, it was shown, were deliberately started by the pestilential gang known as the Sydney Ducks to provide a rogues' festival of robbery and rape. The city was close to anarchy.

Shortly after Walker's arrival, the *Herald* began an anticrime crusade which made it a storm center, and which, as events showed, was largely his work. With his experience of the New Orleans courts, he quickly perceived that the essence of the terrifying situation lay in the alliance of the gangs with the crooked politicians who dominated the city, and who had the police and the judges under their venal thumbs. Nugent gave him a free rein. The first blast of the *Herald* was against the California Supreme Court, which from its seat in Sacramento set the tone of the entire judiciary of the state. "The Supreme Court," said an editorial, "has rendered itself ridiculous," by "flagrant stupidity," and by its toleration of "unprincipled and disreputable hangers-on" and "corrupt practitioners and pettifoggers." To this unexpected attack, the first of its kind to appear in the San Francisco press, the justices of the Supreme Court felt impelled to reply. Using the Sacramento City Council as their mouthpiece, they issued a strong diatribe against the *Herald,* as subversive of justice. Walker was now in his element. Happily he delivered an even harder thrust. On Christmas, 1850, he published an item headed "Personal," to express his feelings about the Sacramento Council. It began on a lofty note: "If an editor were to turn from his course to notice the abuse mouthed by corrupt officials . . . he would indeed be stooping". . . . However, to leave no uncertainty as to his opinions, he added that the Council was "a collection of knaves and blackguards."

For some weeks thereafter, under the heading of "Law Intelligence," the *Herald* published detailed accounts of miscarriages of justice in the courts, and seldom missed an opportunity to upbraid the authorities for failure to act against the criminals of the city. It had plenty of ammunition. The police force was an absurdity. Constables openly consorted with criminals. There was not even a jail in San Francisco. Even if the perpetrator of a crime was identified and brought to court he ran no risk. A little money or the right connection would always uncover a legal technicality to assure dismissal of his case. Or the jury would be packed with friends of the man on trial. Crime had become a way of life for hundreds of dangerous men and women, while the courts looked the other way.

It was a ringing editorial in the *Herald,* "A Way to Stop Crime," that first publicly advocated a vigilante movement, although the word was not yet used. "A band of two or three hundred 'regulators,' composed of such men as have a stake in the town" was needed, said the *Herald,* "to drive the criminals from the city," if necessary with "a few examples of Lynch Law." Twice that week the advice was repeated, with full recognition of its dangers, and a somber warning: "Terrible is the retribution which our citizens will visit on the unworthy public servants who have reduced them to the necessity of defending themselves" against the criminal elements.

Other newspapers took up the idea of a vigilante corps, until alarm at the prospect impelled the ruling politicians to make some gesture to public opinion. At the request of the district attorney, a Grand Jury of respectable citizens was impaneled to try to cope with the flood of crime. Taking itself seriously, it quickly found indictments against a number of known criminals, only to call forth a reprimand from the bench. The Chief Judge of the District Court, Levi Parsons, informed the Grand Jury that it could not indict except on evidence warranting conviction by a petit jury—which meant, for practical purposes, that it could not indict.

It was Parsons' misfortune that this instruction, which might have passed almost unnoticed in the scurry and cynicism of San Francisco life, fell under Walker's legally trained eye. Next day the *Herald* printed a little paragraph, signed "One of the People," and which said, "Whether his Honor, Judge Parsons, in this instance has laid down for the guidance of the Grand Jury, an incorrect rule of law, through haste, inadvertence or misapprehension it is immaterial to inquire." The fact remained, by every precedent of law a Grand Jury need not wait to indict until it had accumulated all the evidence required to convict in an ordinary court.

Judge Parsons, known for his pomposity, replied by an ill-advised blast from the bench. The *Herald,* he said, was a public nuisance and should be prosecuted as such by the county authorities. He then appeared personally before the Grand Jury and urged the indictment of the *Herald* for contempt of court; but the jurors refused to act. Walker seized the opening. In a biting editorial, "The Press A Nuisance," he said plainly that "the District Court instructs the Grand Jury to aid the escape of criminals. . . . No wonder that after laying down the law favorably to criminals the District Judge should declare against the Press." This, Walker concluded, was "judicial madness." As for the charge of contempt, "The courts cannot be reduced much lower than they have reduced themselves. If we were the Guardian Angel of the District Judge we would whisper in his ear, Beware!"

A group of lawyers who were friendly to Parsons promptly held a meeting at which the *Herald* was denounced on the ground that in attacking the Judge it had attacked the courts and the process of justice. Some even called for the paper's suppression. Thus fortified, as he thought, Parsons took direct action. It was common gossip in the city that the attacks on him had come from Walker's pen, and the Judge issued a warrant for his arrest on a charge of contempt of court.

## II

Walker's appearance before the court was reported in great detail by the San Francisco press. The courtroom was crowded with partisans both of the Judge and the accused. Edmund Randolph, already regarded as a leading light of the San Francisco bar, spoke for the defense. Handsome, impressive, combining aristocratic hauteur with a touch of fire, he had the further advantage of being known as an excellent shot—a significant asset in the profession of law in the San Francisco of the 1850s. He began by requesting that the charge against Walker be put into writing. Parsons said, "The objection is overruled," and so continuous were his interruptions thereafter that Randolph was unable to complete a sentence.

Finally he made himself heard, shouting that the Judge stood in violation of the Bill of Rights of the California Constitution. "You are liable to impeachment by the Legislature for your official conduct. . . . The proceeding is monstrous!"

"Mr. Randolph!" yelled the Judge. "The Court cannot sit here to hear itself abused and its proceedings characterized as monstrous!"

Randolph retorted, "I will then call your conduct monstrously illegal, monstrously unjust—" An uproar arose among the spectators, while Parsons, purple in the face, said that he could not tolerate Randolph's "exceedingly disrespectful" language.

"I regret," said Randolph icily, "that the circumstances of the case will not allow me to make an apology."

This was a word full of menace, for it brought the thought of a duel to every mind. Hastily Parsons said, "We do not ask for an apology."

The defense was then permitted to state its case—which was simply that Walker did not stand in contempt of court. If the judge had a proper charge against him, it was libel, not contempt. "I admit that it [the controversial editorial] is a libel; there is pungency in it; and if the statements contained therein are true, the conclusion is inevitable that Levi Parsons is a corrupt man, a dishonest judge." The court rocked at this blast. A fist fight broke out among the spectators. Perceiving the danger of a riot, Parsons sought to terminate the hearing by demanding that Walker admit authorship of the editorial. The room quieted. "Yes," said Walker, "I wrote and published that article to promote—*and not obstruct*—public justice."

Parsons instantly replied, "Then I find you guilty as charged! The fine is five hundred dollars."

"I shall not pay it," Walker said quietly.

"Sheriff!" ordered the Judge. "This man is to be held in close confinement until the fine is paid."

The extraordinary excitement generated by the case reflected the public's awareness that for the first time the scandal of judicial corruption had been brought into the open. Walker had hardly been taken to a cell next to the Sheriff's office and locked up when placards began to appear all over the city: "Justice! Public Meeting! . . .

to express opinions in regard to the decision of the Judge of the District Court." That day 4,000 men gathered on the plaza before the court house and held a mass meeting remarkable for its gravity and decorum. Edmund Randolph was the chief speaker. A great point of law was at stake, he said—the rights of Californians under the Constitution. Let there be no violence. "Mr. Walker has asked me to speak to you of the importance of avoiding violence. He said to me that he will not let himself be set free by violence."

Some of his listeners were disappointed. There were shouts: "Let's bring the Judge out here!" "Parsons resign!" "Set Walker free!" But Randolph maintained his calm and kept the crowd in check. A resolution condemning Parsons' action as "an unwarrantable exercise of power and violation of law" was formally proposed and carried in a voice vote. This resolution, it was agreed, would be delivered in writing to Parsons by a Committee of Ten. Meanwhile, Randolph would apply to the Superior Court of the city for a writ of *habeas corpus*.

For the following week, while the *habeas corpus* proceeding was being argued, most of the San Francisco newspapers allotted whole columns daily to the affair. The case was seen as a major test of the common law, as a defense of the public against judicial tyranny. Walker, from his cell, provided additional editorial matter for the *Herald*, referring to Parsons' "masterly inactivity" in dealing with crime, and adding, "The Judge is a stickler for contempt and he has succeeded in securing to himself an unstinted measure. . . . In trying to snuff out the *Herald*, his Honor has extinguished himself."

The judge of the Superior Court who had to consider Randolph's demand for a writ of *habeas corpus* was in an embarrassing position. To deny the writ would be to defy an aroused public opinion; to grant it would offend the powerful Parsons and his cronies. By this time, however, the case had attracted the attention of the entire state, and steps for the impeachment of Parsons were under way before the Legislature. Ten days after Walker's arrest, the writ was reluctantly issued by the Court, and he was set free. His first action was to publish "A Card" in the *Herald*, thanking those who had rallied to his cause, which was the cause "of the whole people of California." Of Edmund Randolph's arduous efforts he spoke with especial feeling. "It would be idle ceremony for me to return thanks"; this had been an unforgettable act of friendship. The recollection of that act would, five years later, profoundly affect not only Walker's destiny but that of a nation.

As the tumult died away, it appeared that the only real beneficiary of the affair was the *Herald*. Its circulation boomed; it enlarged its page size so as to accommodate more advertising and began to turn out a weekly newspaper in addition to the daily. But Walker was well aware that nothing had yet been accomplished for the city. Crime was unabated. The courts went on their accustomed way. The attack on Parsons and the judiciary, he felt, had to be pressed. Early in April, he appeared before a special committee of the Legislature in Sacramento to present a memorial on Parsons' instruction to the Grand Jury. The committee investigated the charge and recommended impeachment; and the impeachment proceedings moved as far as the floor of the Legislature. There, however, Parsons' political friends were able to intervene successfully; and after some desultory debate, the matter was dropped.

### III

The San Francisco underworld had its own views on "the contempt case," as it was called, and it expressed them with ferocity. On the night of May 4, 1851, simultaneous fires broke out at a dozen points in the downtown business districts, producing a conflagration that totally destroyed twenty blocks of wooden buildings, among them the office and printing plant of the *Herald*. Under cover of the excitement the gangs swarmed into the city and robbed and looted to their hearts' content.

It was a night of terror and despair; and the hope that the Walker case had aroused went up in smoke. The *Herald* lost everything except its fighting spirit. A printing plant which had escaped the fire was put at Nugent's disposal, and he managed to resume publication three days after the fire, with anger bubbling from every page, calling for "a volunteer police." This time something was done, and men armed with rifles began to patrol the city. The entire press of the city was demanding action against the arsonists. The *Herald* went further. On June 5, it came out with an editorial headed, "The Organization of Crime in This State," in which it flatly asserted that the men who had set the fire were known to the authorities, and were receiving the protection of politicians, some of whom were Catilines aiming at nothing less than complete mastery of the city and the state. It was time, said the *Herald,* for "a general war on crime." The shocked and frightened public, however, was in no mood to harken to clarion calls. It was rumored that many respectable people were preparing to leave San Francisco.

The *Herald's* charge of a major political conspiracy resting on a criminal base became more credible when, about three weeks later, with the rebuilding of the ruined district well under way, another great fire broke out, destroying even more of the city, again to the accompaniment of countless robberies. It was this devastating blaze that provided the immediate impetus for the formation of the first Committee of Public Safety, the Vigilantes, who would finally crush the gangs only to impose their own despotism.

## I V

The *Herald* still held to its conviction that, before order could be established, the courts had to be freed from corrupt judges of the Parsons stamp. His docket was crowded with cases, yet he absented himself from the court for days at a time. "How long must we tolerate this man?" Walker demanded editorially. The same question, in reverse, was in Judge Parsons' mind, and he was in the better position to answer it. Among his friends was a notorious duelist, Graham Hicks, known for his deadly skill with the revolver. Several prominent San Franciscans had already fallen to his marksmanship. He was a small wiry man, not unlike Walker himself in build. Walker, said Hicks, had insulted "a friend of his," and would have to apologize or fight. Duelling was the most popular spectator sport in the city, and as soon as the challenge became known and the time of the meeting was set, a huge crowd turned out for the event.

The fact that Walker fought four revolver duels in his life without wounding a single antagonist led some to believe that his marksmanship was poor; but it would have had to be almost incredibly bad to achieve such a record, and other evidence points in the opposite direction. It is perhaps not unreasonable to believe that he had an aversion to this cold-blooded form of killing—that he deliberately shot into the air or the ground in the expectation that his opponents would follow his example. This practice was not unusual among the gentlemen of New Orleans, as a means of satisfying honor without bloodshed. In one of his duels, fought in San Francisco with W. H. Carter in the spring of 1855, at eight paces, Walker was wounded in the foot—an injury sufficiently unusual to suggest that Carter was shooting to miss or to inflict minimal damage after Walker had missed. In the Hicks duel, also fought at eight paces, Walker as usual got his shot off first, without effect. Hicks, however, felt no obligations to *noblesse*. His shot, intended to kill, went through the upper part of Walker's arm, near the shoulder, just missing the bone.

What followed made a great impression on the spectators. Showing no sign of pain, Walker motioned to Hicks that they should take a second shot, but before they could raise their guns again, the seconds intervened, and the duel was declared over.

Some later commentators on Walker's career professed to find in his several duels the signs of a bloodthirsty character, of a desperado, but it is safe to say that they misread both the man and his age. A contemporary of Walker's who sought to explain his outlook to a later generation stressed the atmosphere of the 1850s as an essential factor to be considered. "Men looked upon life from a more romantic viewpoint than they do now. There was more sentiment, more singing of songs . . . grace and gallantry . . . Men had not outgrown the customs of their forefathers, and if they resorted to the *code duello* in defense of their honor, and the honor of women, they were moved by sincerity, and surrounded by traditions still too potent to be cast aside." The way in which a gentleman conducted himself in a duel in Walker's time was taken as a major test of character; the fortitude with which he bore the wound inflicted by Hicks and the anger that made him want to continue to duel gave him an instant reputation as a man among men. "A brave, highly educated and able man" with "a high moral and political position"* on all issues of the time, was the character attributed to Walker in the San Francisco of the 1850's. Men clustered around him.

* F. Soulé, J. H. Gihon, and J. Nisbet, *Annals of San Francisco,* 1855.

# MR. VANDERBILT
# FORGIVES GREAT BRITAIN

◦◦◦ⓦ◦◦◦

Walker in the San Francisco *Herald,* quoting the New York press, commented enthusiastically on Commodore Vanderbilt's great enterprise in Nicaragua. He saw the canal as the key to the Americanization of the Caribbean. The interests of the great capitalist had begun to touch those of the inconspicuous journalist. With the signing of the Clayton-Bulwer Treaty, two new Vanderbilt corporations had sprung into life: the Nicaraguan Canal Company, which was to dig the canal under Anglo-American management; and the Accessory Transit Company, which would carry passengers across Nicaragua until completion of the canal. Talk of war died away. Even the New York *Herald,* which had been virulently anti-British, discovered that in the matter of Nicaragua the United States as well as the British had been at fault, "but an influence of common sense arose from . . . the London Exchange on the one side and Wall Street on the other."

San Francisco heard nothing but favorable news of the venture. Already the Accessory Transit Company was constructing shallow-draft steamboats to operate on the San Juan River and Lake Nicaragua. Yet another Vanderbilt company, the Nicaragua Steamship Line, had ordered ships of unsurpassed size and speed to make the runs from New York to Nicaragua and from Nicaragua to San Francisco. An eminent engineer, Colonel C. W. Childs, had agreed to go to Nicaragua for Vanderbilt to make a detailed survey for the canal and an estimate of cost. And finally it was announced that Vanderbilt would go forthwith to England to negotiate with British financiers.

## II

"The presence of the enterprising and indefatigable Commodore Vanderbilt," wrote Walker in the *Herald,* "will insure the perfection of all arrangements to make the transit connection complete." The tribute was merited. When the *Prometheus* docked at Greytown and Vanderbilt proposed to take the *Director* up the San Juan to the lake, he found himself up against a solid front of pessimism among his own employees. The boat would be wrecked, warned his engineers. No one had ever succeeded in getting a steamboat through the San Juan. Vanderbilt brushed objections aside. With Vanderbilt himself at the wheel, the *Director* headed upstream as if possessed of a devil. "The Commodore," reported one of the crew, "insisted on 'jumping' all the obstacles, and tied down the safety valves, put on all steam, and compelled the little steamer to scrape and struggle over the obstructions into clear water again."

On New Year's Day, 1851, the *Director* completed the 119-mile course of the river and entered Lake Nicaragua. By the time that he returned to Greytown he had laid out the complete transit route.

The Commodore gave orders: construct wharves in all of the Transit's harbors on seacoast and lakeshore; purchase mules and stagecoaches to carry passengers and their baggage; please the Nic-araguans by painting the coaches in their national colors, blue and white; lay wooden planks all along the road through the jungle; buy land outside Greytown and put up company offices—move, act, build! Then he boarded the *Prometheus* and made a record-smashing run back to New York.

From this moment all went as if by magic. Ocean-going steam-ships designed to Vanderbilt's specifications were constructed and sent around Cape Horn to handle the run between San Juan del Sur and San Francisco. He also ordered two small iron-hulled steamers to be built especially for the rocky San Juan River, and he named these, not inappropriately, the *John M. Clayton* and the *Sir Henry Bulwer*. A somewhat larger boat was sent to join the *Director* on Lake Nicaragua. On July 3, 1851, one year precisely after the signing of the Clayton-Bulwer treaty, advertisements appeared in New York newspapers for the "New and Independent Line for California." All New York was excited. What could not Americans do when they put their mind to it?

All the advantage now lay with the Commodore. California-

William Walker (Ed Harris) during the burning of Granada. (*Tom Collins*)

The disastrous battle of San Vicente, Mesaro (Lower California). (*Tom Collins*)

Director Alex Cox in Granada. (*Lynn Davis*)

The entire cast at San Juan del Sur. (*Lynn Davis*)

Wiley Marshall (Fred Neumann). (*Lynn Davis*)

Darlene (Sharon Barr). (*Lynn Davis*)

Bruno Von Nanzmer (Charlie Braun). (*Lynn Davis*)

The church at Rivas. (*Lynn Davis*)

Details of a mural in Granada. (*Lynn Davis*)

The Somoza National Guard entering Managua, September 1978. (*Susan Meiselas*)

Muchachos putting on captured National Guard uniforms after taking over a Managua neighborhood, June 1979. (*Susan Meiselas*)

Sandinistas capturing National Guard arms, Matagalpa, June 1979. (*Susan Meiselas*)

A street fighter, 1979. (*Susan Meiselas*)

A wounded Sandinista soldier after a battle with the Contras in San Juan del Rio Cozo. (*Susan Meiselas*)

A dead Contra being inspected by the Sandinista Army following the battle of Wiwili, 1984. (*Susan Meiselas*)

The townspeople of La Trinidad in northern Nicaragua viewing bodies of Contras after the Contras had attacked the village, 1985. (*Susan Meiselas*)

Mobilized Sandinista troops preparing to counterattack against the Contras in Estelí, 1985. (*Susan Meiselas*)

The founders of the FSLN: Carlos Fonseca, Santos Lopez, Silvio Mayorga, Jorge Navarro, Jose Benito Escobar, Francisco Buitrago, Rigoberto Cruz, Faustino Ruiz, Tomas Borge.

bound passengers soon learned that they could save four days (days in which they might find a gold deposit before someone else got to it!) by traveling through Nicaragua. When Law tried to hold his position by warning the public in print against "melancholy detentions" on the Nicaragua route, Vanderbilt hotly countered with assertions that cholera was rampant in Panama. Law lowered his fares; Vanderbilt lowered his still more. At this stage, loud complaints were heard from passengers about crowded conditions, wretched food, and poor seamanship, but Vanderbilt could afford to shrug; his boats were traveling full, Law's half empty. Nothing could daunt the multitudes eager to reach the promised land of California by the shortest route, and the price war notwithstanding, Vanderbilt's profits were massive. The gross revenues of the Nicaragua Steamship Line and the Accessory Transit Company in their first year of full operation were reported to be over $5,000,000, of which nearly 40 percent was net profit. (Walker in that year of 1852 was lucky if journalism earned him a thousand dollars.)

## III

At one point friction arose with Nicaragua, whose government was so temerarious as to request the share of profits due it under its contract with the company. Vanderbilt claimed that there had been no profits, that a steamboat had been lost, that the outlook was bleak. This the Nicaraguans could hardly credit, since it was public knowledge that Accessory Transit had paid agreeable dividends to stockholders; and they sent two commissioners to New York to press their case. Vanderbilt refused to see them.

To every display of the Commodore's aggressiveness, the public responded with applause, and more than applause, with money. While the price of shares in Law's Panama Line was dropping on the exchange, Accessory Transit stock became a favorite of the bulls, rising in a few months from $18 to $50 per share. At this price, so it was later asserted, Vanderbilt disposed of most of his shares. But this was the least of his gains. It was the soaring of Nicaraguan Canal Company stock that set Wall Streeters agog. Coming on the market at $800 per share, it was first regarded only as an interesting speculation for the wealthy. Then, just at the time when the success of the Accessory Transit Company had made Vanderbilt the darling of the financial community, came the awaited report from Colonel Childs.

The sum of $32,000,000, said the colonel, would be enough to build a practicable lock canal on the Nicaraguan route; and what was more, his plans had been approved by engineers of the British and American governments. A wild rush for Nicaraguan Canal Company shares followed. Although the *New York Times* shook its editorial head, pointing out that the project still existed only on paper, and reminding its readers of the Mississippi Bubble, Wall Street paid no attention. Up and up went the price until in March 1852, it stood at $3600 per share.

The precise details of the subsequent collapse were never revealed, but shrewd guesses were made. As soon as Colonel Childs returned from Nicaragua, Vanderbilt sent him with some financial advisors to London, to arrange for British capital in the venture. A few weeks later he held in his hands a letter, transmitted by Childs, from a partner of Baring Brothers, which knocked the props out from under his hopes. British finance would have nothing to do with the Nicaraguan Canal Company. As planned by Childs, the canal would be too narrow to accommodate large freighters, and the cost was excessive relative to the revenue that could be obtained from small passenger ships.

Whether or not the Barings' calculations were valid, whether or not Childs' plans for the canal could have been modified to meet their objections, hardly mattered. The fact, as George Squier, the American minister, plainly stated, was that all estimates of the cost of the canal were only guesses. He himself guessed $100,000,000 as being closer to the mark than Childs' figure. Any man of common sense, he said, could see that the canal's immense benefits would justify an outlay of $200,000,000, if necessary. Vanderbilt, too, understood this. He perceived between the lines of the British refusal its real significance. England simply did not want the canal. Her policy had not changed an iota; and since the Clayton-Bulwer Treaty, which bound her to nothing, effectively prevented the United States from proceeding without her, there would be no canal.

How long Vanderbilt knew of the Baring letter before he released it for publication no one could find out. The *Herald* made plain its conviction that he kept his information to himself until he had unloaded his shares at some $3600 each. With the announcement came panic. First by hundreds and then by thousands of dollars the price of the stock fell, until buyers could not be found at any price.

While regretting England's decision, Vanderbilt let it be known that he harbored no hostility toward her. Perhaps the reason for his forgiving attitude lay in the profit that he realized from his Wall Street transactions at this period. He was worth, so he told a friend, some eleven millions—which meant that he had doubled his fortune in three years. More, his money was so invested as to yield him a return of 25 percent. He could afford to forgive those who had transgressed against him. In any event his original purpose was achieved. Nicaragua had replaced Panama as the favored route to California, and the stock of George Law's Panama Steamship Line was steadily dropping on the exchange.

Thus, after three years of high diplomacy and even higher finance, England and Vanderbilt were satisfied, but the American government found its position in Central America sadly worsened, and its hopes of a canal blighted. Senatorial inquiry to find out why the plan had foundered had a curious result, for it brought to light the letter from Bulwer that Clayton had hidden away, together with his secret memorandum. Aghast, Congress and the public realized how large Bulwer's diplomatic victory had been; and senator after senator arose to aver that he would never have voted for the treaty if he had known of this "outrageous betrayal." But betrayal or no betrayal, there the treaty stood, a firm barrier against closer relations between the United States and Central America. The one benefit that the nation had gained was the development of the Nicaraguan transit route, through which thousands of California-bound Americans continued to pour.

To Walker, as to many another American, the Clayton-Bulwer Treaty now seemed a terrible misfortune for the nation, an evil which it was the obligation of all men of spirit to resist and overcome. The fact that it may have served to avert a war with England was less important to him than the sharp limits which had been set on the expansion of American power to the south.

# "A RASH AND DESPERATE
# UNDERTAKING"

◥◣◢◤

$A$ new opportunity had come Walker's way. A highly regarded lawyer, Henry P. Watkins, who had a practice in nearby Marysville and was involved in state politics, offered him a partnership. Walker was again restless. He had exhausted the possibilities of San Francisco journalism for challenge and recognition. Without much deliberation, he accepted Watkins' offer and moved to Marysville.

With Watkins looking after the business side of the practice, Walker was able to concentrate on the forensic battles which were the only aspect of legal practice that attracted him. It was not to be expected, however, that his temperament and ambition would permit him to take the slow, steady course to professional affluence and political preferment. Nor did anything in the society around him conduce to a settled life. "Those were the days when the ardor for adventure by land and sea was hot in the breasts of men."

During his year in San Francisco he had met a remarkable personality who, in some ways, so much resembled him that they might almost have been brothers—a French nobleman, Count Gaston Raoul de Raousset-Boulbon. Raousset, like Walker, was a man with a chivalric and romantic stance toward life. Both were idealistic democrats in the French revolutionary tradition; both were imbued with and exalted by the idea of personal heroism. The Frenchman was some seven years older than Walker, similarly short and slender, and with a face distinguished by magnetic eyes. They also matched each other in energy, courage, education, and literary flair. Raousset while in Paris had founded and edited a radical newspaper, *La Liberté,* and had written an emotional novel, *La Conversion,* describing his transformation from aristocrat to democrat.

Early in 1852, the California newspapers began to carry extraordinary news of Raousset. Despite his empty purse, he was the center of the French colony of San Francisco, where one man out of every ten was a Frenchman seeking adventure in adversity. One of their chief topics of conversation was the possibility of wresting from Mexico the southern region of Arizona, then part of the State of Sonora, and reputed to be rich in mineral wealth. A plan to this end quickly took shape in the Count's fertile mind. The population of Sonora was living in terror of the frequent raids southward from Arizona of the savage Apache Indians. It stuck Raousset that if he went to Mexico City with the diplomatic support of the French government and offered to lead a French force into Sonora to suppress the Apaches, he might as a reward obtain from the Mexican government a concession to the gold and silver mines of Arizona. And after that, who knew what his power might become?

By the spring of 1852, it seemed that success was close. The rulers of Mexico were as well disposed to the French as they were resentful of Americans. A company was formed to operate the mines, with a suitable distribution of shares to certain Mexican officials; Raousset formally pledged himself to clear the Apaches out of Sonora; the government granted the new company rights to the Arizona mines; and all went with dreamlike precision. Hastening back to San Francisco, Raousset obtained the aid of the French consul in chartering a ship and raising an expeditionary force of 150 of his compatriots, and in May 1852, sailed for Guaymas, the chief port of Sonora. Since they went nominally as "colonists," and at the invitation of the Mexican government, the American Neutrality Laws were not invoked to prevent their departure.

## II

Walker viewed normal life, with its emphasis on security, with the impatience of a race horse hitched to a milk cart. Raousset's glamorous enterprise made the practice of law in Marysville seem insignificant and tawdry. Life in San Francisco had hardened Walker and the duel with Hicks had left more than a physical scar. His respect for the law had been corroded and cracked. The Neutrality Laws which, in his New Orleans days, had caused him to inveigh against General Lopez' filibustering designs on Cuba, now seemed to him merely a legalistic cover for the weakness and timidity of politicians in Washington, three thousand miles away. Were these ill-advised laws to be obeyed while France took Sonora? Was America, after winning the Mexican War, to stop short of one of the chief prizes of victory, the mines of Arizona? Confident of his vision of the American future, he regarded as ignorant and reactionary those laws which seemed to him to sacrifice the future to the present.

The fact that Raousset already had a contract with the Mexican government did not disturb Walker. It was generally thought that the Sonorans were disaffected and ripe for revolution. Why should not Sonora, like California, be given the benefit of American institutions? Why should not an American company, by making a contract with the Sonoran government, put itself in a position where it could either share Raousset's project or displace it?

Although Walker was for the most part soft-spoken, reticent, and thoughtful of demeanor, he was capable of flashing bursts of excitement that illuminated the projects in which he was interested, and made the people around him regard him as their natural leader. His enthusiasm for the Sonoran venture was so contagious that it won over his partner, Watkins, and several other prominent men. That spring of 1852 a group selected by Walker met to discuss the possibility of an American expedition to Sonora. Agreement was reached, money was found, and two of the men present were designated to go to Guaymas, their purpose to obtain permission from the Governor of Sonora to bring into the state a number of American "colonists." The hope proved futile. Before Walker's agents could reach Guaymas, Raousset had already come to terms with the Governor of Sonora. Owning a substantial block of shares in the French mining company, the Governor had no interest in any other expedition, and certainly not one composed of *gringos*. Walker's agents returned to Marysville disappointed, and he and Watkins had reluctantly to go back to their petty practice.

A few months passed and then the fever returned, as fresh news came of Raousset's expedition. It appeared that the military commander of Sonora, General Blanco, who had more actual power than the state's governor, had somehow been overlooked in the distribution of stock in Raousset's company. A San Francisco banking house, with its eye on the Sonora mines, hastily took advantage of the situation to bribe Blanco to its interest. If he would ignore the Mexican government's contract with Raousset, the bankers told him, he could sign one of his own with a new company to be formed for the purpose. Instantly it became Blanco's chief aim to wreck the French expedition. To this end he kept Raousset and his men dangling in Guaymas, on one official pretext or another, until idleness and disease began to take their toll, and supplies began to run short. When at last the Count was allowed to depart for the north his force was gravely enfeebled; and its situation was made worse by wholesale desertions of Mexican muleteers and guides. The wily Blanco then showed his hand by demanding that Raousset's company submit themselves to him and either become Mexican citizens or work as laborers at the mines under his command. Enraged, the French leader sought to organize a revolutionary movement among the Sonoran people, but without success. Finally in desperation he launched an attack against Sonora's capital, Hermosillo, a city of 12,000 where Blanco had a large garrison. In the battle that followed 243 Frenchmen stormed the adobe walls in the face of musket and cannon fire from 1200 Mexicans, took the town, and almost captured Blanco. But still unable to bring the natives to his side, and suffering from fever, Raousset was compelled at last to come to terms with the Mexican, and to leave Sonora.

If this was failure, San Francisco did not know it. On his return, Raousset was greeted as one of the heroes of the age. He further delighted his admirers when, in accepting the honors heaped upon him, he vowed to go back to Mexico. "I cannot live without Sonora," he said. With that he began to prepare for another and larger expedition.

Not to have been part of so stirring an adventure was more than Walker could bear. Early in 1853, he and his partner Watkins called on Raousset and offered their cooperation and services for the new attempt.

"Together," Walker told Raousset, "we would be far more than twice as strong. There are many in the United States who would stand with us and use their influence in our behalf."

Raousset listened courteously and with appreciation of Walker's intensity. "My friends," he replied, "what you say is perhaps true, but I cannot be associated with you. To be frank, Americans are so strongly detested in Mexico that your presence would destroy my chances."

Walker did not argue. With one of his rare smiles he said, "Then we must be rivals."

"So be it," said Raousset, and they shook hands warmly, while the prosaic Watkins looked on in admiration.

The Frenchman was basing his hopes on a report that a revolution had just brought to the Presidency of Mexico General Santa

Anna, known to be friendly to France. This was the moment for another visit to Mexico City, to make a new and binding contract; and he would soon be on his way. Walker's plan was far more daring —nothing less than to introduce a force of Americans into Sonora, under the guise of colonists, and make himself master of the state, either with cooperation of its politicos or without them. Sonora would then declare itself an independent republic, put itself under the protection of the United States, and give the mining concession to an American company, regardless of any contracts with the French signed in Mexico City.

This was also the reasoning of some of San Francisco's wealthy mining men, who were eager to speculate on the chance of a concession for the Sonora mines. Their need was for a leader who could dominate a fighting force recruited from among the adventurers of San Francisco, and at the same time outmaneuver the Frenchman, Raousset, and the Mexican Governor of Sonora. In the view of the San Francisco magnates, Walker's reputation for bravery, his burning conviction, his power of speech, and his legal and journalistic training outweighed his lack of military experience. They would provide him with the necessary backing and funds, they told him, if he would devote himself to the expedition.

Money was raised by the sale of bonds "secured" by the land which Walker expected to obtain in Sonora.

> The Independence Loan fund [the bonds read] has received of ——
> —————— the sum of $500, and the Republic of Sonora will issue
> to him or his assigns a land warrant for one square league of land,
> to be located on the public domain of said Republic.
>                    Signed, the first day of May,
>                        William Walker,
>                        Colonel of the Independence Regiment *

Sold secretly to selected purchasers, the bonds provided enough money to permit recruitment, the purchase of guns and supplies, and the hiring of a ship. Walker had brought Edmund Randolph and another close friend, Parker Crittenden, also a lawyer, into the project, and together they organized the expedition. He felt, however, that before sailing he needed firsthand information on the conditions that he would have to face; and a few days after Raousset-Boulbon left for Mexico City, the self-created colonel boarded a ship for Guaymas.

* *Alta California*, Dec. 1, 1853.

The effect that Walker made at Guaymas in 1853, as he appeared in his new role as soldier and liberator, is preserved in an eyewitness account. "His appearance was anything else than that of a military chieftain . . . unprepossessing . . . insignificant. . . . but anyone who estimated Mr. Walker by his personal appearance made a great mistake. Extremely taciturn, he would sit for an hour in company without opening his lips; but once interested he arrested your attention with the first word he uttered, and as he proceeded, you felt convinced that he was no ordinary person. To a few confidential friends he was most enthusiastic upon the subject of his darling project, but outside of those immediately interested he never mentioned the topic." *

The San Francisco press knew Walker's intention, and encouraged him. *Alta California*, reporting the murder in Sonora of eighty people by Apaches in a single week, declared. "They cannot protect themselves, and the government cannot protect them." But the American military authorities saw the matter otherwise. On September 30, 1853, Walker's plan came to a sudden halt when the United States Army general in command at San Francisco ordered the *Arrow* seized on suspicion that it was to be used to violate the Neutrality Laws.

With Edmund Randolph as his attorney, Walker instantly filed suit to have the vessel released; but the outlook was dark and he did not intend to submit to any lengthy legal process. Instead, he had another brig, the *Caroline,* fitted out for his purposes and, with as many of his recruits as could be hastily rounded up, secretly boarded the vessel, weighed anchor and stood out to sea before they could be intercepted. Forty-five men were with him. The date was October 8, 1853. Before he sailed he received news which must have heartened him. French rivalry no longer was a threat. Count Raousset-Boulbon had fallen out with President Santa Anna, had been forced to flee Mexico for his life, and was back in San Francisco.

# III

Walker was being driven by idealism and ambition together—an irresistible combination when their thrust is in the same direction. He believed with all his heart that the democratic institutions of the United States offered hope to the peoples of the world and that there

* T. Robinson Warren, *Dust and Foam,* 1858.

was an obligation on Americans to bring the light of democracy to their benighted neighbors. At the same time he held in his heart the heroic dream of world fame. All his secret aspirations were centered on the overcoming of enemies and victory in battle—but in the name of right, justice, and the United States.

He was undismayed by the appearance of absurdity. There was in him just that touch of fanaticism required to ignore public opinion when it ran counter to his own convictions. His true profession was heroism. Like Raousset, another incurable romantic, Walker could no more resist an opportunity to risk everything for a high purpose than a dedicated surgeon could refuse a chance to pit his skill against death. He had become an addict of danger. Regardless of the practical purpose of the Sonoran enterprise as conceived by his backers, to him from the beginning it had always been a personal test, a feat of arms against great odds, by which a man might overnight enter the ranks of glory for the sake of his country. His failure on this, his first try at war and conquest, was abysmal, it was grotesque; and yet it had about it something that was not of the time, a hint of ancient quest and knightly fortitude, a touch of grandeur that men recognized, and that in time caused the laughter and the sneers to die away, and Walker to emerge a larger figure than ever in the eyes of the California public.

In a broad political sense as well, the expedition was by no means fruitless. Although commentators have called it "an inexcusable raid on an unoffending people" and "a rash and desperate undertaking which needs the pen of a Cervantes to do it justice," the fact remains that it played a considerable, if indirect, part in the acquisition by the United States of 45,000 square miles of Mexican territory, an area as large as the state of Pennsylvania, and containing the valuable minerals coveted by California interests, as well as a desirable railroad route. This was the so-called Gadsden Purchase, which a few months later was incorporated with the territories of Arizona and New Mexico.

Walker's original strategic plan called for a landing near Guaymas, but he was compelled to change it. With fewer than fifty men, he could not hope to contend with the strong Mexican garrison at Guaymas. A suitable base of operations was needed at which to assemble additional recruits, promote a native insurrection against the Sonoran government, and finally launch an invasion. For this purpose he decided that his first conquest had to be the sparsely populated peninsula of Lower California, less than a hundred miles across the Gulf of California, from Sonora. The *Caroline* accordingly put in at La Paz, the capital, and Walker landed his force. Without firing a shot they quickly made a prisoner of the Governor of the state, put him on board the brig, hauled down the Mexican flag over his house and raised in its place the flag of the "Republic of Lower California."

To the natives he gave assurance that his purpose was to lead a successful revolution for them against the tyranny of Mexico. Lower California, he stated in a proclamation, was "free, sovereign and independent." Its people no longer owed allegiance to Mexico. He himself would serve as President of the new nation until it was firmly established.

Subsequently his men beat back an attack from a small Mexican force, and captured a Mexican revenue cutter. There was danger that a major expedition might sail against Walker from nearby Guaymas, and not as yet wishing to face such a risk, he sailed north. The port of Ensenada, only one hundred miles south of the American border, struck him as a suitable place at which to marshal the reinforcements that he expected, and from which communication could readily be maintained with the United States. He took possession of the town without bloodshed, and issued a statement for the American people, elaborating his aims. Lower California, he said, had been shamefully neglected by the Mexican government. His purpose in creating the new republic was to develop the resources of the peninsula and "to effect a proper social organization therein." To accomplish this, it was first necessary to achieve independence from Mexico. He had therefore established a government of Americans to begin to administer the country. A list of "cabinet appointments" of chosen officers followed.

This large declaration, coming from a man of twenty-nine years and no military experience, and whose minuscule force consisted in the main of dockside toughs, undisciplined and untried, struck many Americans as ridiculous when they read of it. But it was more astute than Walker's contemporaries realized. He was gambling on sustained support from his backers in San Francisco. To show anything less than complete confidence would have been folly. Everything depended on the reinforcements and supplies that Henry Watkins was supposed to bring him. If the San Francisco newspapers failed to carry word, and bold word, of his achievements and purpose, the entire project might collapse from inattention.

While he awaited Watkins, he had to lead his men in his first

serious battle. Two hundred Mexican soldiers, advancing from the
north, entered Ensenada and laid siege to a house which he had
selected as a fort. The defense was strong and competent, and after
three days of bloody fighting, a bold sortie routed the attackers. The
elation of victory did not last long, however. One morning soon
thereafter the ship *Caroline,* on which most of Walker's provisions
were stored, was seen to be hoisting anchor and making sail. Incredulously Walker and his men saw it put out to sea on a southward
course, ignoring all his signals. Later it appeared that the crew had
succumbed to the bribes of their prisoner, the Governor of Lower
California, who had been left on board.

A few days later, the brig *Anita* put into the harbor, carrying
Watkins and 230 men, full of zeal and expectation. Walker's first
question was, what supplies had Watkins brought? The answer bore
out his fears. The *Anita* carried guns and ammunition, but little food.

This was a terrible blow. As soon as the new men had disembarked, Watkins had to turn around and sail for California; everything depended on the speed with which he could return with a
cargo of provisions. Meanwhile, with so many mouths to feed,
Walker sought a way to obtain supplies without arousing the animosity of the rancheros by raids on their land. His scouts learned
that a noted Mexican outlaw, Melendrez, whose camp was nearby,
had considerable supplies of corn as well as cattle and horses; and
in a surprise attack on Melendrez' camp, Walker seized this booty.
His problem, however, remained acute. Reduced rations consisting
entirely of beef and corn took a toll of his men's morale, already
weakening from idleness and disease. They resented, too, the strict
discipline that Walker enforced, especially his threat to shoot any
man who robbed a house or raped a woman. The signs of impending
mutiny were unmistakable.


# IV


News of Walker's proclamation of independence had gone to Mexico
City, and there it produced political consequences which were to
deprive his venture, in American eyes, of its purpose. The Mexican
government was then being pressed by the American minister, James
Gadsden, to sell northern Sonora for $10,000,000 plus assurance
that the Apaches would be prevented from raiding into Mexico. The
price was felt by Mexican officials to be outrageously low, and the

offer as a whole insulting, but they had to consider whether the United States, if balked, might not use force to compel submission. They had been shocked by Walker's raid on La Paz; now the news from Ensenada that Lower California had been declared independent under American rule seemed to presage disaster for Mexico. Fearing that Walker was secretly abetted by the American government, they came to the conclusion that if they did not consent to negotiate they might lose both the peninsula and Sonora, without compensation. The result was a provisional treaty hastily drawn and signed on December 31, 1853, in which Gadsden's terms were met. A separate letter from him assured the Mexican government that the United States regarded Walker as a violator of federal law, and would deal with him accordingly.

From this point, Walker's expedition lost its appeal for Americans. With the coveted mineral-bearing part of Sonora secured for the United States, who cared about Lower California, or about "effecting a proper social organization" in Sonora?

Adversity now multiplied its forms. A Mexican gunboat appeared off Ensenada and patrolled the coast to prevent further reinforcement of Walker's troops; and almost at the same time an American warship, the *Portsmouth,* anchored in the harbor. Its commander came ashore, met with Walker, gave him news of the Gadsden Purchase, and warned him: he could expect no further aid from his friends in San Francisco, and certainly none from the government of the United States.

The provisional treaty that Gadsden had signed with Mexico struck Walker as altogether unsatisfactory. Its chief defect was its failure to provide an outlet for the United States on the Gulf of California—a limitation certain to hamper the development of the American southwest, Mexico and Central America. Walker thought it barely possible, but nevertheless possible, that a Sonoran insurrection against Mexico could be fomented, would submit to his leadership and bring the Gulf of California under American control. On this remote chance he now staked everything.

V

How does a foreigner make a revolution in a place where his countrymen are hated, where his motives are suspect, and when he is not even there? Walker conceived the idea of beginning with an assembly of disaffected elements in Lower California. Then, bolstered by popular support, he would cross the Colorado River into Sonora and try to win over enough natives to give momentum to his cause. In this hope, he issued another proclamation, asserting Sonora's independence from Mexico, with the status of an independent republic, like that of Lower California.

Food was a major consideration. This time there was no alternative to foraging. The regiment ranged the countryside around Ensenada, commandeering cattle and corn in the name of the revolution, and stirring up hot indignation among landowners. On the whole, there was little violence, and Walker's orders against pillage were respected. But the restrictions that he enforced on his men's behavior became increasingly aggravating to them as their situation deteriorated. Although his officers, who were in daily contact with him and felt the impact of his own conviction, remained steadfast, the morale of the soldiers in the ranks was cracking badly, and they needed only an excuse to show their resentment.

The crisis came when Walker, organizing the transport of supplies into Sonora, gave orders that horses which had been taken from the outlaw Melendrez were to be used for this purpose. A number of his men had come to regard these mounts as their own and they flatly refused to turn them over to their officers. Summoned to the spot, Walker was met by open complaints and even threats.

It appeared that the expedition was about to founder in turmoil and disgrace. Those of the men who were still loyal to Walker waited pessimistically to see what he would do. His response startled them. He ordered the bugler to blow assembly. Hesitantly, the men formed ranks and stood at attention. After a long moment of silence, he spoke to them in a ringing voice, and in courteous, restrained language.

"If any of you wish to leave the expedition, you are free to do so. I shall not compel anyone to remain who wishes to go. Those of you who wish to stay with me I shall ask to signify their loyalty by taking an oath of allegiance to the flag of Lower California. Let there be no misunderstanding. I shall expect the men who follow me to abide by the highest standards of military behavior. Those who wish to go can fill their pockets with rations and leave camp. I shall expect them to be gone within two hours. The American boundary is only a three or four days' march from here. Any of you who do not wish to take the oath of allegiance will step forward, put down your rifles, and go to the supply depot for rations." About fifty of the men left the formation, and gathered in a group to one side, talking among themselves. Some were embarrassed and uncertain, others in a state of intense anger. Finally they decided on a course of action. Instead of accepting Walker's offer, they turned and began to walk away from the camp, their rifles still in their hands.

Walker's aide, Captain Timothy Crocker, known for his courage, rushed after the deserters and ordered them to drop their guns. When no one obeyed, he drew his pistol. A man snarled, "Go on, shoot, Captain. I dare you." Several rifles were aimed at Crocker. At this point, without waiting for orders, another of Walker's officers ran to a nearby howitzer, already loaded, and trained it on the mutineers, ready to fire if Crocker were shot. Walker shouted, "Hold your fire!" For a moment, no one stirred; then the sullen men turned their backs on Crocker and continued to walk away. Walker jumped on a horse, and rode after them. An eyewitness, reporting the subsequent scene, was astonished by the kindliness and calmness of his voice when he overtook them. "Men," he said, "you are going to need rations, and you had better go back for them. I shall not try to take your rifles from you, but you know as well as I do that they are badly needed, and they belong to the regiment. I ask you to leave them behind."

More than half of the men put their rifles down. Two or three expressed their frustration and rage by smashing the butts on nearby rocks before they turned away. Some went back for rations. The entire group crossed the American border safely, and were taken by steamer to San Francisco. It was largely from their bitter testimony that the American press formed its judgment of Walker at this time. He was accused of being excessively harsh with his men, and of believing that "might makes right." But better than anyone else, he had reason to know that might does not make right, for the might was always with others, not with him. In Lower California it was the men behind him who had the power, not he. All they had to do was snap their fingers at him, and he was finished. What he depended on, in the final test, was discipline, or the idea of discipline. In order to hold in check the self-assertive and unruly men who had volunteered for this adventure, he had to focus the full power of his personality on every breach of discipline. Boyish, slight, physically unimpressive, possessed only of an indomitable will and searching grey eyes, he held them by a thin thread. A single lapse in their respect for him would have been fatal. To command them, he had to make them fear, not so much himself, as the disciplined response of their comrades to his orders. In this he was surprisingly successful. The punctilio of military etiquette was not abated for an instant.

Privates were expected to salute their officers. Men stood at attention when addressed by their superiors in rank. All were warned that the death sentence would be imposed on mutineers and deserters. In practice, however, this rule was modified. Of four men who subsequently deserted after having taken the oath of allegiance, only the leader was shot; the others were driven from the camp.

When he finally marched out of Ensenada, Walker had to leave behind him many who had been wounded or were ill. His active force numbered only 130. Finally he convened an assembly of sixty-two Mexicans, who were received in a setting as impressive as ingenuity, in that poverty-stricken land, could make it—complete with a guard of honor, a vestigial military band, and a display of the flags of the new republics of Sonora and Lower California. There were oaths of allegiance, cheers, the firing of field pieces.

When at last, leaving a small garrison in San Vicente, he led his shrunken regiment on the 200-mile march eastward to the Colorado River, they drove a herd of cattle before them. It took two weeks of wearisome struggle to climb up the rugged trails of the Sierras and down again almost to the mouth of the Colorado. By this time they were in rags, and their boots were worn through; Walker himself had lost one boot, and had improvised a kind of sandal in its place, giving a special touch of the grotesque to his emaciated little figure. Exhausted though they were, they had no choice, he said, but to go on. Somewhere in that arid countryside they found wood with which to build rafts. The great question was whether the cattle could be made to swim across the river, which ran wide, deep and swift. An hour later they had their answer; the men and some bags of corn crossed safely, but such cattle as could be driven into the river were swept away and perished.

They were, then, in Sonora, and finished; almost without food, almost without shoe leather, totally without hope. Seventy miles up the river, they knew, was Fort Yuma, under the American flag. Half of the men did not stop for Walker's decision, but deserted and started their northward trek at once. The others waited for their commander to lead them in the same direction. To their considerable resentment, he refused. A skinny hollow-eyed scarecrow standing among scarecrows, he maintained his military dignity, saying that he would give his orders at the right time; and somehow he kept his hold on them.

Three days later he knew that he could expect no aid or comfort from the Sonorans. His half-starved, bearded men lined up at his order, and in silence heard him say that they would march back to

San Vicente, for the comrades who had been left there could not be abandoned to the Mexicans. From San Vicente they would go north again across the desert to the United States. Grimly they listened, and obeyed—recrossed the river, and laboriously began to climb the stony mountain trails behind their leader.

# VI

With the thirty-four men who were all that remained to him, Walker staggered toward the American military post across the border in California. The last thirty miles had been under the hot desert sun, without food and almost without water. Presenting himself to the American military commander at San Diego, and holding himself erect, he said formally, "I am Colonel William Walker. I wish to surrender my force to the United States."

He was arraigned before the Federal Court in San Francisco on an indictment by a Grand Jury, charged with violation of the Neutrality Laws. His partner, Watkins, had already been tried under the same auspices, convicted and fined $1500—a light penalty, as the judge pointed out, since the chief interest of the court was vindication of the law. Filibustering, as seen by public opinion, was a doomed profession. Walker's rival, Count Raousset-Boulbon, had failed in yet another attempt to enter Sonora with a military force, and was soon to face a Mexican firing squad. All the auguries seemed to be against Walker when, with Edmund Randolph again at his side, he heard the clerk of the court read the charges, and answered, "Not guilty."

The trial was put off for four months, and he was set free on Randolph's recognizance. In spite of his failure and the gibes of the newspapers, Walker's reputation, it appeared, was far from shattered. Everywhere he went he was a center of respectful attention. He friends, especially Watkins and Randolph, urged him to enter politics, and sufficiently persuaded him so that he returned to Marysville, as a base of candidacy for public office.

Delegates were then being chosen for the Democratic State Convention of 1854, and "Mr. Walker of Yuba County" was among those elected. When the Convention met in the Baptist Church of Sacramento, on July 18, he was one of its prominent figures, although still under indictment.*

* H. S. Hoblitzell, *Early Historical Sketch of the City of Marysville and Yuba County*, 1876.

# THE
# OPENING OF THE GATE

~~~

**W**alker's first experience in practical American politics was his last. He never ran for office. Soon there entered into his orbit a new personality, who was to have a determining influence on his subsequent career. This was Byron Cole, a well-to-do, ambitious, and sophisticated young man, who had recently come to San Francisco from New England. Cole, who had covered the Democratic Convention for his newspaper, saw in Walker's gift of leadership a magic ingredient which, in combination with his own connections, might achieve great things, and he invited Walker to return to San Francisco as editor of the *Commercial-Advertiser*. The post itself appealed to Walker less than other journalistic openings that were available to him, but Cole was able to add compelling inducements. From the first it was Manifest Destiny, rather than journalism, that linked the two men.

Cole's voyage to California had been by way of Nicaragua, and what he saw there had convinced him that the country was ripe for American intervention. The alternative was sustained chaos. Civil war was almost continuous. The rapid alternation of dictatorship and revolt was like the pulse of a feverish patient, sick with despair. In a period of six years, fifteen presidents had held power, their capitals shifting between Granada in the south, where the aristocratic party known as the Legitimists had its base, and León in the north, the stronghold of the Democrats. The country was beautiful to look upon and rich in natural resources; it had valuable lumber —mahogany, cedar, Brazilwood—in inexhaustible quantities; it produced gold, silver, copper, lead, iron, sulphur; its plantations grew cacao, sugar, cotton, indigo, tobacco, maize, wheat, rice, and a hundred fruits, vegetables, and spices; cattle were abundant; but the people had been ravaged beyond endurance by poverty, war, and disease. Repeated conscription of males into the warring armies of the politicos was a major source of misery. Women outnumbered men three to two, in some villages five to one, while the population remained almost static, at some 250,000.

The situation as outlined by Cole inflamed Walker's imagination, and revived in him the vision of the "column of Progress and Democracy" about which he had written in New Orleans. The United States, and especially California, had a great stake in Nicaragua, with its overland Transit and its potentialities for a canal. If British domination of the isthmus was to be prevented, America could not afford to delay in asserting its democratic leadership. The indifference of President Pierce's administration to England's manipulation of the Central American governments was rapidly destroying the prestige of the United States among them. Neutrality Laws or no Neutrality Laws, the Democrats of Nicaragua deserved American support, and the United States could not afford to withhold it.

What if a band of privately organized American fighting men undertook the task? They might turn the tide of the Nicaraguan struggle, and compel action by Washington. An O'Higgins had rescued Chile from Spanish oppression; a Walker might save Nicaragua from native tyranny. Under friendly tutelage from the North, Nicaragua might set a shining example of economic creativity for the entire isthmus. She might even become the center of a Caribbean alliance with close ties with the United States.

The prospect, with its potentialities of glory and its idealistic aspect, was irresistibly attractive to Walker, as for more practical reasons it was to Byron Cole. If the Democratic effort failed, Cole was aware, the government of Honduras would almost certainly go down with it and be replaced by a pro-British regime. In that event American business interests in Honduras would be imperiled—and Cole was one of the owners of the Honduras Mining and Trading Company, which was about to exploit a large tract of mineral-bearing lands. He was eager for action to protect his interests, and no sooner had Walker accepted the proffered post on the *Commercial-Advertiser,* than the publisher embarked on a ship for Nicaragua, to explore the situation.

II

It was autumn of 1854, and Cole had not yet returned, when Walker stood trial on charges of having violated the Neutrality Laws in his

Sonoran enterprise. He came before the federal court as editor of a respectable newspaper and a figure of considerable prominence. Walker rested his belief that he was not guilty on the moral aspect of his case. The people of Sonora were notoriously oppressed by a corrupt government and were virtually without protection against the raids of the terrifying Apaches. When he had been at Guaymas, Mexicans as well as Americans, women as well as men had urged him to return.

His failure he attributed to the federal authorities. When they prevented the sailing of the whole body of men who had volunteered to accompany him, when they deprived him of needful stores and fieldpieces, all began to go awry. As a result, "I found myself at sea with only forty-five men, and with so few followers I was compelled to land in a sparsely settled region. Some sort of flag had to be raised to protect us." They had been able to sustain their long ordeal in Lower California and their nightmare marches across the mountains and desert only by the consciousness that "right and humanity" were on their side. "The Pilgrim fathers came to a savage land, rescued it from savages and made it an abode of civilization." Was there not always a moral sanction for men who sought to emulate them?

The jury consisted of men in whom the expansionist spirit of the age and the belief in America's Manifest Destiny were stronger than merely legal considerations. After only eight minutes of deliberation, they returned with a verdict of not guilty. Some of the San Francisco newspapers were concerned; Watkins, who was only an agent of Walker's, had been found guilty, while Walker himself was acquitted; was this justice? But the *Herald* replied that Watkins was Watkins, and Walker was Walker, and this seemed to be sufficient answer.

Walker's reputation, which five months earlier had been shattered by failure, now rose intact and brighter than ever. It was rumored that a new Walker expedition, its goal as yet unknown, was in the making, the men eager for adventure sought him out and offered their services in whatever project he might be planning.


## III


By late October, Cole was back in San Francisco, bearing with him a signed letter from the Provisional Director of the Democratic rebel government, Francisco de Castellon. If Cole would bring three hundred men to Nicaragua to serve in the Democratic army, the letter said, they would receive regular pay and land grants after Castellon became head of the national government. To Cole's disappointment, Walker found the letter useless. To attempt to raise an expedition with no better legal ground than it contained would lay them open to immediate arrest for violation of the Neutrality Laws —and with little hope, this time, of escaping conviction. The need, he told Cole, was for a formal grant of a substantial tract of land in Nicaragua and for permission to colonize it—a contractual document which would say nothing of a military purpose. If Cole could obtain such a grant, "something might be done with it," Walker said. Even then, if the federal authorities insisted on probing beneath the surface of the contract, the expedition might not be allowed to sail.

Cole had begun to count heavily on Walker, and he was impelled to make another voyage to Nicaragua. Two months passed. Then, early in 1855, Cole sent from Nicaragua a contract, signed by Castellon, and meeting Walker's specifications. This time his efforts bore fruit. On receipt of the contract, Walker at once returned to San Francisco to prepare for his next adventure.

The decisive question for him was whether, in view of President Pierce's recent proclamation against filibustering, Major General Wool would accept Castellon's colonization grant as sufficient justification for the sailing of an armed force from the port. The prospect was by no means hopeful. District Attorney Inge, still smarting from his defeat at Walker's hands in the trial resulting from the Sonora affair, was not likely to be cooperative. Nevertheless, having gone so far with Cole, Walker was obligated to try to convince Inge and Wool that the fighting men he planned to recruit would be no more than peaceful colonists on their way to a foreign land. Everything would depend on their willingness to let themselves be deceived.

## I V

In the period when Walker was practicing law in Marysville, Commodore Vanderbilt had taken it into his head to go abroad; and the impulse that removed him from New York and from active supervision of his affairs introduced a radical change in the unfolding pattern of events, and gave a dramatic new turn to Walker's life story. The repercussions of Vanderbilt's decision were felt finally in the attitude of District Attorney Inge toward Walker's enterprise.

Between Vanderbilt and total success in life there stood, to his way of thought, only one obstacle—the social barrier. In spite of his great wealth, he and his family had not been able to escape the stigma of the *parvenu,* had never been able to penetrate the high society of the period. Believing that the surest key to the locked door of aristocracy is fame, and that the short cut to fame is publicity, he decided to generate such publicity as no mere millionaire before him had ever received. He would compel the bows of New Yorkers who professed to regard him as a vulgar money-man, by first compelling the respectful attention of the entire world.

For his instrument, he decided on a steam yacht, which was designed to his specifications in 1852. The *North Star,* 2500 tons, 270 feet long, cost him half a million dollars to build and half as much again to operate each year. Engineered to perfection, with an interior in which marble flooring, granite columns, rosewood paneling, and frescoed ceilings created the effect of a luxury hotel, it was by far the largest and most elaborate pleasure craft seen in American waters up to that time. Even before it was completed in 1853, Vanderbilt announced an intention that delighted New York's sensation-hungry newspapers. With his family and a few friends and retainers, he would take the *North Star* on a gala transatlantic voyage such as no American had ever previously undertaken. It was easy to envisage the stir his magnificent boat would make in the ports of England, France, Italy, Russia—tangible proofs for haughty European eyes of the potentialities of American enterprise.

He had to consider, however, that the trip as planned would consume the better part of half a year. What of the companies that he managed? By this time, Vanderbilt had got rid of those in Accessory Transit who were capable of offering resistance to his will, and a puppet board of directors obligingly met his terms. Almost overnight he sold to the company the ships of his Nicaragua Line for $1,500,000, resigned from the presidency, opened his own office as exclusive New York agent for the company, and took as his emolument no less than 20 percent of the company's gross receipts—this for continuing to manage the ships—plus an agent's commission of 2½ percent of all passenger fares.

A problem remained—who could properly manage the affairs of Accessory Transit while he was abroad? Two strong and capable

executives were needed—one in whose hands he could safely leave
the New York headquarters, the other to look after the San Francisco
end of the business. Searching his acquaintance, he turned to
Charles Morgan, a prominent shipowner, almost as well-known as
Vanderbilt himself, and whose Morgan Line dominated the traffic
between New York and the ports of the Gulf of Mexico. When
Morgan, in return for a share in the commissions earned by the New
York agency, consented to serve as Vanderbilt's deputy, the Commodore was flattered. In addition, Morgan had formed a connection
with a redoubtable man of business, Cornelius K. Garrison, who had
made a fortune as a banker in Panama, and who was at that very
time planning to establish a banking house in San Francisco. It was
Morgan's suggestion that Garrison be invited to New York and in-
duced to manage Accessory Transit's affairs on the West Coast. So
it was arranged; Vanderbilt was impressed by Garrison; and a sufficient inducement was found for him in a contract at a salary of
$60,000 per year, placing Garrison among the highest-paid men in
the United States.


## V


The cruise amply fulfilled Vanderbilt's hopes. Admiring descriptions
of his career and his yacht appeared in the British Press and were
circulated throughout the world. The London *Daily News* compared
him favorably with Cosimo de' Medici, and added, "It is time that
*parvenu* should be looked upon as a word of honor. . . . It is time
that the middle classes should take the place that is rightfully theirs
in the world that they have made." In Paris, men of prominence
respectfully approached Vanderbilt with business proposals; in Italy
he sat for a portrait bust by America's most noted sculptor, Hiram
Powers; in Russia the Czar himself took an interest in the *North Star*
and gave Vanderbilt the use of one of the imperial carriages. From
first to last the cruise sparkled like the gem of self-assertion that it
was. But it had its flaw. Letters from New York which came to
Vanderbilt just before he sailed for home told of maneuvers by
Morgan and Garrison to oust him permanently from control of Accessory Transit. Under Morgan's leadership, the company had can-
celed its contract with the Commodore's agency, on the ground that
it had proved "impossible to obtain a statement of accounts" from
Vanderbilt.

In the last days of the voyage Vanderbilt burned with a desire for revenge. Knowing his temper, Wall Street held its breath as the *North Star* was reported steaming back to New York. A few days after his return, Vanderbilt addressed to Morgan and Garrison one of the shortest and most famous letters in the history of business. "Gentlemen," it said, "You have undertaken to cheat me. I won't sue you, for the law is too slow. I'll ruin you. Yours truly, Cornelius Vanderbilt."

The courts of New York soon swarmed with lawyers in *Vanderbilt vs. Accessory Transit Company, C. Morgan and C. K. Garrison.* So numerous were the charges and countercharges, so confused the records of account, so complex the issues uncovered, that the public soon came to agree with the *Herald's* prediction that "no one would ever get at the bottom of this mysterious, mixed-up matter." Vanderbilt himself regarded the litigation merely as a harassing action against his enemies. It was on a direct, frontal attack that he was counting. Early in 1854, he organized a new line of steamships, which included the famous *North Star,* to carry passengers to San Francisco by way of Panama—the very route that he had formerly decried. His new service, called the Independent Line, was designed for one purpose only—to divert passengers from the Nicaragua Line —and it made much of the fact that the transisthmian railroad in Panama was almost completed. The Independent Line offered rates even lower than those which had marked Vanderbilt's earlier price war with George Law. For $100, plus the railroad fare, a man could travel "first class" all the way to California, while steerage cost no more than $30.

From the moment that the Independent Line's advertisements appeared, saying flatly that "passengers will be guaranteed to arrive in San Francisco ahead of the Nicaragua Line," its ships were crowded. Whether it could make money with rates so low was debatable, but Vanderbilt knew more than one way to turn a dollar. Before Wall Street got wind of his scheme he sold short many thousands of shares of Accessory Transit stock. Never was a speculative profit more certain. The falling off of business on the Nicaragua Line was accompanied by a steady decline in the price of Accessory Transit shares on the exchange.

Morgan and Garrison were particularly hard hit when, in the summer of 1854, the Accessory Transit Company, now their property, ran into trouble with obstructive British officials in the port of Greytown. In resentment, the company persuaded the American

Navy to bombard the sleepy little town,* and the news caused a further diversion of the Caribbean passenger traffic to Panama.

The immediate beneficiary of the affair was Vanderbilt, for the price of Accessory Transit stock, already depressed, took a further drop. At this point, instead of selling, he began to buy the stock in large quantities. His purpose now was to regain control of the company; and Morgan and Garrison, alarmed, sought a compromise. Accessory Transit, they said, would pay Vanderbilt's claim for moneys due him under his agency contract, if he in return would sell his Independent Line to the company and agree to retire from isthmian shipping. "A settlement," reported the New York *Tribune*, "has been amicably arranged." "Amicably" was hardly the appropriate adverb. No victory that was less than complete could slake Vanderbilt's thirst for revenge. Morgan and Garrison still had the Accessory Transit Company, which he had founded. Quietly he continued to accumulate the company's shares.

Mayor Garrison, still in charge of Accessory Transit's office on the West Coast, sensed that the Commodore would soon make another attempt to recapture the company. His position was strong, for his contract with the company meant that Vanderbilt could not easily dispose of him; and through a San Francisco banking house in which he and Morgan were partners he had access to considerable financial recources. Given a weapon with which to fight, he could bring to bear enough money and influence to give pause even to Vanderbilt.

The hint that a weapon might be found came to Garrison late in 1854 from a Sacramento publisher who had a slight acquaintance with Walker. This man, Parker H. French, combined an almost total lack of scruple with a fertile imagination, enormous effrontery, and a persuasive tongue. He had learned of Walker's talks with Cole about Nicaragua; he knew of Garrison's struggle with Vanderbilt; and without Walker's knowledge, he appointed himself go-between.†

Garrison was interested, but he was too canny to act hastily or impulsively. He could not afford to have it said that he was in any way connected with a violation of the Neutrality Laws. If Walker could succeed in reaching Nicaragua and establishing himself there —in itself an unlikely assumption—that would be time enough to

---

* *Wheeler Scrapbooks*, Vol. II, p. 10, Congressional Library. W. O. Scroggs, *Filibusters and Financiers*, New York, 1916, Ch. 7.
† William Walker, *The War in Nicaragua*, Mobile, 1860, Ch. 5.

consider an approach to him. He dismissed French with a curt message. He wished "to have nothing to do with such enterprises as he supposed Walker to contemplate." Nevertheless, from this moment, he took a friendly if distant interest in Walker's plans; and his influence in San Francisco being what it was, the danger that District Attorney Inge would stop Walker from taking an expedition to Nicaragua became negligible.


VI


An even more roundabout stream of circumstance, originating in Madrid, played on the mind of General Wool, who had the intention and the physical power at his command to prevent Walker from defying the Neutrality Laws. A few years earlier Spain had raised to aggravating heights Cuba's tariffs on American goods entering the port of Havana and had imposed onerous new rules on American shipping. At that time Cuba was America's third largest export market, taking large quantities of such products as flour, corn, pork, and dried fish; the drastic decline in exports, resulting from the new tariffs, was felt especially by Southern businessmen.

Secretary of War Jefferson Davis, who had inherited Calhoun's mantle as chief spokesman for the South, and who wanted to see Cuba annexed for political reasons, promptly demanded action against Spain, even at the price of war. He did not believe that, in the final test, England or France would stand by the Spaniards.

The specific measure advocated by Davis with respect to Cuba was suspension of the Neutrality Laws. This move in his plan was to be followed by a new and this time powerful filibustering expedition, which, coinciding with a popular Cuban revolution, would drive out the Spaniards, without providing a pretext for British and French intervention. Therefore a friendly Cuban regime would seek statehood in the Union. Davis' great fear was that, unless the island was quickly brought into the United States, Spain might abolish Negro slavery there—a development which could wipe out the political value of the acquisition for the South, and would intensify the agitation over slavery in the United States.

In all the decades during which the eyes of America's leaders, from Jefferson on, had been fixed yearningly on "The Pearl of the Antilles," there had never before been so promising an opportunity for its annexation. That the moment was not seized was due to the peculiar political position in which President Pierce found himself. The Senate was being torn by strife over the Kansas-Nebraska bill,* and the sectional animosities were inflamed to the kindling point. Pierce, who had to think about renomination by the Democratic Party in 1856, had chosen to conciliate Southern opinion by declining to take a firm stand against the dangerous measure, and in so doing had stirred up deep resentment in the North. Under the circumstances, if he had given way to the South on Cuba as well, he would have lost most of his Northern support in the next Democratic Convention.

At one point, in an effort to extricate himself from his dilemma, he tried to use Cuba as a bargaining point with Southern senators. Had they been content to see Kansas and Nebraska enter the Union as free states, under the terms of the Missouri Compromise, their reward might well have been the suspension of the Neutrality Laws and the annexation of Cuba. They were, however, determined to have both the island and Kansas. This was their undoing, and Pierce's. The South's threat to secede from the Union, unless the rich lands of Kansas were open to the slave trade and Southern domination, was met by firm determination on the part of most Northern senators not to move against Cuba.

While the debate raged, the opportunity passed. In May 1854, Spain altered the entire complexion of the affair. Suddenly she announced that thenceforth the slave trade would be banned in Cuba, and hinted at eventual emancipation of the island's Negroes. No move could have been better calculated to harden the split in American opinion and paralyze the administration. Many in the North who had favored acquisition of Cuba so long as the move appeared to be directed against Spanish tyranny now became intensely aware of the moral problem involved, and took a fixed stand against any steps to annex the island.

Walker, then editing the *Democratic State Journal* in Sacramento, also felt impelled to declare himself on the issue. In a revealing editorial he wrote, "Events are justifying the foresight of the Southern men who opposed the Kansas-Nebraska bill. The South . . . has lost instead of gaining by the act. . . . A few hot-headed and narrow-minded men have persuaded the South into a course she already begins to repent of. . . . It is now too late to repent. . . . Ultra-slavery

* Urged by Southerners, this bill left to the settlers of Kansas and Nebraska the decision as to whether slavery should be permitted in their territories. It was generally assumed that Kansas at least would become a slave state. The bill became law in the spring of 1854.

men are the most active and efficient agents abolitionists can have
in the Southern States. The true friends of the South are those who
repudiate the ideas and acts of the South Carolina school."* At this
stage, his views on slavery were identical to those which he had
expressed while editing the New Orleans *Crescent* five years earlier
—against its expansion and against secession.

## VII

The three chief American envoys in Europe were instructed to meet
on the continent and come to a joint recommendation for the administration's policy with respect to Cuba. The meeting took place
in October 1854, at Ostend, Belgium. Out of it came the notorious
document known as the Ostend Manifesto. If Spain refused to sell
Cuba, said the Manifesto, and if the island in her hands constituted
a threat to the United States, "then, by every law, human and divine,
we shall be justified in wresting it from Spain if we possess the
power."

Its effect was to revive the attack of Jefferson Davis and others
on the Neutrality Laws. Although he had been thwarted on the
Cuban issue, Davis now developed a strong interest in the possibility
that one or more filibustering expeditions might head for Nicaragua.
He saw that if a private military force should succeed in Nicaragua,
the entire position of the United States in the Caribbean might be
altered. The Neutrality Laws might be swept into the discard, and
the government compelled after all to seize Cuba and fight Spain. As
Secretary of War, Davis was officially committed to rigorous enforcement of the Neutrality Laws, but as a practical politician he knew
how large the gap is between the avowal of a law and its implemen-
tation. To that gap he now directed his efforts. Rumors of a possible
expedition from California to Nicaragua were already current. A
remarkable letter from Davis to General Wool in San Francisco now
made clear his wish that the general temper zeal with discretion
where the Neutrality Laws were concerned.

This letter was understood by Wool as implying that he was to
invoke the Neutrality Laws against filibusters only if the civil au-
thories requested his intervention. Consequently, when Walker approached Wool early in 1855 to ascertain his views on the

* *Democratic State Journal,* Sacramento, Cal., Aug. 12, 1854.

expedition, the general was suddenly all affability. He declared frankly that the instructions of the Secretary of War left him no authority to interfere unless San Francisco's District Attorney requested him to do so. Privately the old soldier went even further, grasping Walker by the hand, and saying, "Not only will I not place any hindrance in your way, but I wish you the greatest success!"

The train of great events that Commodore Vanderbilt had set in motion five years earlier, when he sought to construct a canal in Nicaragua, had at last intersected Walker's curious orbit. Through the instrumentality of Jefferson Davis and General Wool, through Cornelius Garrison and District Attorney Inge, he was being given a chance to make history.

# "THE IMMORTALS"

The failure of Walker's Sonora expedition notwithstanding, hundreds of the adventurers and soldiers of fortune in whom San Francisco abounded, as well as its derelicts, offered themselves for his service. From among them he chose with a shrewd eye for courage and endurance. His enthusiasm and conviction about his new venture were infectious. He had been studying a detailed description of Nicaragua's history, geography, and people, by the former American minister, George E. Squier, and it significantly aided recruitment. In addition to arresting facts, the book was full of charming little vignettes of Nicaraguan life. Squier had been especially susceptible to the charm of the lissome, glossy-haired native girls, "of all shades from white to ebon black, straight as arrows, lithe yet full-figured, with quick, mischievous eyes"—flirtatious, full of animal spirits, and dressed in vividly colored skirts and scanty blouses that often revealed as much as they concealed when the girls raised their arms to balance red water jars or baskets of fruit on their heads. One passage in this book was picked up by the newspapers—a scene in which Nicaraguan soldiers, seeing some girls swimming nude in a river, sought to scare them to the beach by shouting, *"Lagartos! Lagartos!* ("Alligators!"). Another anecdote described the negotiation of an infatuated young Bostonian with a village priest for the hand of his "niece"—all unaware that it was customary to find in the household of many a *padre* a young and pretty girl designated as the *sobrina*—a niece only by courtesy. A little sketch by Squier of a bare-bosomed beauty rolling tortillas similarly attracted attention by its frankness. In woman-starved California, the sexual possibilities of Nicaragua must have excited almost as much masculine interest as the prospect of winning rich lands in Walker's service. Squier

144

pointed out that the owners of the great Nicaraguan plantations, drawing princely incomes from the land, lived a life of feudal satisfactions such as could not be found in the United States. An aristocrat with a hundred thousand cacao trees or so might obtain from this crop alone some $30,000 per year, free of all taxes; master of his workmen, he would be impeded only by his own conscience of his access to their women folk.

The limiting factor in Walker's effort to prepare his expedition was money. His own meager resources were soon exhausted. Influential friends did their best for him, among them Edmund Randolph, now married and a pillar of San Francisco society. Another favorable voice was raised for Walker by California's favorite son, Colonel John C. Frémont, who, running against Buchanan in 1856, would be the first Republican candidate for the Presidency of the United States. But the funds at Walker's disposal fell far short of his need. A ship had to be chartered; arms, equipment, and food had to be bought. Each additional recruit increased the cost of the expedition—which, it was plain from the first, would have to travel on a shoestring. He was hampered, too, in raising money by the wound in his foot sustained in his latest duel, and which resulted in a painful if temporary limp. When all was done, Walker was unable to pay for many of his purchases; he could afford no better boat than an unseaworthy old brig named *Vesta;* he had no money with which to hire a crew; the only captain available to him was a drunken ne'er-do-well; and he could put aboard only fifty-eight men. It was these men who, a few months later, were celebrated by the entire press of the nation as "The Immortals."

## II

The element of the absurd which was so often present in Walker's undertakings, and which generally arose from his refusal to admit the hopelessness of the odds against him, materialized on the *Vesta* just before it was due to weigh anchor. A revenue cutter, the *Marcy,* came alongside, and San Francisco's sheriff, with a party of deputies, boarded the *Vesta* and ordered it attached for debt. A storekeeper who had extended credit to Walker had changed his mind, and was demanding immediate payment. Until it was forthcoming, the brig might not leave port. To make certain of Walker's compliance, the sheriff seized the *Vesta*'s sails and carried them onto the dock.

One of the newspaper accounts of the incident stated that Walker showed "profound anger"—a display of emotion unusual for him. He suspected that the development was a stratagem of District Attorney Inge, who, while unwilling to block the expedition openly and thus incur the displeasure of Mayor Garrison, might well have resorted to a legalistic trick to express his enmity. Walker acted, however, with restraint and prudence. Cautioning his restive men not to interfere with the sheriff, he limped ashore, sought out the trouble-making storekeeper, and quietly pointed out the hazards that would be run by the man whom his recruits might hold responsible for the failure of the expedition to sail. It was a cogent argument, and the creditor hastily agreed to lift the libel on the ship.

But Walker's problem was far from solved. A more serious threat awaited him on the *Vesta.* The sheriff, in his absence, had prepared a bill of costs for his own part in attaching the brig, and wanted three hundred dollars before he would release it—a sum so far out of Walker's reach as to imply the end of the expedition. At this moment, only one thing was clear to him. The *Vesta* had to sail, and soon. Many of his men, irked by the delay, were becoming unruly and dangerous. Another day's idleness could mean violence, the disintegration of his force, and an end to all his hopes. The sarcasms of the newspapers, too, as they reported his plight, had to be cut short before they weakened the chance of raising future reinforcements.

"It is almost night," he said quietly to the sheriff. "I shall not be able to get the money until morning."

Pleased that Walker had not questioned his exorbitant demand, the sheriff said that he would wait.

"However," Walker went on, "you will not be paid unless the sails are brought back immediately. Legally, you had no right to remove them. If necessary, I shall ask the court for a ruling."

The sheriff, uncertain of his legal position, and with his mind fixed on the three hundred dollars, was not disposed to argue the point. The return of the sails seemed to him to involve no risk. Not knowing that the creditor's libel on the ship had already been lifted, he thought that the cutter *Marcy,* still alongside, would continue to guard the brig; and it did not seem likely that the *Vesta* would sail without a crew. He assented to Walker's request. A deputy, he said, would spend the night on the brig, and he himself would be around to collect the money in the morning.

With the sails once more on board and the sheriff gone, Walker courteously invited the deputy, one Purdy, to join him in a drink. Together they went to his cabin. Once inside, Walker fixed Purdy with a cold gray eye. "The *Vesta* is going to sail, Mr. Purdy," he remarked in the low-pitched drawl that, in him, always signified high tension. As the deputy gaped at him, he pointed to a table. "There sir," he said, "are champagne and cigars." From his pocket he drew a pair of handcuffs which he placed alongside the bottle. "And there are handcuffs and irons. Pray take your choice."*

Purdy, who had been a member of the California legislature, was inclined to be philosophical; and he settled down in a chair with the bottle. Excusing himself, Walker locked the cabin door behind him and went aboard the *Marcy* to show its commander proof that the ship had been cleared to leave port. This done, and finding the officer friendly, he asked a favor of him. Would the *Marcy*'s crew help in bending on the *Vesta*'s sails—a task for which Walker's own men were untrained? Sailors from the *Marcy* came over the brig's side, and by midnight the work was completed.

As soon as the *Marcy* had gone, Walker signaled the shore. A steam tug for which he had previously arranged came alongside, took the *Vesta* in tow, and brought it to a point well outside the harbor. Just before the tug cast off, deputy Purdy was put aboard her, to raucous cheering from Walker's recruits. Then, spreading her sails, the *Vesta* stood out to sea.

## III

Six weeks later (the *Vesta* had sailed a slow, stormy, and erratic course) Walker landed at Realejo, the northernmost port of Nicaragua, close to the revolutionary capital of León. The wild and piratical look of the bearded Americans did not prevent heartening displays of friendliness by the people who lined the streets of the shabby little town. Men cheered, women waved, everyone smiled at the newcomers who were to help the Democrats of the north against their enemies, the Legitimists. A formal welcome from an officer of the Leónese army was followed by the appearance of a gentleman of British birth, Charles Doubleday, who knew Nicaragua well and who offered his services to Walker—a valuable acquisition. Doubleday, who served thereafter as an officer in Walker's army and wrote a

* *Harper's Weekly*, 1857, Vol. I, p. 332. New York *Herald*, June 2, 1855.

book about his experiences, described the impression that the American made on him: "He exercised a magnetic attraction . . . such as is rarely witnessed." Testimony to the same effect came from Joaquin Miller, who in one of his poems spoke of Walker as having "a piercing eye, a princely air, a presence like a chevalier." His appeal for them was obviously much more than a matter of eyes and bearing. Their response and that of many another to Walker was of the kind that idealism alone is able to evoke in educated and sensitive men. Regarding himself as an apostle of American democracy and with unshakable faith in the justice of his cause, Walker radiated the intense glow of the true believer. There was already in him that touch of fanaticism, later to become more apparent, which all men respect as a source of power, and which, in so soft-spoken and courteous a personality, was all the more effective.

## I V

From the first, Walker felt the fascination of the unique Nicaraguan landscape. He had read of the great green plain bordered in the far distance by low emerald hills and a belt of black towering volcanoes, by great blue lakes and a vast rain forest, but everything exceeded his expectation. The brilliant contrasts of raw color under the blazing sun and the dreamlike splendor of the soft tropic night generated in him a sensuous excitement that he never lost. "You felt," he wrote, "as if a thin and vapory exhalation of opium, soothing and exhilarating by turns, was being mixed at intervals with the common elements of the atmosphere." Outwardly he remained altogether the military man—crisp, definite, authoritative. His first order was a warning to his men of stern punishment if they disturbed the peace of Realejo. It is some measure of the respect in which he was held that those hardbitten adventurers, who had been confined to a wretched little vessel for six weeks, and who were now quartered on the town, contented themselves with some drinking of *aguardiente* and a little singing in the taverns (which also served as brothels) and refrained from looting, rape, and street brawls.

The day after his arrival, Walker rode to León for his first interview with the Provisional Director of the revolutionary regime, Castellon. León, a city one-third the size of San Francisco in 1855, was an impressive contrast to that wild boom town. Dignity and tradition were the essence of the Democratic capital. At the center of each municipal district was a church and a plaza, the core of community life and of the markets, while at the city's heart was a venerable cathedral, facing the grand plaza and the government buildings. As he passed the cathedral, Walker noted that its stone walls were heavily scarred with bullet pocks, marks of past revolutions in which the great building had been used as a fortress. A few days later, he would meet the dominant personality of León, the purple-robed Bishop, a man of exceptional intellect and experience, who was well disposed to Walker from the beginning. One of the Bishop's favorite remarks was, "Nicaragua needs only the aid of the United States to become an Eden of beauty and the garden of the world."

## V

Walker could hardly have come at a more fortunate moment for his purposes. The hopes of the Democrats were waning fast. A strong Legitimist army under the most famous of Nicaraguan commanders, General Ponciano Corral, was preparing to march on León from the south. Castellon, gray and anxious, received the American as a drowning man clutches at a log. Through his embraces and compliments Walker perceived a faltering spirit and incipient despair, and he came at once to the conclusion that Castellon "was not the man to control a revolutionary movement or to conduct it to a successful issue." On the surface, however, they established an amicable understanding. Castellon proposed and Walker agreed that the Americans would be constituted a separate corps—*La Falange Americana*—the American Phalanx. To Walker's request that he be given an additional two hundred Nicaraguan soldiers there was no demur. His next and crucial demand, however, produced an immediate crisis. This was for authority to sail south in the *Vesta* and occupy the Transit route. As he himself later wrote in *The War in Nicaragua,* "It was a fixed policy with Walker to get as near the Transit as possible, in order to recruit from the passengers . . . and to have the means of rapid communication with the United States. . . . It was idle for them [the *Falange*] to waste their energies and strength on a campaign that did not bring them toward the Transit road."

It was not Castellon, but his military commander, General Muñoz, who objected. Muñoz was a tall, handsome, and haughty egotist, by no means incapable, but exceedingly jealous of his prerogatives. Resplendent in a blue uniform with red lining and much

gilt, he eyed Walker's drab clothing and slight figure with uncon-
cealed disdain. The *Falange,* he insisted, should remain in the vicin-
ity of León to defend the capital against probable attack. Walker
replied quietly that it would be unwise to submit his men to the
corrosive temptations of garrison life. "Nothing so much tries the
firmness of men like those in the *Falange* as inaction." They had to
an extreme degree, he said, "the characteristic American thirst for
action and movement."

An argument took shape. Muñoz' strategy was based on the
traditional concept of war in Central America, in which victory went
to the side that successfully stormed the enemy's capital. Usually the
hard fighting took place at the very center of a besieged city, its
grand plaza and cathedral. The defenders would sacrifice the countryside and outlying sections of the city in order to entice the enemy
into its heart where fortification and supply gave an advantage to
the besieged. A decade earlier a Legitimist army, having failed to
capture León, had sacked and burned a thousand dwellings on the
outskirts—an atrocity the memory of which still inflamed the passions of the Leónese. Nevertheless, Muñoz saw no alternative but to
prepare for another such campaign.

Walker barely concealed his impatience. The strategy of siege
made for long, inconclusive, and highly destructive fighting, and
was altogether at odds with his temperament. Swift attack, the seizure of lines of communication, the shattering of enemy morale, and
the rout of his army were the essence of military success, his reading
had taught him. The Democratic army had to take the initiative, and
he and his men were prepared to be the spearhead of the attack.

Walker was able to take Castellon slightly apart from the others
and say to him in a low voice, "Let me speak frankly. If General
Muñoz is to give me orders, I cannot serve you."

"But," Castellon protested, "he is the commanding general."

"Perhaps that explains the perilous position of your government," said Walker.

The merits of the case aside—and there was much to be said for
Walker's stand—the urge to rebel against constituted authority was
growing stronger in him. No man had ever commanded him. He had
sprung directly to his colonelcy from the freedom of civilian life,
without ever having served in an army. An order from another was
a sting, arousing all his combativeness. His challenges were invariably aimed at the men who issued orders, men more powerful than
himself. It had been Judge Parsons; now it was Muñoz; soon it would
be Vanderbilt. It had once been his father.

Although he had been in León only a day, already he had generated controversy. But his calculation was sound. Castellon did not
dare risk the withdrawal of the Americans. Reluctantly, apologeti-
cally, the Provisional Director turned to Muñoz and said, "General,
I think we should give Colonel Walker the opportunity he asks."

"As you wish," said Muñoz icily, and making a formal bow to
Walker, left the room.

## VI

A man who had made as many enemies as Walker could not be
unduly disturbed at making another, but from this moment he
sensed that Muñoz' influence would be used to destroy him, and he
was right. Instead of the two hundred Nicaraguans promised him,
he received, after a long interval, only half that number. Supplies
needed at Realejo were so slow in arriving as seriously to delay the
departure of the *Vesta*. By the time Walker landed his force near the
Pacific end of the Transit road, valuable days had been lost, and he
soon had reason to believe that advance word of his plan had gone
to the enemy through an agent employed by Muñoz.

His first objective was the inland town of Rivas, a Legitimist base
near Lake Nicaragua which had to be taken before the Transit could
be held. Simple caution dictated that a surprise attack be made at
night, but his native guides proved untrustworthy and the crucial
hours of darkness were lost in following a circuitous route through
the rain forest. A heavy downpour, with continuous flashes of light-
ning overhead and treacherous mud underfoot, further impeded the
march. When the rain ended, and the moon could be glimpsed
through the thick foliage, the spectral effect of the black gigantic
tree trunks, the heavy branches, the creepers and vines, and a sense
of the wild animal life around them made some of the men uneasy;
and they began to sing, low-voiced, the favorite tunes of California:
"Oh, Susanna" and "Hail, Columbia!" Wearing dark trousers and
shirts, booted, carrying pistols and Bowie knives in addition to rifles,
the Americans formed a sharp contrast to the barefooted Nicaraguans, who wore straw hats and once-white cotton pantaloons, and
were armed with old-fashioned muskets and machetes. Their common purpose showed on their hats, where red ribbons signified their
democratic allegiance.

As a result of the delay, the *Falange* was compelled to advance
on Rivas in broad daylight. Walker's own description of the march

strikes an almost lyrical note. "Every now and then market-women, with baskets on their heads, and just come from Rivas, would gayly greet the soldiers. . . . Such of the men as spoke any Spanish would waste all the terms of endearment they could muster on the girls, who seemed pleased. . . . When, however, the command reached the summit of a hill . . . a scene of beauty and splendor drew them from everything else. Though the order was to march in silence an exclamation of surprise and pleasure escaped the lips of all. . . . The lake of Nicaragua lay in full view and rising from it, as Venus from the sea, was the tall and graceful cone of Omotepe. The dark forests of the tropics clothed the side of the volcano. . . . The beholder would not have been surprised to see it waken at any time. The first glimpse of the scene made the pulse stand still; and the *Falange* had scarcely recovered from its effects when the command was halted in order to prepare for the attack."

At noon on June 29, 1855, as the *Falange* advanced on Rivas for its first battle, it became evident to Walker that he had been betrayed. The enemy force awaiting him behind barricades was far larger than he had been given reason to expect, and it was under the command of a notorious Honduran general, Santos Guardiola, who had come to Nicaragua to aid the Legitimists. Guardiola was known —with reason—to all Central America as "The Butcher," and the terror of his name was enough to weaken the morale of Walker's Nicaraguan troops. At the first fire they fled without making even the pretense of a stand, leaving 55 Americans opposed to over 500 of the enemy.

In the first few minutes of fighting six of Walker's men were killed—among them two of his chief aides, Crocker and Kewen. Hard-pressed, the *Falange* fought its way to a large house and held off the enemy by accurate rifle fire from the windows. The men's fighting spirit was heightened by rage, for they saw five of their wounded comrades, unable to reach the house, done to death on the streets by sadistic bayonets. After four hours of sporadic shooting, the enemy losses exceeded those of the *Falange* ten to one. Now, however, the Legitimists received reinforcements, including a cannon, and with this advantage were able to approach the improvised fortress and set it on fire.

The last hope of the Americans who were still on their feet was to break through the enemy lines, and at Walker's signal, with a wild yell, they charged out of the house by an unguarded door. The movement was so unexpected and their marksmanship so effective that the nearest of the Legitimist troops turned and fled, while the rest were momentarily paralyzed. Retreating through the streets of Rivas, beating back their pursuers with deadly bullets, the Americans were able to make their way into the forest and at last back to the coast. A few hours later, weary and disheartened, they were again on the *Vesta,* sailing north.

Curiously, the defeat at Rivas did not diminish, but rather reinforced, Walker's sense of destiny. Like many a soldier who comes unscathed from a stricken field, he may have gained a kind of strength from the simple fact that he was alive when so many were dead. It has often been noted that repeated survival of great dangers breeds a sense of invulnerability, a secret feeling that one is favored by the gods. After the battle his men saw in him, to their amazement, not chagrin and worry, but a confidence and assurance that sprang wholly from within him, for there was certainly nothing in their circumstances to warrant it. He spent the days of the voyage back to Realejo tending their wounds, seeing that they rested, reviving their morale, and drafting a report for Castellon.

The primary purpose of the report, which he sent by messenger from Realejo, was to break the hold of General Muñoz on the Democratic army. The general, it said bluntly, had acted in bad faith; and he, Walker, would leave Nicaragua with his men at once unless Castellon investigated the sources of the apparent treason which had led to the defeat at Rivas. The response was much as Walker anticipated. Castellon, although unwilling to challenge Muñoz, begged Walker not to leave, but to bring his force to León, where fears of a Legitimist attack were thickening.

In the two weeks of fruitless correspondence that followed, Walker gave the appearance of sulking in his tent, but as soon as his men were fit to march he appeared to yield to Castellon's entreaties, and headed to León and a showdown with Muñoz. Fresh encouragement had come to him in the arrival of Byron Cole, who had just returned from Honduras, and who brought with him another valuable man. This was Bruno von Natzmer, a former Prussian cavalry officer, who knew Nicaragua as well as any foreigner. Their presence made Walker feel a little less the loss of Crocker and Kewen. Natzmer confirmed a point of considerable military importance that had begun to come home to Walker. The ordinary Nicaraguan, though he feared the North Americans, feared even more being conscripted into the armies of his own country, and would take far greater risks to escape the recruiting sergeant than he would ever run in battle.

"There is scarcely any labor a Nicaraguan will not do," noted Walker, "in order to keep out of the clutches of the press-gang." He laughed at the Nicaraguan generals for their "inveterate habit of catching a man and tying him up with a musket in his hand to make a soldier of him." The only natives that he cared to have in his army, from this time on, were volunteers.

## VII

Walker was not unduly surprised, on returning to León, to find that although Castellon's professions of friendship were unabated, he was willing to deliver the *Falange* to the mercies of Muñoz. The general had put forward a new proposal—let the American force be broken into small units and distributed among the Nicaraguan regiments. As soon as Walker became convinced that Castellon was about to support Muñoz on the issue, he decided to take his men out of León to a safer spot. But horses and oxcarts were needed, and when he sent a requisition for them to Castellon, it was ignored. An hour later Muñoz marched a strong Nicaraguan force into quarters directly opposite those of the Americans, as if daring them to attempt a move; and for a time it appeared that the *Falange* would have to fight its way out of León.

Walker then wrote an ultimatum to Castellon: "Remove your troops within an hour or we will consider them a hostile force and act accordingly." The threat succeeded. Rather than face the prospect of battle within his own ranks, Castellon agreed to exert his authority over Muñoz. The Nicaraguan troops were ordered away from the danger spot, horses and oxcarts were provided, and the Americans were allowed to leave the city.

There remained Muñoz to be dealt with. The plan in Walker's mind was open defiance of the general—in effect, a mutiny within the revolutionary army—supported by the populace of the countryside, where Muñoz, as a ruthless conscriptor of men, was highly unpopular. Chance, however, made this drastic action unnecessary. A small Legitimist force appeared south of León, and Muñoz, leading his troops in a raid against it, was mortally wounded. His death freed Walker to develop his own strategy.

He had selected the city of Chinandega, not far from León, as his headquarters, while he prepared his next move, for the Chinandegans were known to be dissatisfied with the do-nothing policies of

Castellon. The people were hospitable enough, but the morale of his own men caused him serious concern. In their view, the expedition had come to a dead end. Supplies of cartridge metal were so low that they were compelled to range the countryside for objects made of lead—a futile search, which they could not even enliven by loot or women without incurring severe punishment. Their interest in Walker's purpose was fading fast. What they wanted was to enjoy such Lotus pleasures as the country afforded—to sprawl in the green tropic shade, pluck fruit from the trees, dally with the Indian girls who preened themselves under their hard masculine stares. Chinandega was one of the many Nicaraguan towns where the dearth of males made women exceptionally responsive. In such an atmosphere Walker's insistence on frequent drill, long hours of duty, and high standards of personal behavior provoked bitter feeling. Two of his men deserted.

Spirits began to revive, however, when a contest between Walker and an English merchant in Chinandega solved the ammunition problem. This gentleman, Thomas Manning, had been a former British consul; and he bore himself so proudly and at the same time was so shrewd a man of business that no Nicaraguan dared oppose him. When it was learned that he and he alone in the area owned enough lead to provide a fresh supply of bullets for Walker's men, and an officer went to his house and proposed to purchase the metal, Manning rebuffed him in strong language. Walker recognized that his reputation among the Nicaraguans and the Americans alike might hinge on the outcome of the matter, and he felt more tension than showed in his own report. "A small guard was sent with orders to take the lead, paying a reasonable price. Thereupon the Englishman declared . . . that if the guard entered his house he would run up the British flag and put his house under the protection of the British government. The officer, uncertain how to act, returned . . . for orders; and being told that no foreign resident, except the representative of the sovereignty of this country, had a right to fly a foreign flag, he was ordered to enter the house; and in case the British colors were shown over it, to tear them down and trample them underfoot, thus returning the insult offered to the Republic of Nicaragua by their display. The native authorities, accustomed to yield to the wishes not only of British consuls but even of British merchants, were utterly astounded at these orders. On the Englishman, however, the orders produced a wholesome effect; for he immediately gave up the lead . . . for the use of the Americans." Manning conceived a considerable respect for Walker, and a little later congratulated him warmly on his successes.

A more important result of his affair was its part in bringing Walker a potent new friend—José Vallé, a pure Indian of vast bulk, robust personality, and great influence, who had been a colonel in the Democratic army before a serious wound forced his retirement. Walker's boldness and vigor appealed to him; intensely loyal to the Democratic cause and a shrewd judge of fighting men, he saw in the American far more hope for his part than in the vacillating Castellon, and gave him undeviating allegiance.

## VIII

Vallé proceeded to recruit a force of Indian field hands and town workers—volunteers, for Walker barred conscripts—to serve under the American with himself as their captain. When word of this activity reached Castellon, he promptly sent Vallé a peremptory order to disband his troop. No one bothered to reply. Instead, Walker led his Americans to Realejo and boarded the *Vesta,* where they were joined a few days later by Vallé and his Nicaraguans. Hot on their heels came another message from Castellon: Walker was to bring the *Falange* back to León.

This was serious, for Castellon was one of those essentially weak public men who need occasionally to taste raw power, as a kind of political aphrodisiac. If disobeyed, he might well use the one effective weapon at his disposal—declare his contract with the Americans void, thus destroying their legal justification for being in the country, and reducing their status to that of mere freebooters. Walker decided that the *Falange* must leave Realejo before such an order could arrive. The moment was hardly propitious, for cholera had broken out on shipboard, and was taking a heavy toll of Vallé's men, but Walker, after imposing stringent sanitary regulations on the American troops, gave orders to sail. Not one of the *Falange* came down with cholera on this voyage, in spite of its presence all around them, and the epidemic among the Nicaraguans was held in check—facts suggesting that Walker's medical training was proving its military value. It was at this time that his men, impressed by his care for their welfare, took to calling their thirty-one-year-old commander—behind his back—"Uncle Billy."

Again the *Vesta* bore southward, and three days later was anchored in the harbor of San Juan del Sur. There Walker heard news which revealed the full extent of the trial that lay ahead. The Legitimist had not been deceived as to his purpose, and 600 of their best troops were approaching under the command of The Butcher, Guardiola, who had sworn a sacred oath to drive the *falanginos* into the sea. Walker had not read his military historians for nothing. It was essential to occupy a favorable strategic position, and one that would command the Transit, without delay. A forced march brought him and his men, now comprising 50 Americans and 120 natives under Vallé, to Virgin Bay, the Transit harbor on Lake Nicaragua. They were eating breakfast and spreading their blankets when the advance guard of Guardiola's army, which had found their trail, attacked their pickets. These pickets, Nicaraguans all, proved the courage and the reliability of the native volunteer, as distinguished from the native conscript. Their cool, disciplined, and staunch defense of their posts gave Walker time to deploy his troops in strong positions, on rising ground, with their backs to the lake, and in possession of the buildings owned by Accessory Transit.

With no retreat possible, and with the knowledge that they could expect no quarter from the enemy, the *falanginos* and Vallé's men made their bullets count. After hours of rifle fire, the Legitimists fled. Sixty of them were found dead after the fight, but not a single American was killed, and only two of Walker's Nicaraguan allies. He himself had a close call, for he was struck in the throat by a spent bullet, and another shot cut through a packet of letters from Castellon, which were in his coat pocket. His readiness to expose himself to enemy fire and the dash with which he led a charge won him unstinted admiration from his men. The Leónese troops were even more impressed, however, by the care that he took to preserve the lives of the enemy wounded—an innovation, for the stricken Nicaraguan soldier left behind in a retreat could usually count on being shot or bayoneted by his captors.

For Walker, the battle of Virgin Bay, his first military victory, was a turning point. He could not know how widely and with what enthusiasm it would be reported in the United States, but the effect in Nicaragua was all that his heart could desire. The country was deeply stirred by the Democratic triumph, which was enhanced by the fact that the dictator, Chamorro, had been stricken by cholera, and was dead—a passing which to many seemed an omen of Legitimist doom.

From León, too, came encouragement. There Walker was hailed

as a hero, the man who had defeated The Butcher. Castellon also had fallen a victim to the cholera epidemic, and his successor wrote Walker that a company of Nicaraguan volunteers was on its way to serve as reinforcement. Even better, in American eyes, was the arrival of a Transit vessel from San Francisco, with 35 recruits for the *Falange;* while local representatives of the Accessory Transit Company, who had viewed Walker with distrust, were suddenly affable and cooperative.

His army now consisted of nearly 250 men—enough, he considered, for a major offensive. The audacity of his next move, if it had not succeeded, would have made him a laughing stock among military strategists. It was nothing less than the capture of the Legitimist capital, the old city of Granada. Using the tactics of surprise, he embarked his force on a steamboat of the Transit Company, landed at night at a point near Granada, advanced under cover of darkness, attacked at dawn, scattered the city's garrison within a few minutes, and took possession of the government offices. There was little bloodshed. "The encounter," said Walker lightly, "could scarcely be dignified with the name of an action." No triumph in battle could have been more effective. Overnight, from being a military adventurer at the head of a tiny force, he had become, for practical purposes, the dominant man of the nation; for the life of Nicaragua centered in the fertile lands that stretched from Granada to León, and to hold both cities was to hold the country.

His first order, as usual, was a warning to his men against looting, rape, and brutality. Resentment among the Americans was multiplied in his Leónese companies, most of whose men had seen their families suffer at Legitimist hands, and who dreamed of revenge. The heavy punishments with which he proposed to enforce his discipline caused mutinous murmurings, and for a time even his staunch comrade-in-arms, the Indian Vallé, was enraged at him.


# IX


Shortly after entering the city, Walker paid his respects to the American minister to Nicaragua, John H. Wheeler, and at the legation found a large number of Granadan women and children who had sought the protection of the American flag. Amazed by his boyish appearance and gentle manner, they begged him for mercy, only to find, incredulously, that he regarded himself at their protector.

Among the women to whom Wheeler presented him was one who particularly caught his attention—Doña Irena Ohoran, an unmarried woman of mixed Spanish and Irish blood (her name had once been spelled O'Horan), who was one of the leaders of Granadan society and a power in Legitimist politics. A few years older than Walker, diminutive, and with a face that radiated intelligence, she touched a responsive chord in him. When she offered her house, one of the finest in Granada, to serve as his headquarters, he instantly accepted. Under her guidance he glimpsed the beauties of Granada. It was a city of only 15,000, much smaller than León, but proud. Through green avenues of palm and orange trees one could see the vast blue sheet of Lake Nicaragua, stretching a hundred miles to the south, and where great seafish, the shark, the swordfish, the tarpon, were found in fresh water. Irena Ohoran pointed out volcanic islands in the distance, inhabited by idol-worshiping Indians, hostile to all whites. There was the beautiful Cathedral of Guadalupe, the grand plaza, and the market place—empty, now; but tomorrow, when the people understood that Colonel Walker intended them no harm, the shutters on the shops would come down and hundreds of market women would appear with their colorful baskets of fruit and vegetables. The shops were the best in Nicaragua, offering cottons from England, jewelry from Spain, silks and wines from France.

The horses and riders were as good as any in the world, and there was many a race in the Nicaraguan style. At the crack of a pistol, two young men would start out holding hands, and race until one was dragged from his horse: broken bones, sometimes broken necks resulted. Of other sports, too, there were plenty—especially cockfighting, the national pastime. Bullfighting was prohibited by law, but bull baiting was permitted—nearly as exciting, when ambitious youths tried to ride the maddened creatures. Men could gamble, too, at a casino, or in the billiard rooms. Theaters were lacking, but sometimes British variety acts—tumblers, singers, clowns—would appear, and one could occasionally ride out to the country to see villagers perform *una sagrada función*—a kind of morality play—very amusing to the sophisticates of the town. In no other small city in Central America did the gentry live so carefree a life. Servants were abundant and cheap. There was much wealth in Granada, derived largely from the great cacao and sugar estates nearby; and every year many Granadans went to Europe to study or travel.

Walker was well aware that the life described by Irena Ohoran was that of a few hundred families only. He did not need to be instructed in the condition of the poverty-ridden workers of the town, or the Indians of the countryside, serfs doomed to incessant labor and to premature death. He had seen their rickety hovels, usually shared with chickens, with dirt floors, mildewed walls, and beds consisting of the stretched hide of a cow. In those dwellings, the chief luxury was the candle. It not only gave illumination but also yielded soft balls of wax, which, when rubbed on the body were a reasonably efficient way of removing the ticks which bored into human skin and were regarded as a worse plague than the scorpions and the snakes.

Among the Granadans Walker became more popular with every hour, the more so because Legitimist propaganda had created an image of him as a bloodthirsty and lecherous buccaneer—and worse, a Democrat—from whom no mercy could be expected. When he set free a large number of political prisoners who had been chained in a medieval dungeon, crowds gathered in the streets to cheer him—crowds composed, it was noted, largely of poor folk who had made their way to the city's center, curious to see their new conqueror, a *gringo* and a Democrat. It was clear to everyone that he was much under Doña Irena's influence, which showed on the very day following his victory. This was a Sunday, and he attended eight o'clock mass at the Cathedral of Granada, where he listened to a sermon counseling "peace, moderation, and the putting aside of revolutionary passions." Afterward he called to his side the parish priest who had delivered the sermon, Padre Augustin Vijil (later to be minister to the United States), and publicly approved his sentiments.

This was the first move in Walker's policy of conciliation toward the Catholic Church. He needed, and knew that he needed, the great influence of the clergy on his side. His enemies abroad, as well as in Nicaragua, spread reports that he encouraged his men to desecrate shrines and churches; there was even a legend that he buried gold and jewels looted from the holy places of the country, but such stories were later found to be fabrications designed to discredit him.

At one point, the Church authorities of Granada granted him a loan of 1000 ounces of silver bullion, certainly without expecting to be repaid. The reality of Walker's relationship to the Church in the early days of his regime is suggested by a letter written to him on November 26, 1855, by the Vicar-General of the See of Nicaragua:

"I congratulate your excellency on the victory obtained in favor of liberal principles . . . I congratulate my country, for she will now come out of the ruins in which she has been sunk for more than thirty years." At the time, the Vicar-General was under the impression that Walker was dissociating himself from the extreme Democratic partisans. Later, when Walker's political activity began to deviate sharply from the preferences of the Church, most of the clergy of the country turned against him, but the issues between them were those of political ideology, not of religion.

Even the British, it would appear, regarded him in those first months as a hopeful figure. A letter from Thomas Manning, with whom Walker had quarreled in Chinandega only a few weeks earlier, and who had been appointed England's Acting Vice-Consul in Nicaragua, said, "As an eyewitness of all the horrors and events which have occurred since May 1851 [the outbreak of the current Nicaraguan revolution], nobody can better appreciate than myself the re-establishment of order and quiet. . . . Be persuaded, Sir, that the government of Her British Majesty will be disposed to sympathize with you." In London, the highly regarded *Economist* was even willing to concede all Central America to Walker and the United States. "We could not hinder the ultimate absorption by the Anglo-Saxon republicans of Central America if we would—and we are by no means certain that we should."

# THE
# HOT SUN OF NICARAGUA

⬥

Whether or not Walker actually fell in love with Irena Ohoran, his men gossiped freely about them. Her popular nickname in Granada was La Niña, the little one, and by the time rumor had worked its way through the ranks of the American force, La Niña Irena had been distorted into "Nila Mairena." Under this name she later appeared as a figure of mystery in American writings about Walker. The men sensed, however, that this was no ordinary affair of the flesh. Between the lines of his own comments on La Niña much can be read. Initially he described her as "a quick and minute observer, with all the gravity and apparent indifference of the native race . . . fertile in resources for sending intelligence to her friends. She had rendered much service to the Legitimist party in days past; and even the stern nature of Fruto Chamorro owned her sway and yielded to her influence, when all others failed to move him."

There soon appears in his account, however, a strong hint of something more than respect for her political talents. He discovered that she had a highly placed lover. "The private relations," wrote Walker in a vein of extraordinary bitterness, "which it is said, and probably with truth, existed between her and D. Narciso Espinosa, a leading man among the Legitimists, enabled her to breathe her spirit into the party after the death of Chamorro." His feelings about Espinosa, whom he described as "a man without principle and without honor," were tinged with a personal resentment such as he displayed toward no other Nicaraguan. It took the form finally of an accusation of complicity in an alleged Legitimist plot against the new regime. What was the evidence against Espinosa? Walker himself admitted that it was only "vague and uncertain," yet he had the man forcibly deported from Nicaragua. Such unusual heat in him suggests emotions at work which were more than political. From this time, the connection between Walker and La Niña became merely formal.

Prior to the Espinosa incident, however, Irena helped to steer Walker though the maze of Nicaraguan politics and to indoctrinate him in the techniques of political warfare, Central American style. In so doing she may well have influenced fundamental decisions. A major strategic problem then confronted him—and more than strategic, for it touched the core of his philosophy. Was he a Democratic partisan, the role implied by his contract with Castellon, or was he seeking to reshape Nicaragua in a new way? There was a common impression in the United States that the partisan armies of Central America represented no more than the personal ambitions of the warlords who led them, and that party programs counted for little, but Nicaraguans knew better. The Democrats had espoused far-reaching reforms in land rents, peonage, and trade, and contemplated a revival of the old Central American Federation. The Provisional Government at León and the Leónese troops in Granada were counting on Walker to secure their control of the country. Anything less than total victory over the Legitimists, in their view, would be an invitation to a renewal of civil war. Similarly the Democrats and Liberals of the neighboring republics regarded Walker with high hope. The San Salvador newspaper, *El Rol,* on January 2, 1856, defended Walker against attacks by conservative elements, stating boldly that "this much-decried invasion of Nicaragua by the North Americans is but an invective and a calumny of the aristocratic party." It was the belief of many throughout the isthmus that unless Walker succeeded in re-establishing the Central American Federation under Democratic rule, nation would continue to fight nation, party would continue to fight party, and the people would be doomed to incessant warfare and inevitable retrogression.

The issue could not be long postponed. Already the Liberal regime in Honduras had been driven from power, and the ousted President, Trinidad Cabañas, who had unhesitatingly sent troops to fight alongside the Nicaraguan Democrats in their time of need, was asking Walker for similar aid. Could he, should he rescue Honduran democracy? This was the question Walker had to decide.

He fully accepted the view that the five Central American republics ought to be consolidated. The Great Seal of State that he designed for the Nicaraguan government showed five volcanoes in a close cluster, with the sun rising behind the first, and the legend

*Dios—Union—Libertad.* In the flag that he adopted (two broad horizontal stripes of azure blue and a white stripe between) the center was dominated by a five-pointed red star. But a political conception was one thing, military reality another. He was less misled than the enthusiastic Democrats by the appearance of his triumph. The Legitimist power could not easily be broken. Its army, under General Corral, still occupied strongly fortified positions on the Transit route, and was much larger than the forces at Walker's command. And throughout Central America, behind the conservatives and the aristocrats, stood not only the prevailing influence of the Church, but also that of England.

It was obvious to Walker that a successful democratic revolution in Central America could take place only if it were strongly supported by the United States. But the administration of President Pierce, far from encouraging the Nicaraguan Democrats, showed a strong bias in favor of the Legitimists; it had recognized Chamorro in spite of his flagrant suppression of democratic rights. The Accessory Transit Company, too, had been content with Chamorro, so long as he did not interfere with their operations. Against this background, Walker took it for granted that a strongly partisan position would invite an attack in overwhelming force from all sides.

In the upshot, the strategy that he chose was a painful disappointment to his Democratic friends. To bring peace to the country was his first purpose, he announced, and this could be done only by compromising the differences between the two parties and establishing a coalition government. His Leónese soldiers muttered, but for the Granadans this was pleasant news. All at once Walker was a favorite of the Legitimists. Receptions given in his honor by Irena Ohoran and others were attended by the wealthiest and most aristocratic families of the city, who now regarded Walker as the only barrier between them and the vengeance of the Democrats. Every honor was accorded him; when he entered a room men and women rose and applauded. The Granadans were in fact awed by his ability to control both the hotheaded Leónese troops and the bearded *gringos.* When one of the Americans in a drunken fog wantonly shot and killed a Nicaraguan boy, and Walker had him court-martialed and executed, the city felt that here at last was a military man dedicated to justice.

# II

The American's driving energy also impressed Nicaragua. His working hours were from six o'clock in the morning until ten at night, his only recreation a daily horseback ride. Confronted with a thousand problems of the moment, he nevertheless found time to plunge into new and ambitious projects, among them the establishment of an official newspaper. One of his Californians had been a printer and editor; they imported a press and some fonts of type from San Francisco, and were able to improvise a remarkably competent weekly, *El Nicaragüense,* partly in English, partly in Spanish. From the beginning it was one of Walker's major tools, through which he interpreted his purpose to the Granadans and the world. Copies went regularly to the United States, inviting Americans to share in the exotic pleasures and bright future of beautiful Nicaragua; and the influence of the paper on the American press, which quoted it extensively, played a large part in bringing nearly one thousand recruits to Walker's service in the year that followed. Political opinion was similarly shaped. *El Nicaragüense* made it clear that Walker was no mere freebooter or dangerous revolutionary, but the "regenerator" of a much abused and unhappy nation.

He was especially successful in surrounding his name with an aura of predestination. There was an old legend among the Nicaraguan Indians, that the people would some day be brought into the light by a redeemer, who would be recognized by his gray eyes. Walker had come across this legend in his reading; under the circumstances, he may even have been inclined to believe it. *El Nicaragüense* left no doubt that he was "the gray-eyed man of destiny." "Last week," reported the newspaper, "we saw in Granada a delegation of Indians, who rarely visit the city, who desired to see General Walker. They were charmed by his gentle reception, and offered to him their heartfelt thanks for their liberation from oppression and for the present state of quiet of this country. They laid at his feet the simple offerings of their fruits and fields, and hailed him as 'Gray-Eyed Man' so long and anxiously awaited by their fathers." Newspapers throughout the United States seized on the story, and for a year it was a rare newspaper article about Nicaragua that did not refer to Walker's gray eyes.

Even the sophisticated European mind was caught by him. British periodicals, which then habitually shrugged at America's politics and public figures, felt constrained to report Walker's actions and statements with close attention, mentioning his name more frequently than they did the President of the United States. The *Revue des Deux Mondes* published a major article on the significance of his achievements, ranking him among the great political figures of the age, "the rival of Washington."

Europe was fascinated not so much by the dramatic fact that, with a handful of men, Walker had swiftly conquered a country and become its dictator, as by the practical implications of his action. Was the United States entering on its imperialistic phase? Accustomed to the ways of their own governments, the statesmen of England, France, and Spain found it almost inconceivable that he could have undertaken such a project, not to say succeeded at it, without undercover support from Washington. The British especially could not believe that he stood alone, and expecting him momentarily to receive recognition and aid from Washington, were tentative and cautious in their first dealings with him.

### III

As the strong man of a Central American republic, Walker suffered from the serious liability of a puritanical upbringing. Instinctively the Nicaraguans felt him to be at the polar extreme of temperament from themselves. He might sympathize with their sorrows, but could never enjoy their pleasures, the stronger force binding men together in daily life. Cockfighting, Granada's favorite sport, he privately considered detestable. He did not even laugh, he hardly smiled. That there was an ironic humor in Walker is shown by many passages in his writings, but to him ready displays of mirth were a sign of weakness. Even the style of Walker's dress struck them as bizarre. Who ever heard of a dictator who wore an ordinary blue coat with cheap dark pantaloons and a black felt hat with a partisan red ribbon, and who moreover carried no arms except in battle?

The chief problem that Walker faced, very simply, was that he wanted to regenerate Nicaragua, and that Nicaraguans did not wish to be regenerated—or, more precisely, the gentry and the clergy wished things to stay as they were, and the unschooled poor, the Indians and half-breeds, aspired to no more than a little more food and clothing. To most of the Nicaraguan people it seemed that the difficulties of their lives could only be made worse by radical change.

Politically, they lived in a jungle world of passion without principle; they were not in favor of anything; they were merely against everything; their attitude might be described as anti-ism. They would follow a revolutionary leader to help him destroy an oppressive government, but as soon as the new government was established, it in turn became their enemy, for it represented the hated power of the law.

Temperament aside, Walker showed himself a shrewd judge of popular feeling. He said little about his plans for the country. When the municipal council of Granada drew up a petition urging him to assume the Presidency of Nicaragua, he reproved them in terms perfectly calculated to allay Legitimist anxieties. They had no right, he said, to make the offer, nor he to accept it; much more appropriate would be the election of such a man as the Legitimist Commander in Chief, General Corral, with a government drawn from the best men of both parties.

This move was highly approved by the Americans in Granada as well as by the Legitimists. Minister John Wheeler was so impressed by Walker's bearing that he offered to go to Rivas, where Corral had his headquarters and to serve as intermediary between the two—and this although Walker had no legal status in the United States. Wheeler was an amiable and impressionable man, himself a former soldier, who regarded Walker as a great man, a rare combination of military virtues and intellectual refinement. Presently his hero-worship would express itself in a remarkable collection of Walkeriana. But in attempting to negotiate with Corral, he exceeded both his authority and his talents. Corral, a man of personal force and conviction, regarded him as Walker's tool, insulted him, and declared his intention to pursue the war against the Democrats.*

More effective than Wheeler's intervention was Irena Ohoran's subterranean influence among the Legitimists. How she persuaded Corral is not clear, but just when the situation seemed most dangerous, a letter from him arrived at Granada, offering to receive Walker for private talks. Doubtless to Irena's surprise, Walker now resisted her. If Corral wished a meeting, he said, it would have to take place in Granada; for he sensed that the first overt move of conciliation on either side would be read as a sign of weakness.

Just when he needed it, a way to exert pressure on Corral was unexpectedly put into his hands by a twisting chain of events. A

* Senate Exec. Doc. 68, 34th Cong., 1 Sess.

contingent of recruits from California had just arrived in Nicaragua, and its leaders, acting without Walker's knowledge, and even before they had reported to him, decided for their own aggrandizement to seek battle with Legitimist forces on Lake Nicaragua. Commandeering a Transit steamer, they fired on a fortress overlooking the lake, and controlled by Corral. The result was disastrous. Not only were they forced by bombardment to scurry back to safety, but they provoked the Legitimists to reprisals in which a number of innocent Transit passengers, including women and children, were massacred.

The crisis was the more serious because Walker needed the services of the American officers who had ordered the attack, and on whose cooperation depended the arrival of future reinforcements from California. With them he went no further than stern reproof; most of his wrath was directed at the Legitimists, on the incontestable ground that their assault on the Transit passengers had been cruel beyond military need. In an angry pronouncement, he called for the punishment of those Granadans who, because of their opposition to the idea of a unified country, had urged General Corral to maintain his armed resistance. These Legitimist conspirators were "morally responsible" for the tragedy of the Transit passengers, Walker declared; and the guilt was especially heavy in the instance of one Mateo Mayorga, a former Legitimist cabinet minister. Mayorga, who had earlier been arrested on suspicion of treason but released on parole at the request of John Wheeler, and was actually living in Wheeler's home, had taken advantage of Walker's indulgence to intrigue against him and encourage Corral. Walker had him taken into custody, submitted the facts to a court-martial which quickly found Mayorga guilty of conspiracy to foment civil war, and turned him over to a firing squad.

When Mayorga was led to the plaza and publicly executed, the Leónese soldiers cheered, and Legitimists trembled. Who would be next? Was this the beginning of the Democratic reign of terror that they had feared? At the height of the agitation, Walker sent a message to Corral. From this moment, he vowed, all the Granadan families of officers of the Legitimist army would be regarded as hostages for the good behavior of Corral's soldiers. The effect was magical. With one voice Corral's officers urged him to make peace; and he went immediately to Granada.

# IV

Outside Granada, Corral was met by Walker with a mounted escort, and at a stately pace they rode together to the city's center. Walker later recalled the enthusiasm of the Granadans at the spectacle. "As they passed, the doors and windows of the houses were filled with women and children, dressed in the bright colors of the country and smiling through tears at the prospects of peace." During the ride, the two men exchanged enough courtesies so that by the time they reached Government House the tension between them had been somewhat relaxed. In the ensuing conference, Walker allowed himself to appear at a disadvantage. Corral was empowered to speak officially for the Legitimist Party, but the American had been given no such authority by the Democratic regime at León, and he was careful to limit himself to such statements as befitted "the colonel commanding the forces occupying Granada." Accordingly, he let Corral "develop freely the terms he desired, saying little by way either of objection or of amendment. . . . The treaty, as signed, was nearly altogether the work of Corral." *

It was a reasonable document. Establishing a Provisional Government, naming as President an elderly and respected gentleman of conservative views, Don Patricio Rivas, making Corral Minister of War, it pleased the Legitimists; while the Democrats were to be satisfied by constitutional reforms, for which they had been contending; and Walker was given the post of Commander in Chief of the army. In the fact that he, who had been totally without military experience a year or so earlier, now assumed the rank of general, his critics in the United States later professed to find proof of unbridled vanity, but it is difficult to see how he could otherwise have commanded an army already loaded with generals.

A few days later word came from León approving the treaty and confirming the peace. All the bells of Granada rang out. The Legitimists especially were elated by what they felt to be a diplomatic triumph, for what, after all, was a mere constitution as compared with the power of administration? Corral was overheard to call out to Irena Ohoran, as he rode past her house one evening, "we have beaten them with their own game-cock!" This piece of gossip filtered

* William Walker, *The War in Nicaragua*, p. 125.

back to Walker from his Leónese officers and widened the rift between him and La Niña.

Corral's jubilation, however, was premature. From the outset, he misread Walker's character. He had expected to find a bully who would attempt to dominate him, trick him, or even humiliate him, in order to gain ascendancy. Discovering instead a quiet and courteous little man, with a profound respect for law, he was unimpressed. He himself had a tall and majestic presence, and this fact may have contributed to his feeling that Walker could be reduced to a subordinate role. His error was soon made plain to him. Walker had based his calculation on the insights which he had recently gained into the mind of the Nicaraguan conscript, and events proved him right. With the announcement of peace, the Legitimist garrisons in the towns, consisting largely of Indians and *mestizos* longing for their homes, melted away; and Walker, as Commander in Chief, did nothing to interfere with their desertion. Within a few weeks Corral's authority over the army had become merely nominal; the real power of compulsion now rested with the *Falange,* and Walker lost no time in exercising it.

A question arose as to the selection of a cabinet officer responsible for relations with the other Central American republics. To Corral's resentment, Walker insisted that the post go to the most celebrated and ardent revolutionary among the Democratic generals, Maximo Jerez, who was also an intellectual with a degree in law, and with whom Walker had conversed at length in León. Such an appointment meant to Corral a major threat to his control of the administration and to the gentry of the entire isthmus. If the extreme Democrats were to have control not only of the army but also of intergovernmental communications, they might well be able to promote revolutions in countries north and south. At all costs Jerez had to be kept out of the cabinet, and Corral said hotly and flatly that he would not serve in the same government with the Leónese. Walker replied simply, "Then we must refer the matter to the President." All Granada by this time was aware that President Rivas regarded the American as Nicaragua's only hope for peace, and never opposed him.

Corral awoke too late to Walker's force of leadership. Although he did not resign from the cabinet, he felt that the Legitimist cause was lost in Nicaragua. His misgivings were strengthened by the evident determination of the Leónese soldiery to maintain their partisan solidarity. Walker had issued an order requiring troops of both parties to remove from their hats the colors of their political faiths, the red ribbon of the Democrats, the white of the Legitimists, and to wear instead the blue ribbon of the nation, with the device, NICAR-AGUA INDEPENDENTE. The Legitimists obeyed, but the red ribbon remained on most of the Democratic hats. This persistence of the revolutionary spirit Corral considered an evil augury. It was, he felt, only through the intervention of other countries that he and his friends could now be saved.

In that conviction, he wrote an impulsive letter to the new dictator of Honduras, and sent it off by secret messenger. Coming from the Minister of War of the Nicaraguan government to the head of another state, this letter was the stuff of treason unmistakable. "My esteemed friend: It is necessary that you write to friends to advise them of the danger we are in, and that they work actively. If they delay two months, there will not then be time. Think of us and of your offers . . . Nicaragua is lost; lost Honduras, San Salvador and Guatemala, if they let this develop. Let them come quickly, if they would find allies here."

Some historians have seen in this letter a warning against seizure of the isthmus by Walker for the United States, but there is more reason to believe that Corral's great fear was the triumph of the Democrats throughout Central America. Unfortunately for him, the messenger whom he chose to carry this dangerous missive had strong grievances against the Legitimists. Instead of taking the letter out of Granada, he promptly put it into the hands of a Leónese officer, and within the hour it was being read by Walker, together with two other notes of the same kind penned by Corral. The situation thus created, while in one way to Walker's advantage, also confronted him with an ugly problem. That Corral had to be exposed and punished was evident, but the man was much loved in Granada. Imprisoned, he would be a center of conspiracy; executed, a martyr to whose memory thousands would rally; while a light penalty would stir bitter resentment among the Leónese troops, who might even suspect Walker of supporting the Legitimists against them.

In a grim mood, Walker notified President Rivas that an emergency demanded an immediate cabinet meeting, and Corral, not scenting danger, attended. To the assembled ministers Rivas said, "General Walker has something of grave consequence to tell us." Walker put the fatal letters in front of Corral and asked, "Did you write these, General?"

Corral turned pale, but bearing himself with dignity, admitted authorship of the letters, which were then read aloud to the cabinet.

"President," said Walker to Rivas, "I charge General Corral with treason, and request you to order his arrest." Rivas nodded unhappily; a Leónese officer who had been waiting outside the door was summoned; Corral gave up his arms and was placed in confinement.

V

Corral's crime, committed as a civilian official, called for a civilian trial. The new government, however, had not yet established a civil court, and it was apparent, moreover, that no Nicaraguan could be expected to be impartial in the matter. The Cabinet therefore decided on a court-martial to be composed entirely of American officers. No time was lost; the trial was conducted fairly, the verdict was guilty, the sentence "death by shooting." But the court was unanimous in urging Walker to show clemency to the prisoner.

The burden was now altogether his. No matter what the decision, it could only harm him; that was evident. In the end he fell back on the principles of John Knox and his Scottish forebears, on belief in the value of the cautionary example. How could the treaty of peace which he and Corral had solemnly sworn to uphold "continue to have the force of law if the first violation of it—and that by the very man who had signed it—was permitted to pass unpunished? . . . Mercy to Corral would have been an invitation to all Legitimists to engage in like conspiracies."

The word went out—Corral was to be shot. Immediately there was a great outcry in the city. Priests and notables begged Walker to remit the sentence. "The night before the fatal day," he himself related, "the daughters of Corral, accompanied by many of the women of the city, came with sobs and anguish and tears" to plead for their father's life. At such a moment a man of Latin blood, a Bolívar or San Martín, might have let himself be carried away by pity, might have commuted the sentence, and endeared himself, at least briefly, to the populace. But Walker, congenitally averse to emotional displays, sought to remain detached. "He who looks only at present grief, nor sees in the distance the thousand-fold sorrow a misplaced mercy may create, is little suited for the duties of public life," he wrote in self-justification. Nevertheless, he was deeply disturbed by "such entreaties as the daughters of the prisoner pressed," and he "closed the painful interview as soon as kind feeling permitted." An effort on Corral's behalf by Irena Ohoran was equally fruitless.

The execution of the Legitimist general, on November 8, 1855, left Walker the undisputed master of the Nicaraguan government. But locks of hair from Corral's corpse and handkerchiefs dipped in his blood were preserved in many a Granada home, symbols of a revenge to come. Where Walker had been feared, he was suddenly hated. A people accustomed to the hot cruelty of rage could not be expected to comprehend the lucid and cool cruelty of reason. If Walker had shrieked out a denunciation of Corral and personally stabbed him they would have understood him better and felt closer to him; but they could not forgive his dispassionate and unshakable judgment that the man had to die.

# VI

So long as Corral lived, the dominant conservative groups of Central America had reserved judgment on the Rivas regime, but with his death they concluded that Rivas was a mere figurehead for the revolutionary Democrats led by the Americans. Walker made earnest efforts to allay their animosity. A circular letter went to all four of the other isthmian republics, declaring Nicaragua's peaceful purposes, and asking for their friendship. Only little San Salvador replied in kind. In Guatemala, Honduras, and Costa Rica the letter was ignored, while their official newspapers made unbridled attacks on the Rivas government. At this stage, hundreds of Nicaraguan Legitimists began to cross into Costa Rica, seeking asylum and offering their services in a war against the Americans; and the equivalent party in Costa Rica, the *Serviles,* demanded that their nation mobilize.

A new decision faced Walker—attack, or wait to be attacked? General Jerez, whose presence in the cabinet had precipitated the Corral crisis, urged him to seize the initiative. Central American democracy was indivisible, he told Walker, and he outlined a bold plan. Rally the Democrats of the entire isthmus. Mobilize a large Democratic army. Send troops, Americans among them, to restore Cabañas to power in Honduras. Move swiftly against the Costa Ricans. Remove the Nicaraguan government to León. Begin to fight. Walker was tempted but unconvinced. To recruit a substantial force of volunteers would take months; he had no faith in Nicaraguan conscripts; he had only a few hundred Americans behind him; and with so small a force he saw only one way to win a simultaneous war against Costa Rica, Honduras, and the Nicaraguan Legitimists.

That was to persuade the United States government to cooperate in sending him recruits and supplies in quantity. "Let the enemy strike the first blow," he told Jerez, for if he appeared to be the aggressor he might alienate the sympathies of the American people, on whom he counted for final victory.

To one concession he agreed. Cabañas was invited to Granada to present his case in person, and was received with all respect. He was one of those dedicated revolutionaries who, out of love for humanity, was ready "to embrace Liberty on a pile of corpses." But Walker remained adamant in the face of the Honduran's plea—a decision that would later rise to haunt him. The high-minded Cabañas and the fiery Jerez felt betrayed. It seemed to them, as Jerez later wrote, that Walker was seeking not a Democratic victory, but personal power, and in this conviction they left Granada angrily and rode north to the protection of León.

Walker was learning some bitter truths of power: that every significant decision of the ruler makes a new enemy, and that every significant enemy imposes a new decision; that although support at best grows only arithmetically, opposition may well grow geometrically. In spite of the confusion of forces around him he saw his situation more clearly than did most of his advisers and critics. In the end, everything would depend on the aid, the men and the money, coming to him from the United States. If that aid were sufficient, he would be able to federate the republics of the isthmus, bring them under "the civilizing influence of the American people," and introduce democratic institutions. Otherwise Central American democracy was a lost cause.

The British government shared this view. As the London press made clear, the big question at the Foreign Office about Central America was whether Walker, in addition to popular and Congressional support, had the backing of President Pierce.

Fortunately, from the British standpoint, the American minister in London, James Buchanan, seemed almost eager to support England's position and was using his influence in Washington to that end. His attitude was especially significant because he was bound to be a strong candidate for the American Presidency in 1856. As an astute politician, he was aware that behind the scenes British influence would be a weighty factor in the presidential preference of the wealthy, conservative and powerful businessmen of New England and New York.

# MEPHISTO AS ENVOY

Two months before Corral's execution, just prior to the battle of Virgin Bay, when Walker's star was flickering uncertainly, an old acquaintance had boarded the *Vesta* in the harbor of San Juan del Sur—the former Sacramento publisher and promoter, Parker French—he who claimed to have the ear of Cornelius Garrison. French had something to say that arrested Walker's attention. If Walker would give him the necessary authority, he would return to San Francisco, recruit seventy-five men, and bring them to Nicaragua on an Accessory Transit steamer, at the company's expense.

Although Walker was aware of a cloud around French's reputation, he knew nothing specific to his discredit—and San Francisco was a city full of forgotten pasts. Whatever else the man might be, he was a personality. One-armed—he had lost the other years before in a Mexican adventure—he cultivated the style of a soldier of fortune. He had a handsome, Mephistophelean head, and wearing a beard like that of Napoleon III, whom he somewhat resembled, and talking with the glib charm of a P. T. Barnum, he evoked so much interest that one almost forgot to distrust him. Dubious though he was of the man, Walker saw no reason to refuse his offer. French thereupon returned to San Francisco, while Walker went on to victory at Virgin Bay.

For some weeks there was no communication between them. Soon after the conquest of Granada, however, French landed in San Juan del Sur at the head of a company of volunteers, as promised. The friendship of Garrison for Walker's enterprise, he said, was not doubted, even though it could not appear on the surface. The Transit Company, eager to see the situation in Nicaragua stabilized, stood ready to carry without charge as many as 500 additional recruits to Nicaragua. What was more, money was available to meet Walker's pressing needs. The new General Agent of the company in Nicaragua, C. J. McDonald, who had just arrived from San Francisco, could put $20,000 at Walker's disposal.

These were magical words in Walker's ears. The problem of pay and supply for his men gave him no peace, for the Nicaraguan treasury was empty. They spoke of French's reward for bringing the company's aid to Walker. If the promised cooperation from Accessory Transit materialized, French said, he would hope to be made Nicaragua's minister to Washington.

Walker was taken aback. He knew how much depended on his selection of an envoy to the United States. His intention was to send a trustworthy Nicaraguan, who might appear to speak for his people. The fact remained that French seemed able to speak for Garrison. Without his good offices the Provisional Government might collapse from sheer inability to pay and feed its troops. Putting first things first, he agreed to French's demand.

Together they went to McDonald, who turned out to be a cautious Scot, carrying credentials signed by Garrison. He confirmed French's statements. The company, he said, wished success to Walker because it wished to see the Transit route kept open. A loan was perfectly feasible. There was at the moment in Nicaragua, on the way to New York, a large shipment of privately owned California gold bullion. If Walker could provide reasonable security, $20,000 worth of the bullion would be extracted from the shipment, and turned over to him. The owners of the bullion would receive instead drafts for $20,000 on Charles Morgan, the Transit Company's agent in New York, whose credit was unimpeachable. As for security, that presented no problem. Under the terms of its charter, the company owed the Nicaraguan government certain sums, the amount still in dispute. Let the $20,000 borrowed be subtracted from that debt. Thus the loan would be instantly repaid.*

A few days later, the necessary papers had been signed, and the gold was turned over to Walker. That it was tendered him in the interest of Garrison and Morgan was obvious, but no effort had been made to commit him. No one could say that he had been bought. There had been no dishonorable bargain. The initiative remained with him, to act as the best interests of the Nicaraguan government demanded. As if to assert this view, he dispatched two Nicaraguan

* William Walker, *The War in Nicaragua*, Ch. 5.

emissaries to New York, to demand that the company settle all remaining obligations due his government.

Now there was French, waiting for his reward. There was only
one honorable way for Walker to extricate himself from his pledge
—by giving the man a post even more attractive to him than that of
envoy. A cabinet seat was open, the Minister of *Hacienda*, with authority over landed estates and responsibility for finding revenue.
This French consented to accept in lieu of the Washington mission.
Almost at once he distinguished himself by confiscating property
and goods on a scale that aroused nationwide resentment. "His ra-
pacity," Walker commented ruefully, "made him dreaded by the
people," and it became urgent to get him out of the country without
delay. Thus, although beset by doubts about him, Walker was forced
back to his original promise.

His hope was that the Pierce administration, even if less than
happy with the appointment of French, would be well disposed.
Although he was being urged by Nicaragua's neighbors to ban ship-
ments of arms to Walker, he had resisted them, saying that he
"would not infringe the sovereign rights" of Nicaragua. How could
this be interpreted, if not as a hint that the Rivas government would
soon be recognized? All that French would have to do would be to
present his credentials, keep quiet, and stand by.

The American press and the people as a whole were unmistakably on Walker's side, regarding him as the avatar of the nation's
destiny. Wherever he looked in the autumn of 1855, the horizon
was rosy with hope. He felt sufficiently secure so that he invited his
younger brothers, Norvell and James, to join him and share his
success.


## II


Some common-sense perceptions that men need in order to function
in a commercial society were markedly lacking in Walker. He had
no talent for the small and continuous compromises that are the
building blocks of security. He did not hesitate to make enemies of
those who might have helped him, if their conduct failed to conform
to his code of gentlemanly behavior. He felt obliged to fulfill his
promises, no matter how inconvenient. The claims of friendship he
regarded as taking precedence over his own interests. It is no wonder that many practical men of affairs were outraged by him.

This attitude, which showed in his unwillingness to break his word to French, almost immediately afterward led him deeper into danger. Not long before, another expedition had left the United States for Nicaragua, commanded by Colonel Henry Kinney of Texas. The colonel claimed the right to colonize a piece of Nicaragua about the size of the State of Maine, and including Greytown and most of Mosquito. This claim was based on a deed which the former Mosquito "King," Robert Charles Frederick, had granted to an American trader, and which Kinney had acquired. Persons close to President Pierce were backing him financially, and worked to have the Neutrality Laws suspended in his favor. The Accessory Transit Company, which was counting on Walker to protect its interests, regarded Kinney as a potential nuisance, and tried to prevent his sailing, but without success; and it fell to Walker to deal with the problem.

Kinney was anathema to Walker—partly because he sought to colonize Nicaraguan territory on the basis of a claim which had no legality in Nicaraguan eyes; partly because Kinney, in Greytown, had power to interfere with Walker's Atlantic communications; partly because his venture, clearly heading for failure, was likely to discredit American influence among Nicaraguans. The hopelessness of his situation was plain to everyone but himself. Finally, his men urged him to seek an alliance with Walker, and the unhappy colonel sent three of them to Granada for the purpose.

Walker greeted them courteously, but on hearing the proposal that he join forces with Kinney, he let his indignation show. Kinney, he told them, had no right to be in Nicaragua. He could only be regarded as an enemy of the Nicaraguan government. "Tell Governor Kinney, or Colonel Kinney, or Mr. Kinney, or whatever he chooses to call himself, that if I ever lay hands on him on Nicaraguan soil I shall surely hang him!"

The threat snapped the slender cord of loyalty that linked Kinney's men to him. They conferred briefly, and then they said, "General, we have no wish to return to Greytown. We would like to join your army."

It seemed to everyone that Walker had scored an effortless triumph. But impotent as Kinney was, he yet had one thing that Walker needed. He could count on the friendship of the White House, and especially of Sidney Webster, President Pierce's private secretary. Another of his financial backers was Caleb Cushing, the Attorney General of the United States. Two of Walker's high-ranking

William Walker (Ed Harris) with his fiancée, Ellen Martin (Marlee Matlin). (*Tom Collins*)

The Immortals preparing to leave San Francisco aboard the *Vesta*. (*Tom Collins*)

The Immortals form a firing squad. (*Tom Collins*)

Walker with Castellon (Paulino Rodriguez), Munoz (Pedro Armendariz), and other Nicaraguan Liberal Party dignitaries. (*Tom Collins*)

The Immortals marching into Rivas. (*Tom Collins*)

The Rivas ambush. (*Tom Collins*)

The charge of the barricade. (*Tom Collins*)

The battle of Rivas. (*Tom Collins*)

The battle of Rivas. *(Tom Collins)*

The battle of Rivas. (*Tom Collins*)

The battle of Rivas. (*Tom Collins*)

Stebbins (John Diehl). *(Tom Collins)*

Dona Yrena (Blanca Guerra). *(Tom Collins)*

Washburn (Dick Rude) with Faucet (Joe Strummer). *(Tom Collins)*

Dr. Jones (Rene Assa) with his pet monkey. *(Tom Collins)*

Colonel Sanders (Jack Slater) with his pet chicken. (*Tom Collins*)

Mayorga (Robert Lopez). (*Tom Collins*)

Hornsby (Sy Richardson). (*Tom Collins*)

Bruno (Charlie Braun), Huston (J. D. Sylvester), Walker (Ed Harris), Henningson (Rene Auberjonois), and Anderson (Bruce Wright). *(Tom Collins)*

Padre Vigil (Del Zamora) giving communion to Walker in the cathedral before the great battle of Granada. *(Tom Collins)*

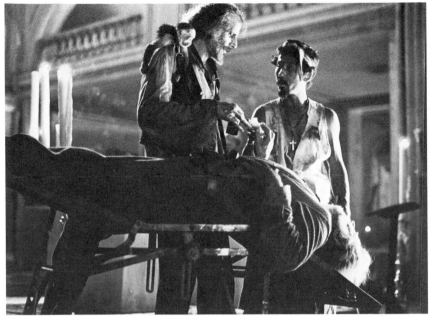

Dr. Jones (Rene Assa) operating on Rudler (Biff Yeader) in front of cathedral altar during the battle. *(Tom Collins)*

Walker and his Immortals fleeing the burning cathedral. *(Tom Collins)*

The victims of the battle of Granada. *(Tom Collins)*

The Managua Cathedral today, with ruins from the 1972
earthquake that devastated Nicaragua. *(Lynn Davis)* →

United States Marines arriving via helicopter to evacuate American citizens from the fall of Granada. (*Tom Collins*)

A funeral at the Granada Cathedral today. *(Lynn Davis)*

The main square of Granada. (*Lynn Davis*)

The back of the set, Granada. (*Lynn Davis*)

The outskirts of Granada. *(Lynn Davis)*

Detail of the facade, Palacio Nacional,
Granada. *(Lynn Davis)* →

Grounded fishing boat, San Juan del Sur. *(Lynn Davis)*

Statue to the anonymous soldier of the FSLN (Sandinistas), Managua. *(Lynn Davis)*

Monument to Pedro Joaquin Chamorro, assassinated editor of *La Prensa*. *(Lynn Davis)*

"Only the Workers and Peasants Will Go to the End"
—Carlos Fonseca Amador, cofounder of the FSLN,
who was killed before the success of the revolution,
Leon. (*Lynn Davis*)

Rigoberto López Pérez, the young poet who assassinated Somoza's father in 1956, Leon. (*Lynn Davis*)

"More Than One of Your Armies, Blond Invader, Will Bite the Dust of My Wild Mountains."
(*Lynn Davis*)

officers, who had known Kinney in the States, came to the conclusion that the interests of both men required an accommodation, and
in this belief they made a journey to Greytown, and urged the Texan
to go to Granada himself and talk with Walker. They would, they
told him, pledge their honor for his safety. Under the impression
that their invitation had Walker's approval, Kinney accepted.

When Kinney entered his office, Walker was cold but not hostile.
It came to him as a shock to hear the proposal that their two governments mutually recognize each other, and that he use his army, if
need be, to protect Kinney in his possessions. Incredulous, he
merely stared. But tenacity was Kinney's strong point, and long
experience in fighting Indians and bamboozling settlers on the Texas
frontier had given him a certain shrewdness and crude verbal power.
"He had acquired," Walker said of him, "that sort of knowledge and
experience of human nature derived from the exercise of the mule
trade." Sprinkling his talk with profanities of which he himself was
unconscious, unaware of the disdain with which he was being listened to, he ignored Walker's rejection of him. He had a right to be
in Mosquito, he asserted. His claim had been paid for in hard cash.
His syndicate had so far spent over a hundred thousand dollars on
the colonization project. How could Walker reasonably expect them
to abandon it?

This argument Walker shrugged aside. "You can't survive another month," he pointed out, "without the protection and aid of
the Nicaraguan government. Why should I help you? What do you
offer in return?"

Kinney's reply was definite. He could bring to Nicaragua a large
number of American colonists; he was in a position to negotiate a
loan in the United States; and most important, he could do more
than anyone else to secure American recognition for Walker.

These were cogent points, and despite his prejudice against the
man, Walker hesitated, adjourning the meeting until next day. For
some hours it appeared that an alliance of sorts might after all ma-
terialize between them. But Kinney was a man who could not even
sniff the fumes of the heady brew of power without losing his common sense. Flushed with hope and lacking in sensitivity, he committed an offense which, in Walker's eyes, was unpardonable. He
had hardly left Walker when he sought a private meeting with President Rivas and set about to discredit his rival. Walker's army, he
told Rivas, would eat up the country like a plague of locusts. Himself
he presented as a man of peace and of business, without political

ambitions. Colonization—agriculture—new blood—these were the needs of Nicaragua. One American colonist was worth five soldiers to the country.

Rivas, unimpressed, answered that Nicaragua, faced with the threat of invasion, looked to General Walker. He dismissed Kinney; and to assure that Walker, if he heard of the meeting, would not misunderstand its nature, he sent him a detailed report of Kinney's remarks and his own replies.

Even now, if Walker had chosen to dissemble he might easily have kept Kinney dangling without a commitment, until he had made use of the man's connection with Pierce, but this he could not bring himself to do. When the optimistic Kinney presented himself the next morning, Walker's voice and words were soft and restrained, but deadly. "I wish no further communication with you, Mr. Kinney," he said. "You have used improper methods in discussing government affairs."

Kinney, a big man, stood for a moment speechless before the slight figure of his adversary, and Walker added, "I have ordered your arrest."

"Arrest!" shouted Kinney. "You can't do that! I came here on a guarantee of safe-conduct."

This was news to Walker, but on inquiry, he found that such a pledge had actually been given. Thereupon he changed his order from one of arrest to deportation, and Kinney was taken back to Greytown ignominiously, under armed guard. He left the country soon afterward.

### III

News of the breach between Kinney and Walker reached Washington some little time before French arrived to present his credentials to Secretary of State Marcy. He came with a great fanfare of personal publicity. Walker was then the darling of the American press, and French was able to bask in his light. People believed, erroneously, that he was one of the fifty-eight Immortals, a one-armed hero, a paladin. His name was heard everywhere. Newspapers in New York and Washington urged Marcy to receive him promptly and with honor. But the ambassadors of England, France, and Spain were making strong representations against recognition of the Walker government, and Marcy felt it advisable to wait. When French requested an audience he was told that "those who were not instrumental in overthrowing the government of Nicaragua were not citizens belonging to it." Marcy's view was that the country should be represented by one of its own nationals. He went on to convey that a free election showing that Rivas and Walker were supported by the Nicaraguan people might influence the attitude of the United States.

Leading publicists at once rallied to French and berated the administration. Walker's own reply, when the news of Marcy's action reached him, was a vigorous editorial in *El Nicaragüense,* praised by the *New York Times* as "reasoning sustained to a high degree of ability." Its essence was a reminder that American independence had been won with the aid of foreigners—Lafayette, De Kalb, Steuben. The Rivas government, Walker said, represented the only hope of Nicaraguan independence and democracy, and was entitled to American aid. As for a free election, the Provisional Government was prepared to hold one in the very near future.

A number of newspapers pressed home the argument, and there were signs that Marcy was beginning to weaken under Congressional prodding. It was plain that the American public cared little about the merits of the Nicaraguan revolution. They regarded it as a kind of athletic competition, and they wanted the Americans to win; that was all.

Still exuberant, French went to New York, where he found the welcome that had been denied him in Washington. His suite at the St. Nicholas Hotel was a favorite gathering place of reporters, for he was lavish of champagne and cigars, and every day he had something new and exciting to tell about the iniquities of the Pierce administration, the bravery of the Immortals, and the importance of his own contributions to Walker's success. In one respect only did he serve Walker. He obtained a promise from Charles Morgan to transport recruits for Nicaragua from New York, as from San Francisco. With an eye on the Neutrality Laws, "emigrants" would be shipped for only twenty dollars per head, and no cash would be demanded. As in the case of recruits carried from San Francisco, the cost would simply be deducted from the company's debt to the Nicaraguan government. This policy was continued after Vanderbilt ousted Morgan from the Accessory Transit Company.

So far as the Commodore was concerned, there was every reason to assist Walker to stabilize Nicaragua. French was encouraged to place advertisements of a seemingly innocuous nature in New York's

newspapers—"Wanted: ten or fifteen young men to go a short distance out of the city. Single men preferred. Apply at 347 Broadway,
corner of Leonard Street, Room 12, between the hours of ten and
four. Passage paid." The same newspapers carried glowing reports
from Nicaragua and excerpts from *El Nicaragüense* on the opportu-
nities awaiting Americans there—the beauty, fertility, and resources
of the country, the broad lands available to settlers, the low cost of
living, and the charm of the señoritas—until the imagination of
Manhattan's footloose males had been thoroughly aroused. Nothing
was said of cholera, dysentery, mosquitoes, flies, or the chiggers that
burrowed into human flesh and were the torment of Walker's troops.

Hundreds of men were interviewed by French and accepted as
"emigrants." Soon all New York knew what was in the wind. Newspapers reported that in California Walker's agents were swamped by
volunteers. A riot broke out at San Francisco's docks, when so many
passengers sought to board a Transit steamer for Nicaragua that
nearly 300 had to be left behind. New Orleans also was bursting
with enthusiasm. There a distinguished Cuban fighter for independence, Domingo de Goicuria, was busily recruiting 250 men, many
of them Cubans, for service in Nicaragua, and Vanderbilt had assured him of a Transit ship to carry them to Greytown.


# IV


The federal government felt compelled to make another effort to
enforce the Neutrality Laws. Attorney General Cushing demanded
that the District Attorneys of the great ports put an immediate stop
to the recruitment and transportation of men for Walker. To assist
them, he gave the press his accumulated facts about French's past.
A startled public learned that French had been incontestably guilty,
not many years before, of forgery and embezzlement. Worse, in the
days of the gold rush, he had defrauded and victimized thousands
of emigrants en route to California by wagon train. A Senate report
bore evidence to his misdeeds, and a pamphlet called *The Sufferings
and Hardships of Parker H. French's Overland Expedition* had been
privately printed in 1851.

Newspapers which had been lauding French were silenced. The
New York *Mercury* spoke the disgust of many when it said, "In
bitterness of spirit, let us exclaim, with Sir Harcourt Courtly, 'Will
nobody take this man away?' " The abuse heaped on French was as

pungent as former praise of him had been saccharine. Heavy criticism was aimed at Walker also for having chosen such a man as his envoy. Nevertheless, to the extent that French was Walker's representative, he still had support. The *New York Times* reminded Marcy that "it is not Captain French, of questionable antecedents, who solicits the ear of our government, but the agent of sovereign power," and the *Sun* commented that "eminently bad men, morally, hold high places in the governments with which we maintain friendly relations. International morals are not so pure that there need be any squeamishness in admitting Colonel French to the diplomatic circle."

French employed all the tricks his ingenuity could conceive, and they were many, to put Nicaragua-bound recruits on board the transit steamships without giving the government firm legal grounds for interference. A favorite device was to have the men come on board singly, and mingle with California-bound passengers, of whom there were always a considerable number, and who were always glad to pretend that Walker's men were their sons and brothers. The frustration of federal officers, who knew the filibusters were there and yet were unable to distinguish them from their companions with any certainty, was compounded by the open derision of the passengers. Steamer after steamer was able to sail from New York loaded with "emigrants" to Greytown, while crowds on the dock cheered the name of Walker and booed any mention of Pierce. New York's District Attorney obtained Grand Jury indictments against French; he even had him put under arrest, but this move proved so unpopular that the order was hastily rescinded.

French, however, had not reckoned on the depth of Walker's anger over his behavior, and especially over his statements about Pierce and Marcy. A curt letter came to him from Granada. His commission as minister was revoked. A new envoy had been appointed to Washington—the Nicaraguan priest, Augustin Vijil, who had steadfastly supported Walker from the beginning. With this news, French lost his hold on all that remained to him of public approval, and when he left New York the newspapers hardly bothered to dust their editorial hands of him. He went to Nicaragua, to hear from Walker's own lips that there was no place for him in the country. French was wise enough not to argue, and boarded a ship for New Orleans. There he gave out that he was on secret business for Walker, and roamed the South, delivering lectures on Nicaragua to large audiences. Returning to New York, he sought to promote a new steamship venture, asserting that in spite of everything he was still Walker's trusted friend. So persistent was he that *El Nicaragüense* was finally compelled to publish a statement by Walker that "French has no connection whatever with this government; . . . he is at present engaged in doing the [Nicaraguan] administration all the injury his genius is capable of."

# MR. VANDERBILT IS
# OUTRAGED

In November 1855, Cornelius Garrison, reading letters from Morgan in New York, knew that the moment of crisis was at hand. Wall Street sources left no doubt that Vanderbilt's purchases of Accessory Transit stock were rapidly bringing the company under his thumb, and that at the next stockholder's meeting he would take over.

Although Garrison's contract with the company had some years to go, he was highly vulnerable, not only because of past opposition to Vanderbilt, but perhaps even more because of certain irregular transactions of the company's San Francisco office—transactions which he was unwilling to submit to Vanderbilt's scrutiny. But in Garrison's philosophy there was always more than one way to skin a tiger, even if his name was Vanderbilt. He and Morgan had sketched out a plan by which the Commodore might be made the butt of Wall Street for a change, instead of its hero, and some of his millions squeezed out of him.

Everything now depended on one man, Walker. Experience as a politician and banker had made Garrison a shrewd judge of character. It was clear to him that Walker's motivations differed sharply from those of the run of men. Conversations in Nicaragua reported by C. J. McDonald and Parker French had so far brought nothing more from Walker than formal appreciation of Garrison's aid. The time had now come to get a definite commitment from him.

With such a man, Garrison sensed, a crude appeal to the pocketbook would not serve. You cannot bribe a knight-errant. But you can always appeal to his knightliness. Garrison accordingly began his campaign by retaining the services of two of Walker's oldest friends, Edmund Randolph and another well-known San Francisco attorney, Parker Crittenden, offering them shares in large future profits if they would go to Nicaragua on his behalf. Their specific assignment was to persuade Walker to seize the properties of the Accessory Transit Company in the name of Nicaragua, and turn them over to Randolph, who would form a new company to be headed by Garrison and Morgan. A legal justification for such a move could be found in the fact that Accessory Transit over the years had refused to admit its sizable debt to Nicaragua.

It was the plan of Morgan and Garrison, if they could win Walker's consent, to sell the stock of Accessory Transit short in huge quantities and make a Wall Street killing when the news broke. But nothing of this was to be said to Walker. Randolph and Crittenden were to emphasize that the new company would accept a charter far more favorable to Nicaragua than that held by Vanderbilt, a contract that would assure frequent and regular shipping service from the United States; and that cooperation in providing the recruits and supplies needed by Walker would be unstinted. He was to be told, further, that if he would not agree, Morgan and Garrison would no longer feel an obligation to make efforts on his behalf. With so cogent an argument, Randolph and Crittenden saw no reason why they should not accept the mission. At the last moment, the Mayor suggested that they take with them his son and trusted aid, W. R. Garrison.

## II

In December 1855, Cornelius Vanderbilt, once more at the helm of Accessory Transit, was feeling expansive. Having accumulated all the necessary stock, he had ousted Morgan from the company and regained the presidency. The company's shares had thereupon bounded upward and had added at least a million to his wealth. With Walker in Nicaragua, the Transit route was secure; and his success might open up not only Nicaragua but the entire Caribbean to American capital. There could be no doubt that the independence of Cuba was one of Walker's major objectives. Why else was the noted Cuban revolutionary, Domingo de Goicuria, recruiting for him in New Orleans? One of Vanderbilt's first actions after assuming command at Accessory Transit had been to confirm an order previously issued by Morgan to send a company ship to New Orleans to transport Goicuria and his men to Greytown without asking cash payment. Vanderbilt expected to begin negotiations with Walker soon over the amount of the Transit's debt to Nicaragua, and he anticipated that his bill for the ocean fares of Walker's recruits, plus the filibuster's gratitude, would offset most of the obligation. Goicuria's gratitude could be expected to have similar dollar value if and when he and Walker succeeded in wresting Cuba from Spain.

At Granada, Walker received a message from Goicuria, who said that if Walker and he were in agreement on future strategy, he would bring Nicaragua 250 fighting men. One thing only the Cuban wanted to determine. Could he count on aid not only in the overthrow of the Spanish tyranny in Cuba, but in support of Cuban independence against any aggressive tendencies that the United States might display?

Walker was able to reply, with complete truth, that to aid in the liberation of Cuba had always been one of his dreams. He believed that the best interests of the United States would be served by the independence of the Caribbean nations, which, under efficient and honest administrations, would benefit from the availability of American capital, business enterprise, and trade.

A memorandum of agreement was drawn up and signed. Goicuria was to aid Walker in "consolidating the peace and the government of the Republic of Nicaragua." Walker on his part would "assist and cooperate with his person and his various resources, such as men, in the case of Cuba and in favor of her liberty." *

# III

While Goicuria and Walker were negotiating for the future of Cuba, Randolph, Crittenden, and young Garrison arrived in Granada, together with a hundred new recruits. It was a joyous moment for Walker, able to receive his oldest friend against a background of power and fame. That evening he entertained the three San Franciscans at a dinner attended by President Rivas and the entire cabinet; and the next day he met privately with Randolph.

Subsequently reporting Walker's action in seizing the Transit, some American newspapers said that in accepting Garrison's offer he displayed impulsiveness and ignorance verging on idiocy. Walker himself made no defense of his action. But his decision was far from

---

* W. O. Scroggs, "William Walker's Designs on Cuba," in *Mississippi Valley Historical Review,* 1914, Vol. I, p. 199.

impulsive or ignorant. Several weeks earlier word had come to him from San Francisco that some kind of stock-rigging deal was in the wind.* There was nothing in this to tempt him. No one could read the New York newspapers, as he had done for years, without being aware of Vanderbilt's tremendous power. That he was wary of any commitment to Garrison and Morgan shows in their recourse to Randolph. He appreciated the aid he had received from Garrison, but he did not misunderstand it or overvalue it. Sooner or later it would all be paid for by Nicaragua through reductions of Accessory Transit's debt.

New York newspapers telling of Vanderbilt's bid for recapture of Accessory Transit reached Granada before Randolph's arrival. The practical question that Walker had to consider was whether he would be better off to cooperate with the legal head of the company, Vanderbilt, or to throw in his lot with the men whom Vanderbilt had defeated. While only that question was before him, he remained neutral. He wanted the good will of the company regardless of the identity of its head. The dangers that would follow defiance of Vanderbilt were unmistakable. But when Randolph came to him, the situation suddenly changed. This was the man of all men to whom he was devoted, the friend who had more than once come to his rescue, helped him, saved him.

A realist, a Napoleon, would have had no hesitation in sacrificing the friendship to political advantage—would have played for time, put off the decision until Randolph grew tired of waiting. Not so Walker. The saying that "a friend in power is a friend lost" did not apply to him. Given his attitude toward life, he could deny Randolph nothing—the point on which Garrison counted.

The press was mystified by what seemed to be a totally irresponsible action on the part of a man who, until then, had conducted his affairs with considerable skill. What it could not know was that, reasoning from Walker's special premises, his decision was in fact entirely logical. His life had never been guided by the canons of success, but the canons of personal honor, in which the claim of friendship was paramount.

He was not unaware of the economic motivations of politics. Rather he rejected them. It was this apparent indifference to the realities of American life that prompted Horace Greeley to call him "the Don Quixote of Central America." The Knight of La Mancha

---

* William Walker, *The War in Nicaragua,* p. 149.

did not seem more wrong-minded and absurd to his contemporaries than Walker in the eyes of the great magnates of the 1850's. It was not merely that he dared to defy Vanderbilt. He was defying the onset of a new age. He was tilting at the unshakable windmill of the money-power.

As Richard III for a kingdom, so for friendship Walker was ready to "set his life upon a cast," and "stand the hazard of the die."

## IV

At the end of February 1856, the stock of the Accessory Transit Company sold at $23 a share, in a rising market. Early in March, the *New York Times* reported that Morgan, "lately in the administration of the company, was selling the stock [short] much as Vanderbilt had done after the latter had lost control." Vanderbilt eagerly grasped what seemed to him a heaven-sent opportunity to corner the stock and squeeze a fortune out of his enemy, and he bought as heavily as Morgan was selling, holding the price close to its peak level. Then, on March 12, news from Nicaragua that Walker had annulled the Accessory Transit charter, and had issued a new charter to Edmund Randolph, precipitated a wild rush on Wall Street to sell Transit shares. That day the price of the stock dropped four points, and it continued to fall until the shares were selling at $13 each. At this price Morgan covered his short sales, for a profit estimated at close to a million.

Incredulous at the first reports of Walker's action, once Vanderbilt was sure of the facts he let out his rage in private and public. The great question in New York's financial community was: what had possessed Walker to do such a thing? Regretfully, the well-informed *Herald* remarked that "the great mass of the American people deeply sympathize with the present government of Nicaragua and will regret that its gallant head has perilled its hitherto bright prospects. It will be seen that it is in Mr. Vanderbilt's power to kill off the new government by opening another route and thus cutting off Walker's communications with San Francisco and New York."

The accuracy of this forecast soon became evident. Morgan had neglected to organize the new line of steamships on which Walker was counting, and for six vital weeks no steamers sailed from New York with the men and supplies essential to Walker's security. Efforts made by Garrison to keep Accessory Transit steamers running from San Francisco to Nicaragua proved fruitless when a Vanderbilt agent arrived with orders that all of the company's ships out of California were to be routed to Panama, where their passengers would be transferred to the Atlantic side by railroad. The Commodore was moving simultaneously on many fronts. When his letters demanding intervention by the United States brought only a cold reply from Secretary of State Marcy, the millionaire promptly turned to England. His agents rushed to London and to the Caribbean to invoke the aid of British diplomacy and warships in blocking the Transit entry at Greytown. Still another agent went to Granada, where he talked secretly with President Rivas, in an effort to produce an open break between him and Walker. Simultaneously Vanderbilt brought suit for $500,000 against Garrison, on a charge of fraud, and another, for $1,000,000 against Morgan, Garrison, and Walker, alleging trespass, conversion, and dispersal of the company's goods, and fraudulent conspiracy to interrupt and molest the corporation.

The force of these moves produced a prompt effect on Morgan and Garrison. Content with their stockmarket killing, they had gone through the form of purchasing the new transit charter from Randolph; now they offered to sell the new charter, with its privileges, to Vanderbilt. He flatly refused. His duty, he replied, was to protect the stockholders of the old company, and he wrote a letter to the New York *Herald* to explain his virtuous stand. "Mr. Garrison called on me and . . . intimated that if I would participate with him and Charles Morgan . . . we could make a good business of it to the exclusion of the Transit Company. I told him he must clear up his character as regards his conduct toward the company. . . ." This was no doubt accurate, but it was far from being the truth. The great financier had in fact found it possible to extract a cash profit from the situation. His order to withdraw his ships from Nicaragua and enter the Panama run created consternation among the other Panama lines. Recognizing his nuisance value, Vanderbilt promptly offered to withdraw his ships from competition, on payment by the Panama lines of a monthly "subsidy" of $40,000 (later $56,000) a month. The agreement was too close to blackmail to be put into writing, but it was made orally, and carried out.*

* *Harper's Weekly*, 1859, Vol. III, p. 114.

# "YOU STAND ALONE"

❦

Walker, in 1856, stood at a focal point of history, where great political and economic forces converged: the need of the United States for a short ocean route to California—the determination of England to prevent the Americans from building an interoceanic canal that would give them an advantage in trade with the Orient—the drive of New York capitalists to control the Central American isthmus—the dream of Manifest Destiny shared by millions of Americans—the urge of the South to annex Cuba and the Caribbean lands—the unending struggle of Central America's peons against feudal serfdom. The importance that the world attributed to his venture is suggested by the enemies that he made. These included, in addition to Vanderbilt, the conservative wing of the American Congress; the Nicaraguan Legitimists; the governments of Costa Rica, Honduras, and Guatemala; England; and less overtly, Spain and France. In the immensity of their power he found a wry satisfaction. He still hoped for victory, but a defeat by hostile forces of such magnitude would at least be no disgrace.

Almost at the moment when his defiance of Vanderbilt was shocking informed circles in New York, a number of speeches sharply critical of him were made in the United States Senate, while British enmity was not confined to words. The chances of intervention on Walker's behalf by the Pierce administration had diminished, England calculated, to the point where her Central American friends need no longer be restrained. State papers which were not made public until many years later revealed that Great Britain's War Office at this time arranged a grant of arms to Costa Rica to combat "the troops under Mr. Walker, against whom you may have to defend yourselves."

These British arms included, in addition to 2000 rifled muskets equipped with sights and superior to those used by Walker's men, a million rounds of ammunition and much other equipment.* To a letter from the Costa Rican government requesting naval support as well, the Foreign Office replied that a cruiser would visit Costa Rica "to protect British interests." Actually, a large squadron comprising some of England's finest warships began to range both coasts of Central America.

Thus encouraged, at the beginning of March 1856, President Mora of Costa Rica issued an order of mobilization calling for an army of 9000 men "to take up arms for the republic of Nicaragua" against what he maintained was an American invasion; and without waiting for a formal declaration of war, a substantial force equipped with British guns advanced into Nicaragua. Advising Mora, it subsequently became known, were agents of Spain and France, as well as of England.

To this invasion the Nicaraguan government responded with a declaration of war. Let the world note, said President Rivas, that his country had been attacked without provocation. More to the point was a statement personally issued by Walker—the affirmation of political principles that Jerez had earlier urged him to make. Throwing off all claims to impartiality as between Democrats and Legitimists, he made a frank appeal to the revolutionary elements of the entire isthmus. He had been invited to Nicaragua by the Democrats, he said, and he and his men had never ceased to struggle for the principle of the revolution. True, he had held his Democratic friends in check, he had sought to conciliate the Legitimists, he had tried to establish friendly relations with the antidemocratic governments of neighboring countries, but all his advances for the sake of peace had been repulsed with scorn. Now the country was being attacked. Let it be so. He and his American followers were joined with Nicaraguan Democrats in eternal opposition to *Servile* governments throughout Central America, and they would resume and wear forever the red ribbon of democracy.

The fact remained that in 1856 Walker's reaffirmation of democratic allegiance was accepted by many Nicaraguans. Native volunteers continued to serve in his army. His popularity among the poorer class was noted more than once. The most dedicated of the Democratic leaders, Maximo Jerez, agreed to join the new Rivas cabinet as Minister of War.

---

* British State Papers, Vol. XVI, pp. 784–5, 794–6.

Horace Greeley might consider him a power-hungry pirate, Wall Street an agent of cunning capitalists, but he thought of himself as the head of a revolutionary army, fighting against the feudal owners of the isthmus in the name of democracy. As proof of his Democratic good faith he not only brought Maximo Jerez into the government, but gave two other cabinet posts to Democrats of Jerez' choice; he authorized the transfer of the seat of government from Granada to León; and he had the government announce an early presidential and congressional election, to be held by popular vote.

To him the shocking thing was that although England did not hesitate to support her reactionary aims in Central America with arms and supplies, the government of the United States, calling itself democratic, refused to see the significance of the struggle that he was waging. *Harper's Weekly* remarked that the treatment of Walker by the American government was very like that of John Knox and John Wesley by the Church of England. It was a comparison the more apt because of the psychological similarity of Walker to the great religious reformers. Like them, he never complained about the injuries inflicted on him by enemies, but the calumnies of his own countrymen left a scar. He had ridden out under the banner of democracy into a world full of danger, seeking dragons to slay, and his feelings about the castigation of him by Marcy and Buchanan were like those of a knight who, while on a great quest, heard that he had been blackballed and barred from the Round Table.

## II

In the ensuing military campaign, which comprised only two battles, Walker's forces lost both, and his reputation as a general was permanently damaged, yet he emerged as the victor and a greater hero than ever in the eyes of the American public. The first battle took place at Santa Rosa, south of Lake Nicaragua, where the enemy vanguard was encamped, and where the Costa Ricans swore death to every American on whom they could lay hands. Walker's situation was deteriorating rapidly. Another cholera epidemic, then in its initial stage, coupled with widespread dysentery and fevers, had reduced his American effectives to only 600. He himself was down with fever and a painful swelling of the face. In an effort to conserve his men for what he could not doubt would be a long struggle, he determined to send against the Costa Ricans initially a battalion of four companies: one composed entirely of Frenchmen recently arrived from San Francisco; one of German immigrants out of New York; one of Nicaraguans, and one of raw American recruits. A question immediately arose: who was to command this polyglot force? Walker's choice could hardly have been worse if he had been delirious with fever, as some thought he was. His attention centered on a German named Louis Schlessinger, an educated and plausible man whom he had previously used on diplomatic missions, and who spoke all of the four essential languages. Totally untrained and psychologically unfit for military leadership, Schlessinger failed to scout the territory into which he was advancing, and was surprised by the enemy in force. At the first fire the undisciplined company of Germans broke and fled, followed by the French, with Schlessinger himself among them. For a few minutes the Nicaraguans and Americans held back the enemy but, after a hundred men had fallen, joined the rout, leaving their wounded to summary execution at the hands of the jubilant Costa Ricans.

News of this shocking defeat came to a Granada already unnerved by the terrors of cholera, and was followed closely by rumors that a Honduran army was about to join in the attack on Walker. The resulting wave of panic swept up many Americans as well as Nicaraguans. Scores of recent arrivals from New York who had not yet enlisted in Walker's force begged to be sent home. Even his veterans were dispirited, especially since a number of his best officers had been stricken by cholera. Efforts to revive morale were unavailing before the despondency evoked by the spectacle of half-starved fugitives from Santa Rosa straggling in with reports of Schlessinger's incompetence and Costa Rican savagery. Schlessinger himself was arrested, court-martialed and condemned to be shot as a coward, but managed to escape, some thought with the secret connivance of Walker, whose own responsibility in having selected so untried a man for a military command was manifest. To his friend and most stalwart defender in the United States Congress, Senator John Weller of California, Walker wrote in a vein of grim realism: "We have great moral odds against us. . . . I may not live to see the end . . . but if we fail, we feel that it will be in the cause of honor."

Most imminent and acute of all the dangers confronting Walker was the likelihood that the enemy, now numbering 4000, would occupy the all-important Transit route and block the way for American reinforcements. To forestall this move, although he was still weak from his illness, he took personal command of the 500 Americans left to him, and led them south to the town of Rivas, the scene of his defeat a year earlier, astride the western segment of the route.

There he put all his energy into a revival of the health, morale, and discipline of his troops.

"Woe betide the luckless wretch who unfitted himself for duty in that dread presence on the eve of battle," wrote one of his officers. It was at this time that Walker publicly reprimanded his brother Norvell, and reduced him from a captaincy to the ranks, for having participated in an all-night carouse against orders. Thereafer he paraded his restive men in the plaza of Rivas, and briefly addressed them. It was a typically Walkerian performance. Thinner than ever, pale and feverish, his drab clothing hanging from him like a scarecrow's slops, he sought to give his men a vision of themselves as heroes.

"Let me try," he said, "to place before you the moral grandeur of the position that you occupy. You stand alone in the world, without a friendly government to give even its sympathy, much less its aid. You have nothing to support you in this struggle except the consciousness of the justice of your cause. Those who should have befriended you have maligned you. . . . I would not conceal from you the great peril and the urgency of the danger in which you stand." They heard him in silence. But "the words . . . had the desired effect and created a new spirit among them," Walker wrote. "It is only by constant appeals to the loftier qualities of man that you can make him a good soldier; and all military discipline is a mere effort to make virtue constant and reliable by making it habitual."

## III

The news grew worse. President Rivas reported from León that in spite of his efforts to conciliate the Hondurans, they were about to invade Nicaragua and attack Granada. Walker now had to consider whether he dared do battle with the Costa Ricans on the Transit route; for even if he won against the heavy odds confronting him, his losses were almost certain to be large, and his army would be unfit to meet the Hondurans. His decision was to return to Granada until Nicaraguan reinforcements then being organized in León could reach him.

No sooner had he reached Granada than further word came: the rumors from Honduras were false. An invasion from the north was not anticipated in the near future. Shaken by this disclosure of the weakness of President Rivas as a source of intelligence, Walker turned back toward the Transit, but too late; the Costa Ricans had taken advantage of his withdrawal to occupy the towns of Rivas and Virgin Bay, where they seized the buildings of the Transit Company and wantonly killed nine of its American employees.

In such a situation, failure to attack would be equivalent to slow suicide. As Walker saw it, his only hope lay in forcing the Costa Ricans out of their strong position in Rivas. The first hours of the battle went well for him, but he lacked the manpower needed to maintain his advantage, and his casualties, killed and wounded, rose to 120, one quarter of his total command. The fall of night enabled him to withdraw his men, the movement being carried out in utmost silence, and when with daylight the Costa Ricans prepared to resume the battle they found to their astonishment that the Americans were gone, carrying their wounded with them.

Some of Walker's own associates thought the end had come, as they again retreated northward toward Granada, but they did not reckon on the imponderables of war. Costa Rica soon began to hear the truth about her heavy losses at Rivas, and after General Mora's bombast the long casualty lists came as a shock. Even worse was the appearance of the cholera in his army, in an especially virulent form. It was not to see thousands of its young men destroyed within a fortnight that his nation had heeded the call to arms; and the epidemic, which had begun to spread throughout Costa Rica itself, was blamed on the war. When a spontaneous demonstration demanding the return of the army and verging on revolt broke out in San José, Mora decided to hasten back to his capital with such troops as were fit to march.

Suddenly, amazingly, the Americans heard that Rivas, Virgin Bay, and the Transit once more lay open to them. There came a note from the commander whom Mora had left in Rivas, begging the indulgence of Walker for the stricken hundreds of Costa Ricans whom he would find there. The first reaction in Walker's camp was a roar of protest; was the shooting and bayoneting of wounded Americans to go unrequited? Nevertheless, when Walker issued an order that the troops respect the conventions of war among civilized peoples, it was obeyed. The enemy sick were tended; those who recovered were repatriated, and those who died were given formal burial. Even the most anti-American of Costa Rican historians had to admit, "In regard for the truth, we must say that Walker treated with humanity the soldiers whom he found in Rivas." *

* J. Perez, *Memorias*, II, p. 51.

This display of humanitarianism in the midst of despair and horror caught the imagination of the American people, and proved to be Walker's most effective political instrument, more than offsetting his loss of military prestige. The press, which had begun to grow cool at news of his defeats, took him again to its editorial heart, praised him for his forbearance and generosity, rejoiced in the fact that the tide had turned for him, and even saw in the ravages of the cholera, which had brought Mora's campaign to its abrupt end, the beneficent favor of Providence for Americans, recalling the fate of the Assyrian when he came down like a wolf on the fold.

In May 1856, Walker, regarded as doomed two months earlier, was again in full command of the situation. Costa Rica and Honduras appeared to have lost their stomach for war. Legitimist insurrectionists had been put down by Nicaraguan troops under the command of Vallé and Goicuria. Some reinforcements and supplies from America were again reaching Greytown on a steamer belatedly supplied by Morgan. And most important, American sentiment for Walker was making itself heard more and more loudly in political circles.

# I V

Like any political man, Walker was perpetually striving to make rational decisions in an irrational framework. Whether his judgment was good or bad in a given instance mattered less than the ever-changing and unpredictable pattern of circumstance in which he worked and which more than anything else determined the outcome of his actions. A man shooting from the hip at a mile-high eagle had as good a chance of hitting his target as Walker to overcome the hostility of the Pierce administration by anything that he might purposefully do. Only great luck, some favorable concatenation of events could change the President's attitude toward him. That luck was his in the spring of 1856, when his mercy to the Costa Ricans at Rivas was affecting American sentiment. The Platform Committee of the Democratic Party was then at work drafting the principle on which the party's choice of a presidential nominee would presumably be made. Prominent in the Committee was Pierre Soulé, who had never forgiven Marcy and Pierce for their "betrayal" of him in the matter of the Ostend Manifesto. Regarded as a leading light of the American expansionists, he was determined to revive the spirit of the Manifesto in the Democratic platform. The soaring of Walker's reputation—"the noble Walker," Soulé called him—provided the former ambassador with precisely the opportunity he sought, and almost singlehanded he drafted a plank for the platform that, he hoped, would alter the nation's policy not only toward Walker's effort in Nicaragua, but with respect to Spanish and British provocations throughout the Caribbean.

Soulé in effect said that only a candidate who would agree to back Walker and the Ostend Manifesto would get the majority of the Southern delegations at the Convention which was to assemble in Cincinnati in June—a warning to Buchanan, and an invitation to other hopefuls. Buchanan was playing a subtle game. To Southerners he spoke of his satisfaction in his part in the Manifesto, to which he had made considerable contributions. But in the North and in British circles he let it be known privately that Soulé, "a regular bird-charmer," had hypnotized him into signing the document, and that he was in fact out of sympathy with it. No one could be sure precisely where he stood in the matter.

The first candidate to yield to Soulé's pressure was President Pierce, who still dreamed of succeeding himself in the White House. For once overriding Marcy, and ignoring protests from Costa Rica, Honduras, and Cornelius Vanderbilt, on May 14, 1856, he recognized the Rivas government of Nicaragua, in the person of its new minister, Padre Augustin Vijil.

No one could have been more surprised by the new turn of events than Padre Vijil himself, who from the moment of his appearance in Washington had been subjected to insults and vilification. A gentle and idealistic soul, a former lawyer turned priest, eager to serve the cause of peace and the popular welfare, he was dismayed by the intensity of feeling against Walker that he encountered wherever the influence of Great Britain, the Central American conservatives, or the Catholic hierarchy was felt. Most of Washington's diplomats ignored him, the Vanderbilt-oriented press abused him, and the Archbishop of Baltimore rebuked him: "Is it possible that a Catholic priest should come to this country to labour against his Church and his native land?" It took the President's acceptance of his credentials to make Vijil realize that Walker's strength lay not in Washington but in the country at large.

In New York City a mass meeting, attended by thousands, was held to celebrate the recognition of Walker, with gigantic signs reading NO BRITISH INTERFERENCE ON THE AMERICAN CONTINENT! and

ENLARGE THE BOUNDS OF LIBERTY! At this meeting, another contender for the Democratic nomination joined the pro-Walker camp—Lewis Cass, United States Senator from Michigan. In a letter read to the cheering crowd he said, "I am free to confess that the heroic effort of our countrymen in Nicaragua excites my admiration. . . . The difficulties which General Walker has encountered and overcome will place his name high on the roll of distinguished men of his age. . . . A new day, I hope, is opening upon the states of Central America. Our countrymen will plant there the seeds of our institutions, and God grant that they may grow up into an abundant harvest of industry, enterprise and prosperity."

These developments were not lost on the British, who supposed that recognition of Walker would be followed by open American aid to him. It was the easier for England to believe this, since she herself was secretly aiding his enemies. As evidence of the seriousness with which he viewed the situation, Lord Palmerston ordered 20,000 troops to Canada, and staged a great naval review, to which the American minister in London was pointedly invited. A wave of war talk rose again on both sides of the Atlantic.

Most of the Southern delegates at the convention gave their votes to Cass or Pierce. The Northern states, however, felt safer with the always-uncommitted and exquisitely cautious Buchanan, and as many had foreseen, he emerged with the nomination. With the ineffectual Millard Fillmore as the American Party (Know-Nothing) candidate, and the newly born Republican Party gambling wildly on General Frémont of California, it was not difficult to foresee where the victory would lie in the coming November. At this stage there was still a widespread impression that once Buchanan was in the Presidency he would reveal himself as an expansionist, call what was generally assumed to be Palmerston's bluff, and give Walker all possible aid and encouragement.

# THE PRESIDENT

ᘛᘚ

In Nicaragua, too, 1856 saw a presidential contest, and it achieved a degree of turbulence remarkable even for Latin America. In the early spring, when southern Nicaragua was in the throes of war, there was an election in the region around León. A head of state was chosen from among three candidates—Rivas, standing as a moderate, Jerez, representing the radical wing of the Democratic party, and Mariano Salazar, a wealthy merchant turned army officer, who had achieved considerable popularity by fiery speeches and judicious expenditure. The returns favored Salazar by a slight margin. After Walker had re-established order in the south, however, Rivas demanded that Granada and the districts to the east and southwest of Lake Nicaragua, where most of his strength lay, be polled. Instantly trouble began.

The Granadans were agitated by the realization that no matter which of the three candidates was elected, they would be subordinate to hated León. Even Rivas was committed to the northern center as Nicaragua's capital. The alarms of war had not abated the rivalry of the two cities by an iota. They had been brought into uneasy truce only by the American, Walker. If there was to be a new President, said many in Granada, let him too be a candidate. Let there be a completely new election.

Against this proposal Rivas, Salazar, and Jerez all three took a firm stand. They had no doubt as to the outcome of an election in which Walker was a contestant. Not only the Granadans but even some of the Leónese could be expected to vote for him. Withdrawal of the Costa Rican troops had made him a national hero. In Granada he was followed by cheering crowds wherever he went. When he visited León with some of his American troops the city went wild with enthusiasm. Feasts were given, songs were written in his honor, "women of every age and condition" thronged around him with blessings for having protected their homes. News of Padre Vijil's recognition by President Pierce added to his stature in the public eye. He was the successful man, and the people, realizing that further attacks on their country from south and north were probable, looked to him and his *gringos* to protect them.

The intensity of feeling with which Rivas opposed the idea of a new election took Walker aback. He came to the conclusion that pressure from Vanderbilt's agents and from the British-dominated Guatemalan government had begun to sway Rivas. In no other way could he account for the proposal that the elderly President blurted out during their meeting in León—that Walker, in order to appease Nicaragua's neighbors, reduce by half the size of his American force. Sensing conspiracy in the air, he replied only that he would consider such an idea when Nicaragua was able to pay the men discharged, in accordance with their contract, which promised them substantial grants of money and land at the end of their service.

Walker noted, too, that "the face of Jerez had a cloud over it." One evening Jerez came to Walker's residence in León to discuss the future of the Nicaraguan legation in Washington, for Father Vijil had asked to be relieved of the post. Thinking that Jerez wanted the appointment for himself, Walker promptly offered his approval, and Jerez seemed pleased when he took his leave. Within the hour he returned, however, to ask uneasily, "My appointment to the United States is then decided on?" Walker caught the intimation. The offer, Jerez felt, might be designed to get rid of him. To reassure him, Walker said, "I will support the appointment, Don Maximo, only if you desire it." But Jerez still showed suspicion, and Walker realized that no words of his could restore their former amity.

Salazar also became a potential source of trouble, for it transpired that he had used his army position to make profitable contracts for himself as a merchant, at the expense of the state. Walker, calling him to account, turned him into a powerful enemy. "There were many," he wrote of this period of tension, "desirous of exciting popular passions and prejudices against the Americans . . . to destroy the confidence of the people in the naturalized Nicaraguans." He and most of his men had long since become citizens of their adopted state.

## II

At a cabinet meeting, when Rivas' ministers debated whether or not to call a new election, all except one of them stood opposed. Walker listened in silence. Central American historians, dealing at length with this moment in his career, concluded that he was animated wholly by ambition, but this view misses the fact that he could have made himself President long since had he so chosen. He himself had established and maintained the Rivas government in power. The presidency, for him, was certain to be an embarrassment, giving fresh ammunition to his enemies in Washington. There is no reason to doubt his own statement that his motive in insisting on a new election with himself as a candidate was to assure the protection of his American followers. "All things tended to show that in case Nicaragua was invaded . . . the Americans might find the machinery of the government they had created and sustained turned against themselves," he wrote. "Hence, unless disposed to carry Rivas off a prisoner—and thereby the whole moral force of his government would have been lost—it was necessary for the welfare of the Americans that a new election should be called." He could no longer control the government from behind the scenes—and not to control it would have been to betray the army that had loyally fought for him.

At the decisive cabinet meeting, having listened patiently to every opinion, he turned to Rivas and quietly requested him to decree a new election. Threats were unnecessary; all knew that the issue had been reduced to a test of power, and there could be no doubt as to where the power lay. Yielding, the President signed the decree.

The next day, leaving an American garrison under Natzmer in the city, Walker rode south toward Managua, midway between Granada and León. He had not gone twenty miles when the political storm hanging over León broke. Suddenly the unfounded rumor spread that the entire cabinet was about to be arrested by Natzmer, and as if convinced of its truth the President and several of his ministers took horses and fled northward. Chief fomenter of the trouble was Salazar, who rode through the city proclaiming that the Americans were about to assassinate the Nicaraguan leaders. The unfounded accusation was especially effective in the poorer sections of the city, where the poverty-ridden were easily stirred to demonstrations and riots. Large numbers of ragged and perpetually hungry men came out of their huts, some of them armed, and began at Salazar's urging to throw up barricades in the streets near an arms depot guarded by American troops.

The crisis mounted fast. Natzmer, believing his soldiers were about to be attacked, ordered his small force to occupy the towers of the Cathedral of León, and prepare to defend themselves. Promptly an order came to him from Jerez, as Minister of War: the Americans were to evacuate the Cathedral, and would be replaced by Nicaraguan troops, who would maintain order in the city. Natzmer hesitated. Disobedience might be construed as mutiny, but he feared to expose his men to attack in the streets. Hastily he sent a fast rider to Walker with Jerez' order and a request for guidance.

As Walker saw the matter, "the designs of Rivas and Jerez were now apparent . . . Jerez had given the order to Natzmer, supposing it would not be obeyed, thereby hoping to make the movement against the Americans turn on their disobedience to a lawful authority." Unwilling to have the breech between himself and the Leónese occur on such an issue, he ordered Natzmer to withdraw his men from León immediately, and join him on the road to Granada.

## III

In a bitter proclamation Walker told Nicaragua that Rivas had betrayed his faith as President by inviting the troops of other nations, Guatemala and San Salvador, into Nicaragua. Of this there was factual evidence. "Conspiring against the very people it was bound to protect, the late Provisional Government was no longer worthy of existence. In the name of the people I have therefore declared its dissolution."

A new Provisional President was appointed—a Nicaraguan who had held responsible government posts and whose headquarters were in Granada. Rivas, from León, replied in kind, calling Walker a traitor, depriving him of his command and summoning the country to take arms against the Americans.

Sunday, June 29, the election was held. As tabulated in *El Nicaragüense,* the ballots gave Walker an overwhelming majority—almost 16,000 out of a total vote of 23,000, and out of some 35,000 eligible to vote in the entire nation. These figures were obviously incredible, since no ballots were cast in the heavily populated area in and around León. In this respect, the Granadans who ran the election for Walker followed the national custom. Nicaraguan elections were traditionally almost as dishonest as those held in New York or San Francisco at the same period. Of the country's small male population only a small fraction had the qualifications and the interest needed to vote. Most of those who did vote were townsmen of the middle class, shopkeepers and artisans, for few in the rural districts would make the tedious journey to town merely to replace one politico by another. The total vote was generally too small to be convincing, and the standard procedure of the controlling party was to inflate the size of its victory, so as to create the impression of a popular choice.

To the Granadans the outcome of the election was a relief; what would have happened if a Leónese had become their ruler? The city turned out *en masse* for the inaugural, and the streets were filled with cheering multitudes. *"Viva el Presidente! Muerte a los enemigos del orden!"* To the splendor-loving Latin American multitude Walker's drab personal appearance must have been sadly disappointing. The thirty-two-year-old undersized President was dressed in a rusty black coat, baggy trousers, and a black felt hat—looking, in the words of a reporter for the *New York Tribune,* like "a grocery keeper from one of the poorer localities of the Sixth Ward." Nevertheless, there was a sufficiency of pomp—a parade, martial music, flags, a church service, a solemn ceremonial oath. Later Walker addressed a great crowd assembled in the plaza of Granada. A rumor that he would utilize the occasion to seek to annex Nicaragua to the United States had been widely circulated, and representatives of the press and consuls of the great powers were present in considerable numbers. To the general surprise, the crux of the speech was a warning of Nicaragua's intention to control her own destiny at any cost, and a denial of the rights of other powers, "either neighboring or distant," to occupy or dispose of any part of her territory. The firing of a twenty-one-gun salute put exclamation points after this proud asseveration.

An inaugural banquet, attended by fifty leading Nicaraguans and Americans was equally a success. In deference to Walker's personal preference, all toasts were drunk in light wines—a sensible precaution, since no fewer than fifty-three were offered. Walker himself proposed a toast to President Pierce, but the most enthusiastic response greeted a toast by one of his officers to "Uncle Billy." It brought a hearty laugh from Walker—a phenomenon sufficiently rare to cause comment in the press.

# IV

Two days later he announced the formation of his cabinet, consisting entirely of Nicaraguans—who were backed, however, by American deputies. As reform followed reform, it was quickly seen that his intention was to Americanize the country, even while retaining its independence. English was introduced into the courts as a legal language "of equal value" to Spanish. Currency values were brought into line with the American dollar. Bonds bearing six percent interest were printed, to be offered for sale through agents in the United States. Military scrip in dollars was issued to meet current expenses. But the most important changes came in fiscal policy. The Nicaraguan government had in the past drawn its chief revenue from high tariffs on imported staples, such as cloth, wines, knives, plows, and the like, an arrangement which had made prices oppressive for the poor. These commodities Walker put on the free list, while duties on other items were sharply limited in order to encourage trade.

The government, Walker declared, must henceforth look for income to sources which previously had been exempt from taxes. All retailers were to be licensed, and to pay a licensing tax to the government. Manufacturers (the chief, almost the only, "manufactured" product of Nicaragua was the national alcoholic beverage, *aguardiente*) were similarly required to pay heavily for the privilege of doing business. Lands which had been in the possession of disloyal persons—those who had assisted the enemies of the Republic—which meant Nicaraguan Legitimists who had supported the Costa Rican invasion—were to be confiscated and sold. Of such estates there were several score, including some of the richest in the country. These announcements, reminiscent of measures introduced by Robespierre in the radical years of the French Revolution, brought howls of pain from Nicaragua's conservatives, and considerable criticism in the United States.

The seizure of the estates outraged Nicaragua's propertied class, but it also deeply disturbed the tenant farmers and hired hands of the countryside. Whatever the hardships of their lives, they had no desire to exchange their familiar masters for strangers and *gringos*. The unpopularity of Walker's land policy was evident from the first. He was not in a position, however, to alleviate the blow. Time was running out. With the Leónese against him and troops from San Salvador and Guatemala likely to join them at any time, and with England prodding Costa Rica to a resumption of the war, prompt

American support more than ever was his only hope. If money, men, and supplies were not soon forthcoming from the United States in quantity, defense against the impending odds would be hopeless. The rich farms of Nicaragua were bait which he deliberately dangled before the eyes of Americans in order to lure them to Nicaragua and the defense of his government.

V

He was seeking to strengthen his army, and he even established a rudimentary navy. This initially consisted of a single schooner, owned by Walker's Leónese enemy, Salazar, who had begun to trade with Costa Rica under an American flag to which he had no claim. When the schooner put into the harbor of San Juan del Sur, Walker's men promptly seized it. Two small cannon were put on board, it was renamed the *Granada,* and was placed under the command of a remarkable young sailor of fortune, Lieutenant Callender Fayssoux, a handsome, bearded young Missourian who had distinguished himself with the Cuban expeditions of Narciso Lopez five years earlier. Resembling Walker in pride of bearing and determination, Fayssoux quickly justified Walker's faith in him. A British man-of-war, the *Esk,* hailed him on the seas, and its captain, Sir Robert McClure, ordered him to come aboard and exhibit the commission under which he sailed the *Granada,* "flying a flag unknown to any nation." Fayssoux bluntly refused, and threats to sink his ship could not make him obey McClure's order.

Walker, reading Fayssoux's report of this incident, resolved not to let it pass. Some days later McClure visited him in Granada to arrange for the safe departure of some British subjects then in the city. Walker did not rise or even suggest that the Englishman be seated. Instead, looking at him coldly, he said, "I hope, sir, that you have come to apologize for that affair of the schooner. Your conduct to Lieutenant Fayssoux was unbecoming an Englishman and a British officer. I shall make a report of it to your government, demand an investigation, and insure an explanation."

McClure found that he would be unable to transact his business until he apologized, and he finally consented to do so. From this time on, Fayssoux was Walker's favorite among his officers.

Another temporary lift to Walker's prestige came from the American minister in Granada, Wheeler. A belated letter from Secretary

Marcy informed Wheeler that the credentials of the Nicaraguan minister Vijil had been accepted, and instructed him to establish diplomatic relations with the Nicaraguan government. So far as Marcy knew when he wrote this letter, the President of Nicaragua was Rivas. Wheeler did not bother to wait until the Secretary could reconsider the matter in the light of Walker's assumption of the Presidency. Instead, he hastened to Walker with the news that he would immediately recognize his government on behalf of the United States. At a subsequent ceremony, Wheeler took it on himself to threaten Great Britain, by implication, with war. "The government of the United States," he told Walker, "hopes to unite cordially with you in the fixed purpose of preventing any foreign power that may attempt to impede Nicaragua's progress by any interference whatever. The great voice of my nation has spoken. Its words must not be unheeded."

# VI

The hopes kindled by Wheeler's action soon fizzled out. Its chief effect was to precipitate an open break between the Pierce administration and Walker. Pierce, now a lame-duck President, no longer had any motive to support Walker against Marcy's wishes. Marcy was thus able to rebuke Wheeler in caustic terms, and recall him to Washington; and he was equally sharp in denying an interview to the new minister whom Walker had sent to replace Vijil.

So far as the American government was concerned, Walker was now an outlaw whose head was forfeit to any one of his myriad enemies who could capture him. Was there then any hope? One man on Walker's staff thought there was—the Cuban, Domingo de Goicuria, then a brigadier general in Walker's service. Nearly sixty years old, a man of broad experience and common sense, he was impatient of Walker's romanticism. He himself cut a romantic figure —he wore a flowing grey beard he had vowed never to shave until his country should be free from Spain—but the idea of compromise did not disturb him. Walker's willingness to fight Vanderbilt and his determination to make no concessions to British power struck Goicuria as unreasonable in a man whose own country had abandoned him. Why should Walker not abandon the United States? It seemed possible to Goicuria that England could be made to see Nicaragua under the new regime, not as an American bastion, but rather as a buffer against any move by the United States into the Caribbean. Only a month earlier Benjamin Disraeli had made a speech in the House of Commons, suggesting that England might cease to contest the Americanization of Nicaragua if the United States would give up the aspiration to Cuba—an idea full of encouragement for the Cuban independence movement.

Walker believed that if he could hold out for some eight or nine months, until Buchanan won the Presidential election and assumed office, all might yet go well. He had received no indication that Buchanan would ignore the plank in the Democratic platform calling for support of the American effort in Nicaragua. His need was for time, and any expedient that might win him time was worth trying. In this frame of mind, he agreed to let Goicuria make a diplomatic effort on his behalf, and appointed him minister to England with a twofold mission: first, to negotiate a loan in the United States; and thereafter to proceed to London to see what he could do. In further-ance of his approach to England, he gave the Cuban a letter carefully concocted to produce the impression that, as between England and America, he was neutral. "Make them [the British] see that we are not engaged in any scheme for annexation. You can make them see that the only way to cut the expanding and expansive democracy of the north is by a powerful and compact southern federation based on military principles."

This was one of those letters, familiar in diplomacy, which, while ostensibly containing secret instructions, are actually intended to be shown privately to statesmen on the opposite side, in order to carry conviction—a card in the diplomatic game, accepted by Goicuria in this sense. Walker evidently felt the need to reassure Goicuria's Cuban friends as well as the British of his intentions with regard to Cuba, for he added, "Cuba must and shall be free, but not for the Yankees. Oh, no! That fine country is not fit for those barbarous Yankees. What should such a psalm-singing set do in the island?" This was the tone in which Latin Americans were accustomed to talk of the *gringo;* the style is curiously inconsistent with Walker's, and it is not unlikely that the idea and phrasing were suggested by Goicuria.

## VII

In his first port of call, New Orleans, Goicuria was badly jolted. The public might feel enthusiasm for Walker, but Southern men of means felt none whatever for Nicaragua's bonds. Aside from the precariousness of Walker's situation, they could not overlook his unsatisfactory stand on slavery. Such hope as remained of raising money on the requisite scale lay in New York, and Goicuria went north without delay. But there the situation was even more disillusioning. Financiers merely smiled at the suggestion of a loan for Walker. With Vanderbilt to contend with? And with Morgan and Garrison already backing away from their contract to supply ships for the Nicaragua run? No one would touch the proposition. The men with whom he talked showed moreover a distressing cynicism about Walker's motives. It was well known in Wall Street that Randolph stood to gain a personal fortune from the deal with Morgan and Garrison. Would anyone in his right mind doubt that Walker himself was to be similarly paid? Goicuria defended his chief against the imputation; on this ground, at least, he knew his man. Walker might be corruptible in other ways, it might be that the need to hold power was already corrupting him, but no one cared less for personal wealth.

The Cuban was seized by a tremendous idea. Since Walker's government could not survive without a loan, and since a loan could not be obtained against the weight of Vanderbilt's enmity, there was only one way out. He would approach the Commodore. Impetuously, without waiting for instructions from Granada, he called on the millionaire and boldly stated his proposition—restoration of Vanderbilt's privileges in the Transit route, in return for a loan.

The Commodore was interested—more, amenable. The destruction of Walker was turning out to be a costly business—and his admiration had been stirred by the man's courage and persistence. All he wanted was Walker's capitulation; that assured, he was disposed to be generous. A loan of a quarter of a million dollars to Walker was discussed—one hundred thousand to be paid on the day when Vanderbilt restored ship service to Nicaragua, the balance within a year thereafter.

Overjoyed, Goicuria hastened to write Walker the great news. He could not resist, however, adding to his letter the reports that he had heard of Randolph's personal stake in the deal with Morgan and Garrison. This proved a fatal error. He did not understand that where Randolph was concerned Walker would hear no criticism. A month of uncertainty followed while the letter went to Granada and was answered. The reply when it came was like a whip across Goicuria's face. "You will please not trouble yourself further about the

Transit Company. As to anything you say about Mr. Randolph, it is entirely thrown away on me."

So curt a rebuff the Cuban could not endure, and he wrote Walker in terms which put them still farther apart. It was evidently useless, he said, for him to proceed to England. If the comparatively friendly American government had refused to receive Walker's envoy, there could hardly be hope of British recognition—until at least the present Nicaraguan government had proved its stability by a decisive victory over its military enemies. In icy language, Walker responded that if Goicuria chose to resign from his mission, another would go in his place; and he spoke bluntly of his concern over rumors that the Cuban had become an agent of Vanderbilt's.

At the same time, Walker revoked Goicuria's commission as a brigadier general in the Nicaraguan army, and an item to that effect appeared in *El Nicaragüense*. New Yorks' newspapers, especially the *Herald,* pressed Goicuria to explain, and unable to contain his anger, he released for publication that part of his correspondence with Walker which bore on his attempt to regain the good will of Vanderbilt. The entire nation focused on the controversy. The Vanderbilt faction gleefully cited the letters as proof that Walker was either a fool or a hireling of Morgan and Garrison's, while friends of Walker denounced Goicuria as Vanderbilt's cat's-paw. Edmund Randolph, who was then seriously ill and confined to his bed in the Washington Hotel on Broadway, published in the *Herald* a paid notice which delighted readers: "In the Transit business Don Domingo de Goicuria is an intruder, with a dishonest and treacherous intent, and knowing the import of the language I use, I shall remain here until one o'clock tomorrow and longer if it is the pleasure of Don Domingo de Goicuria."

The duel of pistols was averted, but the duel of words went on. It was at this stage that the wrathful Cuban scored his most telling blow, by publishing Walker's secret letter of instructions for his mission to England. Readers of the *Herald* learned that, contrary to the general expectation, Walker had no intention of bringing Nicaragua and Cuba into the United States—that he intended rather to bar the way to American expansion—that he regarded Yankees as "a psalm-singing set" not fit to control the Caribbean lands. The purpose for which the letters had been written was not explained.

Some years later the Cuban privately expressed regret at having allowed the Walker correspondence to be published, for its effect on Walker's reputation was enduring and deadly. The floodgates were opened to vicious abuse of Walker from American, as well as from British and Central American sources. He was condemned as unpatriotic and false to the interests of the United States. He was called a cold-blooded martinet indifferent to human suffering. The *Atlantic Monthly* published a savage piece by a deserter from Walker's army, who, writing under a pseudonym, complained that General Walker, "instead of treating us like fellow-soldiers and adventurers in danger . . . bore himself like an Eastern tyrant—reserved and haughty—scarcely saluting when he met us, mixing not at all." A scurrilous pamphlet called "The Address of the Seven Prisoners," ostensibly written by seven of Walker's soldiers "captured by the Costa Ricans at Santa Rosa," received wide attention. As Mora's captives, asserted the authors, they had been freer and better treated than as Walker's soldiers. Later it was learned that only three of the seven signatories were Americans, and that one of these, a drummer boy, knew no more of the document than that it had been shown to him by a deserter, that he had refused to sign it, and that his name had been used without his knowledge.

# THE
# MOMENT OF FALSEHOOD

❧

With the November election coming closer, James Buchanan, as the candidate of the Democratic Party, had to make up his mind about Walker and Nicaragua. The scope of the decision went far beyond American interests in Central America. In the words of an authoritative interpreter of the diplomacy of Buchanan's administration, the President recognized that "the only way to avert civil war . . . was to unite North and South by a common foreign policy of a nature to arouse national feeling."* There was one means by which he might hope to rally North and South to a common cause— abrogation of the Clayton-Bulwer Treaty and reassertion of the Monroe Doctrine. This was precisely the policy for which Walker stood. But it was not easy to predict how the British would react to such a challenge; and Buchanan, aside from his anglophilia, was temperamentally incapable of taking the risks inherent in an adventurous foreign policy.

There was also another reason, one which came to light only later, why he preferred to adopt a hands-off policy toward Nicaragua. His close friend and political manager, Senator John Slidell of Louisiana, and the junior Senator from Louisiana, the financier Judah P. Benjamin, were actively interested in promoting an interoceanic railroad and canal route across the Tehuantepec Isthmus of Mexico. Buchanan himself certainly had no financial interest in this venture. He was a wealthy man, scrupulous in the observance of proprieties, patriotic in every ordinary sense. He had a habit, however, of convincing himself that expedients comfortable for himself coincided with the nation's benefit. With Slidell and Benjamin op-

---

* L. Einstein, "Lewis Cass," in *American Secretaries of State*, (S. F. Bemis, ed.), Vol. VI, p. 302.

posed to governmental support for Walker and the Nicaraguan Transit, it was not to be expected that Buchanan would move in the opposite direction.

Only one card remained in Soulé's hand, and he now played it. Announcing that he was going to Nicaragua to confer with Walker, he boarded ship in New Orleans and on October 20, 1856, arrived in Granada. The main reason for his visit, as stated in *El Nicaragüense,* was to advise Walker as to methods of floating a loan in the United States. So far as it went, this statement was accurate. It was Soulé's advice, which Walker accepted, not to attempt to combat Vanderbilt's influence in New York, but to handle the loan entirely through agents in New Orleans. Twenty-year bonds, paying six percent, in the amount of $500,000, and secured by one million acres of public lands would be issued; and at the same time Walker put on the market other public lands at low prices for purchasers in the Southern states. It was obvious, however, that these formal moves in themselves meant nothing. The wealthy men of the South, the great majority of whom were plantation owners, had no interest in acquiring lands or making investments in a country which excluded slave labor. In their view efficient cultivation of the tropical crops which Nicaragua produced was possible only with slaves, either Negroes brought into the country, or Nicaraguan Indians. The burden of Soulé's message was that if Walker wanted Southern support, he would have to pay for it in the one form which the South's aristocracy would accept—the introduction of slavery in Nicaragua.

If Parker French was Mephisto to Walker's Faust, Soulé was Lucifer himself. A man of fiery temperament, vivid imagination, and great verbal power, he had a gift for evoking dreams and inspiring visions. The temptations that he put before Walker must have been grand of scope and eloquent of description. Anyone could foresee that the South would separate from the Union before long. On which side would Walker be? From which country, the Northern rump of the United States or the Southern confederacy, could he expect support? To which would he, a Southerner, want to give support? Nicaragua and the Caribbean might well become the key to the survival of Southern civilization.

In his journalistic days Walker had taken what was then termed the "conservative" position on slavery—against its expansion, and less overtly, in favor of its gradual elimination by law and economic measures. Of some 125 antislavery societies in the United States in the 1820s, nearly three fourths were south of the Mason-Dixon line. Many Southerners hoped to prevent the frightful economic and social problems of sudden emancipation by encouraging state-by-state abolition. In the North, too, gradualism had vigorous support. Several prominent businessmen urged that Northern capital be used to construct railroads and factories in the South, to demonstrate the benefits of free labor while breaking down dependence on a plantation economy.

When all the pious oratory was vaporized, it could be seen that the residual choice offered the South was in reality no choice at all —or, more accurately, a choice of evils so appalling that rational selection between them was impossible. Southerners could sacrifice themselves for the higher morality and the nation by giving up their slaves and voluntarily plunging into bankruptcy and social chaos, or they could continue to oppose the entire trend of world thought and eventually fight against the superior military force of the North. The human paradox was—and is—that men so closely identified their own survival with the persistence of their institutions, that they preferred to die rather than submit to changes in their way of life. The institution, becoming a symbol of life, invited death for its sake. As usual when the only chance of peace depended on the willingness of men to give up an institution that they had been taught to revere, there was no chance of peace.

The voices of peace and good will grew faint. By 1856 the Southern "ultras" and the militant Northern abolitionists were dominating public opinion. It was becoming rare to find any informed American who did not grimly believe that the time had passed for a peaceful solution. As the threat of civil war came closer, Southern gradualists were faced with the wrenching need to choose between beloved Dixie and the claims of an uneasy social conscience. For most of them loyalty to the homeland was the stronger emotion, and they found themselves struggling to preserve an institution that in their secret thoughts they regarded as an evil and a misfortune.

In Walker's case the issue was even more painful. His last hope of success in Nicaragua was at stake. The situation as Soulé presented it must have been crystal clear. Walker could maintain an antislavery stand and go down with his men to sure disaster, or he could flee Nicaragua and seek discreditable asylum abroad, or he could abjure his former political views, link himself to the land of his origins, and perhaps rise to further triumphs with the aid of his own people.

## I I

He was being torn apart by the same forces that were tearing apart his country. He had to fight the Civil War within himself five years before it began. His effort to preserve his intellectual integrity showed in the weeks that it took him to make up his mind. His first response was an attempt at compromise. Early in September he issued a decree which, in effect, established a system of forced labor for all Nicaraguans who were adjudged guilty of vagrancy, or who failed to fulfill the terms of their labor contracts with employers. In effect, Walker was reassuring American purchasers of Nicaraguan estates as to the availability of workers.

If he hoped to avoid further concessions, he was mistaken. A change in the military situation forced his hand, when word came that a strong army, representing Guatemala, San Salvador, Honduras, and the Leónese Nicaraguans was being mobilized for attack on him. On September 22, he issued the decree which was to brand him as a slavery man. It did not mention slavery. Its essence was a declaration that certain provisions of the Nicaraguan Constitution were null and void. One of these had prohibited the introduction of slaves into the country.

The thing being done, he had to find a justification with which he could live. The poorest and most numerous class in Nicaragua, the Indian workers of the Nicaraguan plantations, he wrote in a letter to an American Congressman, had been exploited by the great landowners and the town tradesmen until their economic and social condition was worse than that of most slaves in the United States. Slavery under the American system would actually be a step upward for them, the best way of freeing them from perpetual indebtedness.

But when all was said, he knew what he had done to his moral position in the eyes of the Nicaraguan people. He had been popular among the Indians largely because he spared them from the horrors of military conscription. Now he was bound to lose them.

Some of his antislavery admirers were loath to believe that their hero could overnight shift his position so radically. The former American minister to Nicaragua, George Squier, wrote a letter to the London *Times* denying that Walker really intended to introduce slavery in Nicaragua. But from this time on, Walker's chief allies were Southern ultras. He who had refused to be served by conscripts and who had never owned or wished to own a slave could find support only among the slavery men.

It was later rumored that he had from the first been an agent of the slavery interest, and he deliberately lent credence to this notion. Rather than admit that he had changed his politics and chosen survival at the expense of principle, he preferred to appear as a man who had always been secretly dedicated to the Southern cause. Once he made his fundamental concession, he went to extremes to have it thought that in his heart he had never doubted the virtues of slavery, and so had no need to be convinced by Soulé. To his earlier writings on the subject he never referred.

## III

The concerted attacks on Walker in the United States, resulting from his slavery decree and the Goicuria affair, came at a time when his military position was rapidly worsening. Over 2000 troops had been put into the field by the alliance of the Northern republics. Costa Rica was preparing to renew her war on Walker from the south. Thirteen British warships manned by 2500 men had arrived in the harbor of Greytown. Against these forces Walker had only one ally —the cholera, which, while it depleted his own ranks, took a much heavier toll from enemy troops, and temporarily paralyzed them. In every other respect—with only 600 men, with no new recruits to be expected, facing serious shortages of food and ammunition—he was at a hopeless disadvantage. For readers of American newspapers the allied advance toward Granada in September and the first reports of the fighting presaged his imminent doom. At Masaya, on the allied route to Granada, his troops suffered a severe repulse, and had to fall back on the capital; but before he could reach the city, a strong Guatemalan column had invested it, murdered a number of American civilians, and seized all the munitions and food supplies they could find.

Everyone thought he was finished. It came both to Nicaragua and to the United States as a stunning surprise when, in a battle on October 13, exactly one year after his original seizure of the city, he drove the enemy out of Granada, inflicting heavy losses, and reestablished his authority in the capital.

# MR. VANDERBILT
# TAKES HIS REVENGE

After Walker's unexpected recapture of Granada, a strange rumor began to circulate in the financial district of New York. Behind the scenes a powerful and unexpected well-wisher was working for him —the only man perhaps capable of coping with Walker's enemies at home—the great "Liveoak" George Law, Panama shipping magnate, railroader, multimillionaire, and a man who harbored heavy personal grievances against Vanderbilt. It had struck Law that neither the Garrison-Morgan combine nor Vanderbilt's company any longer had a firm legal hold on the Nicaraguan Transit route. If aid initiated by himself were to enable Walker to win his war, would he not reward his benefactor with the privileges of the Transit, and would not Vanderbilt writhe? This appears to have been the reasoning behind the moves made by Law in the summer of 1857.

He knew, or thought he knew, how to rescue Walker from his dark military situation. Among Law's friends in New York was one of the world's most renowned soldiers of fortune—the Swedish-born Charles Frederick Henningsen, a blond Viking of a man, scarcely forty years of age, who had distinguished himself in wars in Spain, in Russia, and notably in the Hungarian revolution, where he had become one of the chief officers and close friends of the famous Kossuth. The author of several much-praised books on military strategy, his talents went still further: he was an able journalist, a novelist of wit and repute, and the husband of a wealthy and aristocratic Georgian beauty. Henningsen had from the first taken a deep and admiring interest in the youthful Walker's struggle and had come to the belief that with a few hundred more men, some mortars and howitzers, better rifles, and adequate supplies, the American could yet beat back his foes and conquer the isthmus. When he mentioned his views to Law, the financier instantly proposed that they join forces. It was the kind of adventure that Henningsen could not resist. Law had bought several thousand army muskets with a view to their use in Nicaragua, and he offered these to Henningsen together with $20,000 for the purchase of artillery and ammunition.

The landing of Henningsen in Greytown early in October, 1856, was widely acclaimed by the American press as a possible turning point in Walker's fortunes. Boats of the Accessory Transit Company brought him and his armament to Granada, where they were joyfully welcomed by Walker and his men; within two weeks the Swede had organized and trained two effective companies of artillery and one of sappers and miners. His impact on the little army was considerable, and Walker wrote that he "never had reason to regret the confidence" that he placed in Henningsen. From the first his knowledge, skills, and competence were so manifest that even when his commission as Major General put him above other veteran commanders in rank, jealousy was diluted with respect.

Henningsen willingly accepted Walker's leadership, and later wrote articles for New Orleans and Nashville newspapers, paying high tribute to Walker's intelligence, modest bearing, and force of character. The curious composition of the little army also impressed the Swedish adventurer. In explaining the ability of Walker's soldiers to sustain battle against appalling odds, he wrote, "Such men do not turn up in . . . everyday life. All military science failed, on a sudden field, before assailants who came on at a run, to close with their revolvers, and who thought little of charging a battery, pistol in hand."

The very same qualities that made practical men of affairs turn from Walker drew to him the idealistic youths, the poets, and the soldiers of fortune. The small band of Americans who followed him to Nicaragua produced no fewer than six books about his venture, as well as numerous articles and a considerable amount of poetry.

The army's morale was remarkable, and contrary to statements by Walker's Northern critics, he was revered by his men, who recalled an occasion on which he had given his horse to a wounded soldier, while he himself trudged thirty miles on foot. Similarly, Henningsen praised the discipline of the army, and discounted frequent charges of pillage and rape against Walker's troops. Much of the adverse criticism aimed at the Americans on this score was due to the depredations of thirty men, who in July 1856, arrived from Texas in a body, and who turned out to be a robber gang urgently wanted by United States authorities. Deserting almost immediately after arrival, and wearing the uniforms of Walker's Rangers, they wandered through the Nicaraguan countryside in search of loot, leaving a trail of misery behind them, and carefully avoiding Walker, who had sworn to hang them if they fell into his hands.

Another striking feature of Walker's operation observed by Henningsen was the good will shown him by the poorer folk of the countryside. Even the "slavery decree" did not materially affect the attitude of the Nicaraguan Indians toward Walker in the first months of his war with the allies. Their feeling was undoubtedly due mainly to the fact that, unlike their native commanders, he never conscripted them for military service—a dispensation which filled them with gratitude amounting almost to reverence. The company of Nicaraguans who remained in his service to the end, and whom he regarded as equal to any of his troops in courage and loyalty, were all volunteers.

It was the propertied and their retainers, the calzados, the wearers of shoes, numbering perhaps one tenth of the Nicaraguan people, who regarded Walker as their natural enemy. The change that took place in the popular attitude toward him came only in the late stages of the war, when appalling shortages of food compelled his men to forage. Unlike Walker himself, who ate sparingly and almost indifferently of whatever rations came to hand, they were accustomed to consume far more provender than did the typical Nicaraguan. Not content with a diet of tortillas and plantains, they seized grain, cows, horses, mules, and chickens as they found them, ravaging the countryside for miles around their camps. Word of such depredations spread quickly, and before the war's end country folk and town dwellers alike had come to regard the appearance of Walker's bearded Rangers as a disaster. When Henningsen first came to Nicaragua, however, his chief's reputation among the common folk was considerably higher than that of any Central American general.

## II

Three weeks after Henningsen's arrival, a strong Costa Rican army crossed into Nicaragua and moved north to occupy the Transit route west of Lake Nicaragua. Simultaneously a Leónese column marched south to join the Guatemalans and Salvadoreans for another attack on Granada. With 600 men Walker had to fight a war on two fronts against nearly 5000. A sudden attack drove the Costa Ricans out of San Juan del Sur, but this did not help him much. Compelled to leave a garrison of 250 men to hold the Transit route, he had only 300 effectives with which to resist the northern allies, who were strongly fortified in the town of Masaya, some twenty miles north of Granada.

The allied army had every advantage except one—artillery. The great question for Walker was how far mortars and howitzers could offset weakness in numbers. His only hope lay in a bold strategy. The enemy had to be shattered in a single battle. He and Henningsen wasted no time before beginning the attack on Masaya. Within an hour, however, they realized that their main asset was hollow. The fuses of their mortar shells were too short, and the explosions were taking place harmlessly in the air, instead of on the ground. To retreat would have invited pursuit in force; they had no choice but to try to take Masaya by assault, relying on Henningsen's trained sappers and miners to dislodge the allies from their strongholds. For a time success seemed possible. In three days of sleepless effort they pushed the Central Americans into the center of Masaya, and pressed them hard. A few hundred fresh troops, had they been available, could conceivably have compelled the surrender of the entire allied army, and made Walker the master of Central America. But exhaustion was taking its toll. With a third of his men killed or wounded, and the rest staggering from weariness, there was nothing for them to do but abandon the attack and drag themselves back to Granada. A strong sortie by the enemy would have finished them. It was their good fortune that the losses of the allies were so heavy, and their commanders so shaken by their close call, that they did not follow up their advantage.

There was worse to come. Although a few days of recuperation somewhat restored the morale of Walker's men, their extreme fatigue and the primitive conditions of their hospitals, where flies and vermin abounded, made them excessively vulnerable to the most dangerous enemy of all, cholera. An epidemic broke out, raging at a new peak of mortality, and claiming as one of its victims Lieutenant James Walker, the filibuster's youngest and favorite brother. As each day took the lives of two or three percent of his force, Walker's surgeons warned him that unless he evacuated Granada every American there would be dead within six weeks.

Granada had to be abandoned, and under Walker's personal

direction the sick were moved across Lake Nicaragua, first to one desolate place, then to another, in an effort to find safety and tolerable conditions. Their miseries and fatalities increased with each day. The horrors of this hopeless flight from disease shook Walker as had nothing before in his experience, for among the evacuees were a number of women, some of them wives of Americans who had come to Nicaragua as to a promised land. He, the defender of womankind, had no internal defense against their sufferings and reproaches—any more than he could forget that he had lured his brother to his death.

It was at this point of psychic turmoil that he had to make a decision which was bound to confirm to the outside world his reputation for ferocity. The allies, anyone could foresee, would soon occupy Granada, and the moral, as well as the military effect of the move would be disastrous. Holding both Granada and León, they would hold the core of Nicaragua. No hope would remain for Walker's army. To destroy the city would be to send up cries of horror from all Central America, but to leave it intact would be suicidal. So, at least, Walker and Henningsen reasoned. It fell to Henningsen, with 300 men, to undertake the task of razing Granada after first evacuating the native population. Amid further scenes of misery and tragedy, the shocked and wretched Granadans, such as still remained in the city, were removed by boats of the Transit Company to points along the shores of Lake Nicaragua, while the grim work commenced.

Part of Granada was still intact when the allied army surrounded the city and commenced a three-sided assault on Henningsen's small force. Through four days of incessant fighting, firing from adobe houses and public buildings, the Americans stood them off, their marksmanship taking a great toll of life. An illustration of the battle in an American magazine suggests the scene: the plaza under the pale blazing sky, everything starkly outlined in sunlit white and angular black shadow, a wretched rubble of buildings in the background, puffs of musket smoke coming from the few that remained standing, and white-clad Guatemalan corpses sprawled in the tawny dirt.

Henningsen's problem was complicated by the fact that the strongest position in the city, Guadalupe Cathedral, had been seized by the enemy. To leave it in their hands, he realized, would be fatal. It had to be taken by storm; but could he afford the resulting losses? To make matters more difficult, his men uncovered in one of their improvised fortresses a large store of liquor, and their discipline, already faltering from exhaustion and desperation, disintegrated. In the middle of the battle, half of them were stupefied by drink. Nevertheless, at a lull in the fighting the tireless and inspired Henningsen was able to rally enough volunteers to drive the enemy out of the cathedral. A few hours later he had crowded into it his entire force, now reduced to 200 men able to fight, together with the mutilated, the sick, the drunk, and some scores of women and children, many of them Americans, who still remained in the city. Their ordeal, marked by instances of extraordinary heroism and self-sacrifice on the part of women as well as men, provided sensational material for American journalists.

Presently General Zavala, the Guatemalan commander, realized that Henningsen was depending on supplies brought to the wharves of Granada by Walker's lake boats, which were also his only means of escape. For a time Zavala was deterred from attacking the wharves by uncertainty as to the size of the force which had been left to protect them, and which was strongly barricaded. Then fortune played into his hands. One of the defenders of the all-important area was a Venezuelan whom Walker had rescued from a Granadan dungeon a year earlier. Since then his gratitude had thinned away, and now he deserted and revealed to Zavala that there were only 27 men between him and command of the lake front. The storming action that followed wiped out the Americans in the little garrison to a man, and isolated the remainder of Henningsen's force.

With Walker's boats unable to reach the city, food supplies in Guadalupe Cathedral soon ran so low that men and women had to subsist on small rations of mule meat and decayed flour. Ammunition reserves also were dwindling fast. To provide shot for their field pieces Henningsen's artillery officers made holes in the sand, filled them with scraps of iron, and poured melted lead over them to form an approximate ball. Their situation seemed beyond hope. Zavala, however, was not in a position to follow up his advantage. His losses had been staggering, and in order to regroup his forces he temporarily broke off the attack. Instantly Henningsen ordered his men to proceed with the firing of Granada. Their effort culminated in a final explosion of powder trains which demolished the center of the city. Simultaneously a successful attack by Walker regained command of the wharves, and Henningsen was able to withdraw his troops and the noncombatants under his protection. His flair showed in his last gesture on leaving the ruined city, when he raised an improvised flag in the rubble, bearing the legend AQUI FUÉ GRANADA—"Here was Granada."

The unexpected success of the Americans in sustaining the siege, the burning of the city, the terrible mortality among the allies, the rejoining of Henningsen's force with Walker's, and the continued ravages of disease so shook Zavala that he hastily ordered a retreat to Masaya. The Costa Ricans also thought it wise to pull back, relieving the pressure on the Transit route. Quarrels between the allied commanders still further diminished the possibility of an effective attack on Walker. All at once his generalship, which had been sharply questioned by the American press, seemed vindicated.

Of major importance was word from San Francisco that a hundred well-armed recruits were on the way to join him. At this stage, he had to meet a new threat, when a large and well-armed brig of British origin appeared outside the harbor of San Juan del Sur, flying the Costa Rican flag, and manned by a large Costa Rican crew. Its obvious purpose was to blockade the port and prevent the landing of reinforcements. Walker's hopes rested on the little schooner *Granada,* with its 28 men and two guns. A two-hour sea fight ensued, in which Captain Fayssoux, by brilliant seamanship and accurate gunnery, sank the enemy vessel, and added compassion to victory by rescuing from the Pacific nearly half of the brig's 114 sailors. Almost immediately afterward, the ship from San Francisco arrived with Walker's recruits.

The Americans were further heartened by word that several hundred fighting men were on their way to Greytown from New Orleans. In spite of everything that England, Vanderbilt, and the Central American coalition had done to destroy him, it still appeared possible that Walker might re-establish control over Nicaragua.


# III


To Vanderbilt it was unthinkable that his aims should be frustrated by a few hundred Americans led by the man who had dared to confiscate his property, and who was supported by his commercial foes. In his opinion Walker's Central American enemies had failed to grasp the strategic realities of their situation. To try to defeat the man's army of daredevils in direct battle would take too long and cost too much. The way to break Walker's resistance, he was certain, was simply to cut his lines of communication across the isthmus. So long as the filibuster held the Transit route and the boats of the San Juan River and Lake Nicaragua, he could be supplied by Law or by Morgan and Garrison; but without the route and the boats, he could soon be starved out and put at the mercy of the Central Americans.

Late in November 1856, two of Vanderbilt's men traveled on his fastest ship to Costa Rica, where they held secret talks with President Mora. One of them was an American, Sylvanus Spencer, an old-time employee of Vanderbilt's, eminently suited to the task before him. He had at one time served as engineer on the Transit boats, understood every detail of their operation, knew their crews personally, and had navigated the San Juan River many times. With Spencer was an enigmatic Englishman, William R. C. Webster, an agent of the British government who apparently was assigned to Vanderbilt for the mission to Costa Rica, and who coordinated Spencer's operations with those of Captain Cauty, the chief British military officer in Costa Rica, and with the Central American army in the north.

In their arrangement with Mora, Spencer and Webster agreed to aid him to recapture and hold the Transit route while the northern allies destroyed Walker's army. In return, Vanderbilt would expect Mora's influence on the next Nicaraguan administration to be used to grant him anew the title and privileges of the Transit. Word of the agreement went to Vanderbilt from Spencer, and on December 25, 1856, the financier gave a Christmas remembrance to stockholders of the Accessory Transit Company, in the form of a notice in the New York *Herald:* "Present appearances indicate a realization of my hopes that the company will be speedily restored to their rights, franchises and property upon the isthmus of Nicaragua."

Action followed swiftly. Within two days, Costa Rican troops led by Spencer, in a series of cleverly planned surprise attacks, had seized most of the Transit steamers and Spencer had assured the loyalty of the boats' officers and crews for his service by judicious use of a fund provided by Vanderbilt. Another Costa Rican column under the command of Captain Cauty invested a key fortress on the eastern shore of Lake Nicaragua, where Walker had not been able to leave more than a skeleton garrison. At Greytown, a British man-of-war prevented 400 well-armed American recruits who had arrived from New Orleans from recapturing one of the riverboats and steaming upstream to join Walker. Across the isthmus, at San Juan del Sur, British ships bottled up the harbor where the ship *Granada* rode at anchor. The joy of the Costa Rican government over these events spilled into a proclamation to its army: "The main artery of filibusterism has been cut forever. The sword of Costa Rica had severed it."

Under the Costa Rican flag, the Transit steamers swiftly concentrated the forces under Spencer and Cauty near the Transit route and they seized the crucial lake town of Virgin Bay before Walker, in his camp at nearby Rivas, had even been informed of the invasion. At the same time, the allied army at Masaya again advanced southward to form the upper jaw of the pincer movement in which he was now almost trapped. But in spite of their enormous advantage in manpower, they did not attack in force. The new plan was to bring the Americans to their knees by starvation. For four bitter months the siege continued, while hunger, thirst, disease, and boredom sapped the strength of Walker's men. And this was not the whole tally of his burden. He was concealing from his men two pieces of disastrous news. A letter from California had revealed that Garrison and Morgan had surrendered to Vanderbilt, and would no longer provide any aid for Nicaragua; and the effort of one of his trusted officers, Colonel S. A. Lockridge, to bring in the Americans stranded at Greytown had been conclusively thwarted by the British.

Walker fell sick of a fever, and to his sickbed came word, in March 1857, that 160 of his men, who might in other days have fought off a thousand of the enemy, had been routed by a body of only 200 allied troops on the road west of Rivas. This demonstration of the extent to which the army's morale had deteriorated was more than he could bear. Dragging himself to his feet, he assembled his men on the plaza of Rivas and tried with words to revive their courage. "We are engaged in no ordinary warfare. . . . We have come here as the advance guard of American civilization. . . . Are we to be driven from the country merely because we were not born on its soil? Never! Never!"

His hold on them was still strong, for a few days later 400 of them followed him into a desperate attack on 2000 Guatemalans. In this battle his wild and reckless exposure of himself to enemy fire awed even those who thought they knew him. He seemed to be saying, with Marc Antony, "I'll make death love me!" But the bullet that might have honorably extricated him from his dilemma did not strike. In spite of feats of extraordinary valor on the part of his men, the attack failed, and Walker had to move back swiftly to Rivas. At one point during the retreat, he was thought to be wounded when a burst of musket fire from a house made his horse rear; but he relieved the alarm of his troops when he brought the horse under control, and drawing his revolver, fired a few deliberate and, as it were, symbolic shots at the window from which the bullets had come. Then with a wave of his hand, he motioned the column forward.

Twice his troops repulsed attacks by the Costa Ricans, but the victories were empty. The situation worsened from day to day. Rumors of the Garrison-Morgan betrayal had begun to spread among his men. Provisions were steadily diminishing, and foraging raids on the countryside had become unproductive. Henningsen, looking at the small hunk of mule meat that was counted as dinner, remarked "A little more of this and we'll have to eat the prisoners." Walker's own mood had become fatalistic. He no longer cared to submit his men to pitched battles which, even if won, could not save them; and daily exchanges of fire with the enemy were producing more casualties than he could stand. In a letter to Edmund Randolph, Walker told him that of some 800 men in Rivas, only 332 were fit for duty, and 224 were sick or wounded.

The last battle came on April 11, 1857, when Zavala, having learned of conditions in Rivas, grew overconfident, and mounted a surprise assault with nearly 200 men, most of them raw conscripts from the farms of Guatemala. The result proved that Walker was still to be reckoned with. The open advance of the enemy was met with such withering rifle fire from behind barricades that 700 of the attacking force were killed or wounded, as against 9 American casualties. "It was with a feeling almost of pity for these forced levies," wrote Walker, "that the Americans were obliged to shoot them down like so many cattle. The Guatemalan officers cared no more for their men than if they were sheep."

Even now he still nourished a last secret hope of victory. The cholera, which had saved him before, was again decimating the enemy. Both the Guatemalan and the Costa Rican troops camps were daily losing scores of men to the disease. He felt that in another few weeks panic might yet compel them to lift the siege. Everything depended on such spirit as remained in his own army. It was dwindling fast. No longer was Walker "Uncle Billy" to his troops; many, especially among the recent arrivals, had begun to see him as a heartless fanatic, forcing them to fight in a lost cause that was meaningless for them. Eating their repulsive mule meat, they muttered to each other, where was the high adventure, where the rich lands, where the beautiful women for which they had journeyed to Nicaragua? In the period of inaction that followed the slaughter of the Guatemalan conscripts, morale steadily sank.

It was at this stage that General Mora of Costa Rica executed his most telling stroke. Recognizing that the struggle had become one of morale in both camps, he proclaimed that his former "no quarter" policy had been abandoned. Instead, he offered protection, food, liquor, and free passage home to any American who would come across the lines and give up his arms. Nothing could have more painfully shaken Walker's men. Not only a number of soldiers in the ranks but several officers stole away from their quarters on the very night of Mora's proclamation. One of the officers even appeared the next day on the enemy barricades, calling to his former comrades to join him and share in the meals, tobacco, and *aguardiente* that Mora was providing.

Daily the wave of desertions mounted until as many as twenty men a day were being lost. What followed was pure Walker. Calling his remaining force together, he told them that any soldier who wished to leave his service would be given his passports, so that he could cross the enemy lines without being regarded as a deserter. Probably no other tactic could have stiffened the backs of those unhappy men. Five soldiers among them who asked for their papers were hooted by their comrades as they left; and one who tried to turn back was intercepted by Walker himself, and was made to go on. The remaining troops, fewer than 200, laughed, cheered, and returned to their weary routines and wretched rations.


# I V


Early in 1857, President Buchanan found himself under increasing pressure to bring the Central American embroilment to an end. Senator Benjamin and his associates were eager to begin active negotiations with Mexico for the Tehuantepec route, and were handicapped by the uncertainties over Nicaragua. Commodore Vanderbilt was disturbed by indications that the Costa Rican government, having put its flag on the Transit steamers, had no intention of letting them go. Action was needed, and it took the form of the arrival at San Juan del Sur of a powerful American sloop-of-war, the *St. Mary's,* and Commander Charles N. Davis, with official instructions to "take such steps as circumstances required for the protection of American citizens" in Nicaragua, and perhaps unofficial instructions to put an end to the war by any means that came to hand.

A shrewd man, Davis began by negotiating with General Mora to allow the removal of American women and children from Rivas to under the protection of the American flag. A truce was declared for this purpose, and while it was still in effect, he suggested to Mora and the northern allies that they permit at the same time the departure of Walker's army. They were delighted to comply. Subsequently Mora admitted that in another twenty days his losses resulting from cholera would have compelled a cessation of the war. The only stipulation that he made was that he was to receive all of Walker's artillery and munitions. On April 30, Davis wrote Walker a letter, carried to him under a flag of truce by one of Mora's officers. Its essence was that the situation was hopeless, and that Walker would be well advised to surrender himself and his men to the United States, represented by Davis. If this offer were not accepted, Davis went on, he would seize the *Granada* at San Juan del Sur, thus cutting off the last marginal hope of escape.

The threat infuriated Walker; at the same time it made him see the futility of further resistance, and he replied that he was ready to negotiate the terms of capitulation. Conferences followed, distinguished chiefly by his determination to assure the safety of those Nicaraguan soldiers who had continued to serve in his army; he would sign no agreement that did not allow them to go peacefully to their homes. Nor did he have any intention of letting the Costa Ricans benefit from his artillery. The articles of surrender, while calling on him to deliver his field pieces, did not say that they had to be in firing order; and Henningsen and his officers proceeded systematically to wreck all mortars and howitzers, as well as an arsenal that they had constructed.

On May 1, 1857, at five o'clock in the afternoon, Walker addressed his men for the last time. His brief remarks were in a vein not likely to give much comfort to his dispirited and hungry followers. The tone was defiant, the ideas remote from their present miseries. One suspects that it was only by remoteness and detachment that he had been able to sustain his own morale during the siege; if he had identified himself with his men, their misery would have destroyed him. Now he told them that he and they must part "for the present." They had "written a page of American history which it is impossible to forget or erase. From the future, if not from the present, we may expect just judgment." He then thanked the officers and men who had served under him, and stood aside while General Henningsen explained the terms of the surrender and the order of march. Walker and his staff would go to San Juan del Sur, and deliver themselves to Commander Davis aboard the *St. Mary's*. The remainder of the army and the noncombatants would be taken over the Transit route to Greytown, to board another United States warship, the frigate *Wabash,* Commodore Hiram Paulding in command.

The fact that Walker and his higher officers were Davis's prisoners apparently did not come home to many of his men. Nor were they interested in the plans already in his mind for the future, and which required his return to the United States at the earliest moment. To the newer recruits especially, those who knew him least and had not felt the impact of his personality, the overriding fact was that he was leaving them at the low point of their lives. His departure, abrupt and seemingly unemotional, was to them the climax of a nightmare. From the moment when they saw him ride away their accumulated resentments gathered force. They felt toward him as the remnants of Napoleon's Grand Army felt when he left them on the retreat from Moscow. High politics meant nothing to the disheartened men in the ranks of Walker's army. They had endured hunger, festering wounds, fevers, flies, chiggers, lice, dysentery; they had lived in a miasma of blood, foul smells, fear, and disease; they had seen their friends, and even American women and children, suffer and die in Nicaragua; and now their leader, the man for whom they had risked everything, had deserted them: so they felt. He and his officers rode horses; they had to walk—or hobble, if they were wounded—the miles that lay between Rivas and Lake Nicaragua. He was in the hands of Americans; they were left to the mercies of the Costa Ricans. Rage grew in them on the slow boat journey across Lake Nicaragua and down the San Juan River to Greytown. Although Mora's troops refrained from obvious violence, they missed no opportunity to pilfer such belongings as the Americans still had, and to humiliate them; and such food as was offered them was barely edible. When at last they staggered on board the *Wabash,* the ship's officers were shocked and filled with pity by their plight, and the voyage home, through a stormy sea, was a long hymn of hate to Walker.

## V

A crisis developed after Walker boarded the *St. Mary's,* for Commander Davis insisted on the surrender of the *Granada.* This had not been provided for in the articles, but when both Walker and Fayssoux demurred, Davis threatened to sink the vessel then and there, and trained his guns on the little ship. After a bitter protest, Walker wrote an order to Fayssoux—"Deliver the *Granada* to the United States." The sense of injury that he felt was compounded when Davis turned the vessel over to the Costa Ricans, and he subsequently expressed grim satisfaction when incompetent seamanship under the Costa Rican flag caused the doughty little schooner to be wrecked and lost.

In all, 2500 American fighting men had served under Walker in Nicaragua—never more than 800 in any one engagement—against enemy forces estimated by Henningsen at 17,000. Of the total American enlistment, 1000 had died of wounds or disease, 700 had deserted, 250 had been discharged, and 80 had been captured by the enemy. Henningsen, a trained military observer, believed that about 5800 Central Americans must have been killed or wounded in battle during the war, but how many had died of disease he could not guess.

The next moves on the Washington chessboard were predictable. The Costa Rican minister announced that his country had a legitimate claim to the Nicaraguan Transit, and planned to participate in its future control. Vanderbilt protested. Buchanan said that legality must be observed. Senator Benjamin and an associate left Washington for Mexico City, with the intention of concluding a contract for the Tehuantepec Transit route.

At this point, as so often during his administration, Buchanan's hopes of achievement collapsed at the first challenge. Neither he nor Benjamin expected that Pierre Soulé would forestall them in Mexico. Savagely indignant at the wrecking of his hopes for Nicaragua, the father of the Ostend Manifesto was determined to frustrate Buchanan by every means at his disposal. The Mexican officials responded to his political skill and eloquence, and Benjamin's negotiation swiftly lost momentum and came to a stop.

Here was a new embarrassment for the President. If an American transit could not be established in Tehuantepec, then the Nicaraguan route took on renewed importance. Belatedly he raised the question of its future with England. An almost plaintive letter went to his friend Lord Clarendon. "I think you ought to keep your protégés in Central American in better order. I wish I could induce you to believe that the interest of the United States in that region is the very same with your own. Your special favorite Costa Rica is now endeavoring to convert her patriotic assistance to her sister state against the filibusters into a war of conquest, and she modestly claims the right to sell the Transit route to the highest bidder."

Buchanan then added, in his first draft of the letter, as preserved in his files, the sentence, "To this I shall never submit." However, he characteristically struck out the word "never," and the letter as it went to Clarendon read merely, "To this I shall not submit." Then, on a sighing note, the President lamented, "Both of our countries and the world would have been better off if the Clayton-Bulwer treaty had not existed."

# A NAME
## TO CONJURE WITH

❦

He had gone to Nicaragua in the name of democracy and the Nicaraguan Democrats had turned against him. He had begun with a sense of America's mission to the world, and the government of the United States had rejected him. He had stood for the gradual elimination of slavery, and now the world knew him as a slavery man. His purpose had been twisted until all the idealistic essence had been wrung out of it. He could no longer hold on to his Byronic conception of himself. But to the average American he was still the hero of heroes. This fact first came home to Walker in the wild welcome that awaited him at New Orleans, where he landed on May 27, 1857. Word had come from Washington that, on order of the President, no charges would be preferred against him for violation of the Neutrality Laws; he was a free man. A cheering crowd was on the wharves; men surrounded him, lifted him to their shoulders, bore him to a waiting carriage, formed a procession, and marched behind him to the sumptuous St. Charles Hotel, where rooms had been reserved for him. So numerous and persistent were the people in the street outside that he was compelled to appear on the balcony of his apartment and make a short speech. This was not enough; his admirers entered the hotel and refused to leave until they saw him again.

At the mass meeting, held in the open two nights later, he stood on a platform surrounded by flags of the United States and Nicaragua, and spoke for two hours, making no secret of his intention to return to Central America and complete the task he had begun. The New Orleans press reported his oration as a *tour de force,* an oral history of his career on the isthmus, and an explanation—pointing bluntly at Secretary Marcy, Commodore Vanderbilt, and the British government—of the reasons why he had not succeeded. In speaking of President Buchanan, however, Walker was reserved; already arrangements were being made for a talk between them at the White House. One newspaper wondered whether he was planning on a political future in the United States. If so, the popular base for it was established. His was a name to conjure with.

## II

Walker could not have been unmindful that all the cheering was being done by men whose politics he had opposed a few years earlier. Like others whose guiding principle has crumpled under pressure, he could achieve forgetfulness only by doubling the intensity of his new conviction, and hypnotizing himself with its repetition. Journeying northward, he asserted in every speech not only that the introduction of American civilization in Central America was the road to salvation for the United States, but that Southern institutions had to prevail there. It was Walker's position that if it had not been for Davis's interference, the Central American armies would have disintegrated, while the morale of his own men would have been sustained by the knowledge that a route of retreat was open to them. He made these charges first orally, then in writing.

Some months later, in a speech at Mobile, Walker said that the President in this meeting had not only heard him with attention but had actually encouraged him to make another attempt to conquer Nicaragua. It would have been nothing for Buchanan to drop hints of sympathy and understanding without actually committing himself—hints that would have been the more effective because Walker as yet knew nothing of the President's commitment to the Tehuantepec project.

With a strong revival of inner confidence, Walker went on to the culminating point of his triumphal tour, New York. There even New Orleans' hullabaloo was exceeded. A committee of admirers met him in New Jersey and escorted him by boat to Battery Park, where in spite of rain a large crowd awaited him, and where he accommodated them with a short speech. When he finally got to his hotel, it was to discover a brass band waiting for him, and he had to submit to an hour-long serenade.

So ruthless an invasion of his privacy was more than he could

bear. Three days after his arrival he secretly left the hotel and se-
cluded himself in a friend's house, the address of which was known
only to a few intimates. There he set about the business on which
he had come. This was nothing less than the formation of a secret
"Central American League," with branches in the main American
cities, each under the charge of a trusted officer, to raise funds,
recruits, and supplies for a second expedition to Nicaragua. Henningsen was in charge of the New York branch. One after another
his key men took their instructions from Walker, as from the general
of an actual army, and departed. "We meet again at Philippi," Henningsen was reported as saying to them.

Walker's decision to hide himself from New York's reporters did
him no good in their eyes. Perhaps he had forgotten that the fury of
a journalist frustrated exceeds that of a woman scorned. Now the
press readily seized the first opportunity to turn against him. Several
newspapers criticized him sharply for impugning the motives of
Commander Davis, who after all "had saved him." The fact was that
he had become indifferent both to popular praise and journalistic
condemnation. Events would speak for him, or nothing would.

# III

It was not a good time in which to raise money. A financial panic
which had shaken the City of London was suddenly echoed in Wall
Street; stock prices collapsed, credit tightened, business fell off, men
lost their jobs, and a cloud of pessimism settled over the country.
The Dred Scott decision and reports of violence between slavery
men and free-soilers in Kansas added to the general disquiet. Many
promises of support came to Walker, but they were seldom backed
with cash. Nevertheless, he made some progress. He had gone to
New Orleans, where, keeping out of the public eye, he found enough
money to enable one of his secret agents to purchase a steamship,
the *Fashion,* and a cargo of arms and military stores. Recruiting was
no problem; many young Southerners were eager to serve under
Walker, despite all the hardships his previous army had endured.
The essential question was that which he had faced two years earlier
in California—whether the Neutrality Laws would be enforced
against him. It was soon answered. Buchanan's administration
showed every sign of antagonism. Particularly significant was the
fact that the new Secretary of State, Lewis Cass, who a year earlier,

when he hoped for the Presidency, had backed Walker and "the rights of Americans to emigrate and take their arms with them," had reversed his stand. In subservience to Buchanan, Cass now ordered federal authorities in all port cities to be on guard against the departure of any filibustering expeditions.

On November 10, 1857, federal marshals appeared at Walker's house and arrested him. He made no protest. In the court hearing that followed, the New Orleans federal attorney showed evidence that the *Fashion,* which was advertised to depart for Nicaragua, had taken on board an extraordinary quantity of supplies such as would be required in a military campaign. That the passengers would be filibusters recruited by Walker was the prosecution's case, and the judge thought it good enough to remand Walker for trial, setting bail in the amount of $2000. There was no actual proof, however, that the *Fashion* had violated any law. Walker being ashore, and none of his men on board, the ship was allowed to weigh anchor and steam away.

With Pierre Soulé as his lawyer, Walker found bail and, released from custody, proceeded to execute a plan carefully devised for that very situation. Mobile, even more than New Orleans, was sympathetic to his cause, and it was unlikely that any federal officer there would seriously seek to stop him. Ignoring the fact that he was on bail, he and a few members of his military staff boarded the daily mail boat from New Orleans to Mobile. At every stop they were joined by additional small groups who had quietly left New Orleans well in advance, and by the time they reached Mobile Bay the boat was crammed with Walker's men. Among them were six of the original Immortals.

They found the *Fashion* anchored far out in Mobile Bay, where it had taken on a cargo of arms, and they boarded her without interference. The final test lay ahead. A cutter drew alongside and federal officers came on board. They had been instructed, they said, to inspect the steamer, its passengers, and the cargo. Solemnly they performed their duty, but carefully managed to see no arms, no sign of Walker or his officers, no suspicious circumstance of any kind. With 270 men on board, including such famous veterans as Colonels Hornsby, Anderson, Natzmer, and Henry, and Commander Fayssoux, the *Fashion* was given her clearance for Nicaragua; and a telegram from Washington, ordering pursuit of the ship, was mysteriously lost before it reached the federal officer to whom it was addressed.

## IV

Buchanan was then engaged in an attempt to persuade England to scrap the Clayton-Bulwer Treaty—something that England was determined not to do. Walker's flaunting of the Neutrality Laws not only made the President look foolish, but was interpreted by the British ambassador, Lord Napier, as proof that the United States had imperialistic designs in Central America, and stood in violation of the treaty. Otherwise would Walker not have been prevented from sailing? Buchanan hastily assured Napier that he intended to uphold the treaty until it was abandoned by mutual agreement. He then declared war on Walker. An order went to his Secretary of the Navy, Isaac Toucey: intercept the *Fashion*. Soon afterward, Buchanan sent his first annual message to Congress, and urged the enactment of legislation which would "be effectual in preventing our citizens from committing such outrages" as Walker had perpetrated. Walker's expedition could "do no possible good to the country" but was certain to "injure its interests and its character."

The unaccustomed vigor of the President's attack on Walker had a shrewd political purpose. Although Buchanan professed personal aversion to slavery on moral grounds, he had found it politically expedient to favor the slavery interest in Kansas. To justify his policy, the President had arrived at a strict and sterile interpretation of the Constitution which enabled him to maintain that the slavery problem in Kansas and elsewhere could be dealt with simply by "proper administration of the law." His position in Kansas had excited unrealistic expectations in the South and extreme abolitionist agitation in the North. Irreconcilables on both sides were increasing their power. But having won over the Southerners in Congress with his Kansas policy, Buchanan had to deal with the heavy fire then being aimed at him by the Northern press. His need was to show himself to the North, if he could, as, after all, neutral on slavery. Walker provided the perfect instrument. He was backed by slavery men; in attacking him, therefore, the President seemed to be attacking slavery, a position calculated to mollify Northern critics. And it was a safe tactic in the South, for Southern leaders in Congress were so eager to keep Buchanan's Kansas policy unchanged that they were unwilling to make a strong effort on Walker's behalf. It was politic and it was easy for Buchanan to condemn him unrestrainedly.

Walker, who foresaw that some such move would be made,

seemed to his companions on the *Fashion* strangely unconcerned, as if he had an inner knowledge of events to come. So certain was he of success that he had even brought with him the editor of *El Nicaragüense,* John Tabor, several new fonts of type, and the Great Seal of Nicaragua, which he had carried away with him. The nine days of the voyage from Mobile were spent in organizing his force and drilling his men. His strategy had been thoroughly worked out. The first essential was the capture of the Transit steamers on the San Juan River and the small fort, Fort Castillo, which dominated the entry from the river into Lake Nicaragua. To try to move up the San Juan from Greytown, however, was hopeless; the Transit boats would be forewarned and would simply escape to the lake. Surprise was of the essence, and Walker knew how to achieve it. A fork of the San Juan known as the Colorado, which reached the sea at a desolate spot some miles south of Greytown, was known to be unguarded. Before attempting to land at Greytown, the *Fashion* would put down a company of picked men under Colonel Anderson at the Colorado, with three boats; this force would row upstream, seize the first Transit vessel encountered, capture the other steamers as they came down the San Juan, disembark at Fort Castillo under cover of the Costa Rican flag, and disarm the unsuspecting garrison. The steamers would then be sent back to bring the rest of Walker's troops up the San Juan and across Lake Nicaragua. Before an army could be mobilized against them they would take Virgin Bay, Rivas, and San Juan del Sur. By that time reinforcements already being organized by Henningsen in the United States would have arrived, they would sweep north to Granada, Masaya, Managua, and León, and Nicaragua would once more be in American hands.

True to this plan, the *Fashion* skirted Greytown harbor and in a drenching rain reached the mouth of the Colorado unobserved. After seeing Anderson and his men on their way, Walker ordered the ship to stand out to sea, and cruise slowly along the coast through the night, timing its approach to Greytown for broad daylight the next morning—an hour when, presumably, no filibustering ship would dare to run the *Saratoga*'s guns.

V

At seven o'clock on the morning of November 24, 1857, Commander Chatard of the *Saratoga* saw the steamship *Fashion* come into Greytown harbor, with fifteen passengers or so on deck. When he hailed the ship, an officer on the vessel called back something that could not be distinctly heard, except for the word "transit." Knowing that the Vanderbilt interests intended to reclaim the Transit property, Chatard came to the conclusion that this was the purpose of the party on board the *Fashion,* and he made no effort to interfere with its progress. A few minutes later, when the steamer tied up at a wharf, he had the shock of his life. All at once the *Fashion's* decks were crowded with laughing men, carrying rifles, and leaping ashore.

Chatard's orders gave him no right to use force against the filibusters once they had landed. Only if they offered violence against members of his ship's company could he justify the use of his guns to coerce these Americans on foreign soil. To provoke some hostile action by Walker now became the purpose of the humiliated Commander, and in this he showed considerable ingenuity. Sailors went ashore to prevent Walker's men from occupying the buildings of the Transit Company, thus compelling them to bivouac in the open, exposed to the steady tropical rain. Officers of the *Saratoga,* disregarding Walker's sentries, strolled through his camp, some of them not even in uniform, inviting a challenge. More malevolently, the ship's gunners were ordered to use an area only a few yards from Walker's camp for cannon practice.

At Walker's camp, days of incessant rain passed with no word from Anderson. Mud, insects, boredom, and anxiety were telling on the men. Walker himself began to sit up of nights at a campfire, waiting for a signal from the river. On the afternoon of the twelfth day, when confidence was ebbing fast, a native canoe appeared on the San Juan, with one of Anderson's men sitting comfortably in the stern with a rifle, while two Costa Ricans, his prisoners, worked the paddles. The news that he brought sent the camp into a wild demonstration of joy. Anderson's expedition had been a total success. Without the loss of a single man, he had captured the river steamers and Fort Castillo; and although navigational problems had delayed the steamers, they were on their way to Greytown. In a day or two Walker and all his men would be able to start up the river.

The revival of spirits did not last long. Before a river boat could arrive, the frigate *Wabash* steamed into the bay, and anchored as close as it could to Walker's camp. Shortly it was joined by another American ship, the *Fulton,* and by two British men-of-war. With the *Saratoga* these ships among them carried over 200 guns. Pinnaces plied back and forth and the commanders were entertained at dinner by Commodore Paulding aboard the *Wabash*. The Commodore, a large, robust, and ambitious man, had been excessively aggravated by the thought that a United States Navy vessel, and a ship of his own squadron to boot, should be held up to derision. When British officers suggested that the ships of both nations join in taking Walker prisoner, he refused; he wanted Walker's scalp for himself.

His first move was to have small boats from the *Saratoga* go up the San Juan, ostensibly for fresh water, but actually to establish a blockade of the river. When two of Walker's chief aides, Hornsby and Fayssoux, arrived on board the *Wabash* to make a formal protest against this proceeding, he shrugged their words aside, and gave orders that they were not to be allowed to leave ship. They would be joined, he told them, by Walker and all his men, whom he would shortly make his prisoners.

Three hundred marines were sent ashore to take up a position that would prevent the filibusters from moving inland, and the ships swung their broadsides toward the camp. Walker could clearly see the gunners take their battle stations and train their cannon. Some of his men, unable to bear their disappointment, begged him to fight, but he refused to permit so senseless a sacrifice of life. He still bore his head high; no one observing him could have guessed that all his hopes had become ashes in his mouth. When a boat put off from the *Fulton,* in it one of Paulding's officers, Captain Engle, Walker went courteously to meet him. They shook hands, and Walker listened quietly while Engle read a note from Paulding. He and his men would board the Navy ships and be taken back to the United States, or they would be fired upon by sea and by land. As a sign of his surrender he was to lower the Nicaraguan flag that flew over his camp.

Walker merely said to Engle, "I surrender to the United States," and ordered his men to break camp. Of the two, Engle appeared the more emotional. "General," he said to Walker, "I am sorry to see an officer of your ability employed in such a service. Nothing would give me greater pleasure than to see you at the head of regular troops." The cup of Walker's bitterness ran over when, at that very moment, one of the delayed river steamboats appeared with some of Anderson's men aboard, ready to begin the movement of his troops upstream. He had to watch while the boat was seized by Paulding's marines, and the men taken prisoner.

Having carried the day without opposition, Paulding was dis-

posed to be considerate. Another officer came ashore to reassure
Walker that, once on board, he and his officers, instead of being
treated as prisoners, would have quarters suited to their rank. A
polite oral reply from Walker acknowledged this gesture, and added
that he did not seek privileges beyond those given his men. This
message, garbled in transmission, came to Paulding as a blunt rejection—"General Walker asks no special benefits"—and deeply offended him. His next communication was a sharp command to
Walker to embark immediately on the *Fulton,* to which the Commodore had transferred his flag.

A few minutes later Walker stood in Paulding's quarters, hearing
himself addressed in a tone and in terms that no man had dared to
use to him since he had been a boy in his father's house. He and his
men were a disgrace to the United States. They had dishonored their
country. They were no better than pirates and murderers. For the
first time Walker's self-control cracked under the edge of suppressed
rage and the weight of failure. With a curious mingling of satisfaction and sympathy, the tall, handsomely uniformed Commodore
saw tears come to the eyes of the shabby little man whom all the
world knew.

Paulding's uneasiness at the possible consequences of his actions
grew when the *Fulton* arrived at its Panama base. He had accepted
Walker's pledged word to proceed to New York by passenger ship
and give himself up to the United States marshal there; and his
desire to conciliate his prisoner before they parted expressed itself
in numerous courtesies. Pointing out that five days would elapse
before the next steamer would leave for the United States, he invited
Walker to remain for this period in his comfortable cabin on the
*Fulton,* rather than take up quarters in a flea-infested hotel of the
town. Walker declined; he would not even share another meal with
his captor. It was too much to expect that he could forgive the only
man who had pierced the armor of his self-control. From this moment they resumed their enmity.


# VI


Two distinguished lawyers and an Army general, all friends of Walker's, accompanied him when he offered himself for arrest to the
United States marshal in New York. An ironic aspect of the situation
lay in the fact that the marshal himself was one of Walker's great

admirers—Captain Isaiah Rynders, a leader of Tammany Hall who had taken a large part in organizing public support for Walker. An arrest, Rynders said, was out of the question, since he had neither warrant nor official instructions. A conference followed, and out of it came a decision that he and Walker would go to Washington and present the problem to the administration. By that time impatient reporters were pushing their way into the marshal's office and demanding a statement from Walker. He gave them one that made headlines the next day. Paulding had invaded the territory of a friendly nation and insulted its flag. The government of the United States had an obligation to remedy his gross error. This it could do by returning him, Walker, and his men to the place from which they had been forcibly removed. On this note, leaving the reporters agape, he departed with Rynders for Washington.

Walker's departure had infuriated Buchanan; his return embarrassed him. Paulding had unmistakably exceeded his authority. Southern indignation promptly flared into mass meetings where Paulding was denounced in passionate terms and his condign punishment demanded. A resolution passed in New Orleans urged that the government not only return Walker's expedition to Nicaragua but indemnify it for losses "sustained from capture, detention and privation of liberty and property," and several senators volunteered to initiate Congressional action to that effect.

Increasingly the issue took the form of a personal contest between Walker and the President. As always, Buchanan moved with great caution. When the filibuster appeared in Washington, Cass quickly announced that there was no reason to keep him in custody. Walker staked his case on a long letter to the President, which he made public. His expedition had been justified, he insisted, in law and morality. He was the president-in-exile of a foreign government which had been recognized by a former President of the United States. It was his right and his duty to Nicaragua to seek to reestablish that government in power, with or without the aid of the United States. "Some have told you, I know, that I am a man 'without faith and without mercy'; but from the beginning to the end of my career in Nicaragua, I challenge the world to produce a single violation of public faith."

The day on which this letter appeared, January 4, 1858, the Senate passed a resolution calling on the President for "the correspondence, instructions and orders to the United States naval forces on the coast of Central America, connected with the arrest of Wil-

liam Walker and his associates." Buchanan was now compelled to
reply, and he did so in a communication of considerable ingenuity.
"In capturing General Walker and his command . . . Commodore
Paulding has, in my opinion, committed a grave error. It is quite
evident, however . . . that this was done from pure and patriotic
motives." The President, having thus made clear his intention to let
the Commodore off lightly, quickly moved to safer terrain. On a
note of reassuring, if empty, prophecy, he said, "The tide of emigration will flow to the South. . . . Central America will soon contain
an American population which will confer blessings and benefits
upon the natives and their respective governments." Therefore, he
implied, Walker and his methods were not needed. He went on to
say he believed in the "Manifest Destiny" of the American people to
dominate in the Western Hemisphere, but "no administration can
successfully conduct the foreign affairs of the country in Central
America . . . if it is interfered with at every step by lawless military
expeditions set on foot in the United States."

A tumult of debate followed in both Senate and House. Conflict-
ing resolutions were introduced, one calling for official punishment
of Paulding, another for the presentation to him of a gold medal for
his action in Nicaragua. For days all other business stood still while
Walker and Paulding were each roundly criticized and staunchly
defended. Fifteen senators made speeches, covering every aspect of
the controversy. The question was raised, how was it that Paulding,
if he regarded Walker and his men as "outlaws who had . . . left our
shores for the purpose of rapine and murder"—the Commodore's
words in his own defense—how was it that he had made Walker his
close companion on the *Fulton,* taken meals with him, addressed
him always as "general," and accepted his parole of honor for his
return to New York? The question went unanswered.

In the end, the weary senators and the President arrived at a
compromise. All resolutions were dropped. While Paulding was
mildly censured by the Secretary of the Navy and temporarily relieved of his command, Walker was given no encouragement. When
all was done, the administration still stood firmly against him; the
Congress was divided as before.

# VII

From the reception that he received as he journeyed South from
Washington, one would have thought that Walker came with re-

newed laurels of conquest, instead of as a man who had twice failed
of his purpose and had been roundly castigated by the President and
many senators of his country. In Richmond and Montgomery, where
every honor was heaped on him, he reminded his audiences that
before leaving New Orleans for Nicaragua he had been arrested and
put on bail; he was returning now to insist that he be tried for
violation of the Neutrality Laws. At Mobile, he made a major address
on the issue between Buchanan and himself. It was in this speech,
delivered on January 25, 1858, that he brought into the open Buchanan's support of the Tehuantepec scheme, and Soulé's part in
thwarting it.

The style of the Mobile speech and of the letters which Walker
wrote on the Davis and Paulding affairs suggests the profound psychological change that had taken place in him. The former note of
high-mindedness, the alleviating flashes of ironic humor have given
way to hot indignation and cold legalism. While he regarded himself
as a missionary for Americanism and democracy, his personality had
color and warmth, but he seemed motivated now mainly by a de-
monic drive to fulfill "his destiny." At the age of thirty-three the only
possibility of life that interested him was his return to Nicaragua.

But perhaps for that very reason his power to lift an audience to
its feet was never greater. The Mobile speech was an immense success, a devastating exposure of Buchanan's inconsistency. The President's stand, Walker asserted, had nothing to do with principle.
Surely the co-author of the Ostend Manifesto was not the man to
defend the Neutrality Laws! It was not filibustering as such that
aroused Buchanan's wrath, said Walker. What the President really
resented was his, Walker's, alliance with Soulé, who had blocked
the Tehuantepec project. The administration was perfectly willing
to encourage filibustering attempts elsewhere than in Nicaragua.
The Secretary of War, John B. Floyd, had actually urged Henningsen
to aid a revolution in Mexico and incite a war with Spain, so as to
provide a pretext for the annexation of Cuba. Therefore Buchanan's
attacks on Walker had nothing to do with principle. They were to
be understood simply as a matter of low politics to serve the interests
of the President's friends in Tehuantepec; and Walker was fully
justified in his defiance.

The public seized excitedly on this revelation. Floyd, who could
not deny that he had met with Henningsen, contended that the
statements attributed to him were false. The abolitionist North believed him; the South preferred to believe Walker, and became even
more convinced that he had spoken the truth when Henningsen

went to Mexico to offer his services to a revolutionary movement in that country.

The practical result of the Mobile speech promptly showed in the Alabama legislature. Deeply impressed by Walker's arguments, the state granted a charter to the Mobile and Nicaragua Steamship Company, known to have been incorporated by Walker's supporters. Simultaneously the Central American League was revived, under the name of the Southern Emigration Society, and its branches throughout the South again took up the task of raising funds and finding recruits for Walker. Contributions were at first slow, for even ardent supporters now understood the weight of the odds against Walker. He had finally to undertake an extensive lecture tour, and this proved more successful. Listening to him, Southern audiences became convinced that Nicaragua was the key to their future security, and they responded with substantial donations to the cause.

Even after two failures he still retained his luster. It was not the sad loyalty for a fallen idol, not the loyalty of nostalgia, that Southerners gave him, but a vibrant faith that he would yet achieve his purpose. When he stood trial in New Orleans he made the federal prosecutor appear feeble. An impassioned speech in his own defense outweighed in the minds of the jury both the evidence against him and an adverse charge by the judge; ten jurors out of twelve voted for acquittal. Intent on complete vindication, he demanded a new trial, but the government declined to prosecute further. On leaving the courtroom he declared openly that he would soon return to Nicaragua and "eat Christmas dinner in Granada."

# THE DARK LIGHT
# OF HOPE

❦

The strategic moment, Walker felt, could not be far away. Knowing Central American politicians, he was convinced that it would not be long before Costa Rica, holding the Transit, and the new Nicaraguan government were at daggers' points, and that a determined invasion would find only faltering and feeble resistance. In the early months of 1858, the press was astir with rumors of another Walker expedition, and this time it seemed that Buchanan would be unable to stop it. The President's hold on the Southerners in Congress had been seriously weakened by events in Kansas. In spite of his inclination to favor the Southern interest in the territory, resistance to slavery by "free-soil" settlers from the North had become so vigorous and so much blood was being shed, that Southerners had begun to lose hope. Kansas was no longer an effective lever with which Buchanan could push the South into acceptance of his anti-Walker measures. A major split in the Democratic Party and a revolt in Congress threatened the President if he sought to interfere with the new and powerful Walker expedition which, as widely rumored in the press, was in preparation. Walker himself went to Washington, where, after conferring with senatorial supporters, he wrote enthusiastically in a private letter that the administration would either "yield to the voice of the country in regard to our affairs," or face catastrophic Congressional reprisals.*

Buchanan, however, had by no means exhausted his repertory of political devices in his contest with Walker. There was yet one way in which criticism of his Nicaraguan policy could be silenced and Walker frustrated once and for all. That was to send to Nicaragua,

---

* Fayssoux Collection (ms.) No. 66, Jan. 5, 1858.

with the consent of its new government, a strong force of American marines, who would occupy the Transit route and render meaningless and hopeless any attempt by Walker to land an expeditionary force. To this end Buchanan, through Secretary of State Cass, now addressed himself. The fact that his new policy ran counter to everything he had said and done in connection with Nicaragua since taking office did not trouble him.

The first step in Buchanan's plan was to aid an American company to gain control of the Transit concession. No one was any longer sure where legal title to the Transit lay. Nicaragua owned the route, Costa Rica held it; but the positions of Vanderbilt, and of Morgan and Garrison were obscure. The latter two made a bold effort to reassert their claim. It seemed to them that since Costa Rican troops held the boats and occupied most of the route, the key to the outcome lay with President Mora, and their problem was only to find an agent who could exert the necessary pressure on him. W. R. C. Webster, who had been instrumental in organizing the alliance against Walker, was an obvious choice; he had the advantage of being British and had a claim of sorts on Costa Rican gratitude. The fact that he was in Vanderbilt's employ was not a serious deterrent for Morgan and Garrison, who knew the uses of money. Webster broke with Vanderbilt, entered their service, traveled to Costa Rica with ample funds at his disposal, and within a short time was able to report success. Mora, always generous with his signature on documents that could be repudiated, had given him the desired contract.

Buchanan, however, did not trust Morgan and Garrison, largely owing to their previous connection with Walker. He quickly wrote to Lord Clarendon in London that Costa Rica "had got hold of the greatest scamps as purchasers" of the Transit route and plainly conveyed his feeling that Mora should be discouraged from any thought of executing the contract he had given Webster. England cooperatively intervened, and from this time Morgan and Garrison ceased to be serious contenders for the prize.

Vanderbilt had bitterly, hotly, and publicly protested the Morgan-Garrison contract, and it was generally thought that their failure would be his success. He, after all, controlled Accessory Transit Company, which held a contract with Nicaragua for the route; but with his innate contempt for the law, he was unwilling to take his stand on a merely legal claim. He wanted to get physical control of the Transit first, and argue about legality later. To this end he began a secret intrigue with a high-ranking Costa Rican general. This proved a poor tactic. Agents of the State Department reported the plot to Washington, and Buchanan was incensed to the point where he refused to give the Commodore diplomatic support. Instead he turned to a new contestant for the Transit—Vanderbilt's former associate, Joseph L. White, godfather of the Clayton-Bulwer treaty, and a political manipulator of great skill and experience. With some wealthy associates, White had accumulated the worthless shares of the old Atlantic and Pacific Ship Canal Company. Thus he had acquired the original canal concession granted by Nicaragua, which gave his claim to the Transit a certain air of legality. More important, he had persuaded the new Nicaraguan government to grant him secretly a provisional contract covering both overland transit and canal. Here was the opportunity that the President sought to put an end to filibustering and regain popularity among the expansionists. He set Secretary of State Cass to work negotiating a treaty with Nicaragua under which the United States would have the right to use military force, if necessary, to protect "persons and property conveyed over the route," as operated by White. Objections from Vanderbilt were disregarded.

To Lord Clarendon, Buchanan wrote that British interests would be protected, that the new treaty, known as the Cass-Irissari Convention, in no way threatened her rights or violated the intent of the Clayton-Bulwer treaty, and that the Costa Ricans would have no cause for complaint. "Great Britain and the United States, while treating them [the Costa Ricans] justly and even liberally, ought to let them know that this transit shall be kept open and shall never again be interrupted."

## II

At this juncture the Nicaraguan kaleidoscope was shaken again, and a totally new pattern emerged. To Buchanan's consternation, Nicaragua at the last moment rejected both the Cass-Irissari Convention and the White contract, and announced that the concession for the canal and Transit route had been granted, not to an American, not even to an Englishman, but to a Frenchman, one Félix Belly; and that in this grant Nicaragua and Costa Rica had acted in concert, as joint owners of the route.

The American press and Congress howled with anger. The weakness of the American government had lost the greatest prize in the Western Hemisphere, the isthmian canal route, to a European power —with all that that implied for the Monroe Doctrine and the future of the United States. There was talk of war with France. Was it for this that the President had rejected Walker? Buchanan was scourged even by newspapers which had been friendly to him. To make matters worse for the President, the tone of the Nicaraguan announcement was offensive in the extreme. Monsieur Belly, who represented a Parisian syndicate, was trading on the anti-*gringo* sentiment of the isthmus. Fluent in Spanish, vivacious, eloquent, with a talent for bravura, he was able to excite and persuade the Central American mind as could no Anglo-Saxon. He knew how to convey, without actually saying, that he was a trusted agent of Napoleon III, and that the wealth and arms of imperial France stood behind him. Why, he asked President Mora of Costa Rica, and the new president of Nicaragua, Martinez—why should they yield the Transit to the *gringos?* Instead, let them confer the rights to the route on a company of Europeans who shared their religion and their culture. Assured of protection by the French, and of a large share in the profits, their countries could grow rich, put an end to American pressure, and be free at last of William Walker.

This last point especially carried great weight with Mora and Martinez, who lived in dread of Walker's return. Most sensational of their productions was a joint Manifesto declaring the belief of the two Presidents that a new filibustering expedition against Central America was being organized in the United States, and requesting England and France not to leave them "at the mercy of barbarians." A separate declaration empowered Belly to arrange for the stationing of "European vessels of war" on the Central American coast.

But like everyone else in the tangled business, he was doomed to disappointment. The French government shrugged him aside, partly because it was then deeply involved in a European crisis, partly because Belly's backers were out of favor at the imperial court, and partly because Napoleon III was thinking vaguely of promoting his own long-dreamed-of Nicaraguan canal company. The one hope for Belly now lay in the possibility that American financiers and the Buchanan administration, recognizing his hold on the Central American leaders, would overlook his previous attacks on the United States, come to terms with him, and give him support. In this feeble hope he embarked for New York; but at the very moment of his arrival, the Herald was running a front-page dispatch from Paris under the headline DISAVOWAL OF M. BELLY. The myth of his power was exploded, and with it went all expectation that he would ever dig his canal.

## I I I

With Belly's failure, every advantage in the contest for the Transit reverted to Vanderbilt. The bewildered Nicaraguan government was easily persuaded by his agents to declare invalid all previous contracts for the route, and to restore the concession to the original owner, the Accessory Transit Company.

But weeks went by, and Vanderbilt took no action. When queried as to the causes of the delay, he referred gravely to the physical deterioration of the Transit route. New steamboats would have to be built and bridges restored. Silting at the mouth of the San Juan River had seriously impaired the channel at Greytown harbor. The road west of Lake Nicaragua was in need of repair. Large new sums of capital would have to be invested—and the company was already in debt to Vanderbilt personally for loans made in the past. He would of course do what he could, but it was all very, very difficult.

Then, in June 1858, light dawned on the press and the public, when word leaked out of Vanderbilt's arrangement with the Panama lines. Merely for withholding his ships from competition on the Panama run, he had been receiving $480,000 a year. Now he had yet another lever, the threat of renewed service to Nicaragua, with which to squeeze the Panama shipping magnates even harder. Rather than compete again with the Nicaraguan Transit, they had agreed to raise their payment to Vanderbilt by 40 percent, to $56,000 a month.

Prodded by the government and by public opinion, the Panama lines finally terminated their arrangement with the great financier. But it was plain to Vanderbilt that the importance of the Nicaragua overland route was diminishing. Its troubles had created public suspicion of it, and California-bound travelers had become accustomed to the Panama service. Accessory Transit could never again be the bonanza it had been a few years earlier. As for a canal, the chances that it could be dug in the face of British opposition, and with the Clayton-Bulwer treaty still in effect, were as poor as they had ever been.

Besides, Vanderbilt's own interests were shifting. Now in his midsixties, he was still eager to prove his powers, and his mind was turning to great new ventures—transatlantic ocean liners, the railroads of the northeast, Wall Street warfare on a grand scale. He was through with Nicaragua. Those who continued to dream of a Nicaraguan canal and of the Transit route's revival recognized that everything would depend on Walker's next expedition.

## IV

The leaders of Central America had come to believe the legends they had helped to create, in which Walker was seen as another Tamerlane, combining an insatiable thirst for blood with military genius—the implication being that they, having triumphed over this "military tactician of epic proportions," were the more deserving of their people's gratitude. In Nicaragua especially dread of Walker had been so sedulously cultivated by officials and priests that the prospect of his return evoked a nationwide shudder. When the New Orleans *Delta* erroneously stated that Walker was in San Francisco, recruiting a thousand men for an invasion of Nicaragua's west coast, President Martinez was seized by panic. Bitter against America and disappointed in France, he turned to England for aid. Would she provide naval protection for Nicaragua's coasts and cope with Walker if he landed? The British were glad to comply. The opportunity was ready-made to extend their control of Central American resources and markets at the expense of the United States. All that was necessary was to keep the Clayton-Bulwer treaty in operation, Buchanan in his customary permissive state, and Walker out of Nicaragua, while British diplomats made the necessary arrangements.

The first move in their gambit was an interview with Buchanan, solicited by Lord Napier, the British ambassador. The insight of the British into Buchanan's psychology had been shown in their selection of Napier as minister to his administration. He was an aristocrat of great astuteness and much charm; and the President was highly susceptible to displays of friendship by England's titled diplomats. With a light and delicate touch, Napier shaped Buchanan's mind to the views of Whitehall. He began by referring to the agitation in Congress for unilateral abrogation of the Clayton-Bulwer treaty. What were the President's views in the matter? Buchanan replied that he considered the treaty "a fruitful source of misunderstanding" but on the other hand it was a binding agreement, and "no attempt by Congress against it would have any countenance from him."

So far, so good; Napier now advanced another pawn. In recognition of the purport of the treaty, his government contemplated certain territorial concessions, long urged by the United States, to the republics of the isthmus. England was prepared at last to give Mosquito back to Nicaragua, and to return to Honduras certain islands off her Atlantic coast, seized by the British years earlier. Assuming that the President would welcome these moves, London would like to send out a special commissioner "to carry the Clayton-Bulwer treaty into execution . . . by separate negotiation with Central American republics, in lieu of negotiation with the federal government" of the United States.

Buchanan, if he felt a touch of skepticism within him, was not so inconsiderate of Lord Napier's feelings as to voice it. Instead, he expressed satisfaction at England's attitude. Napier doubtless understood the willingness, even eagerness, with which the President accepted his proposal. Although both houses of the Congress were Democratic, antagonism to Buchanan was then so intense as to threaten the collapse of his legislative program. He urgently needed to be able to show the Congress and the country some constructive result of his statesmanship that would restore his prestige. If the people would accept England's concessions as a retreat on her part, the President would receive credit for it, and be strengthened accordingly.

It was not long, however, before Buchanan was smitten by misgivings, for the British in Central America negotiated treaties so favorable to themselves as gravely to prejudice American interests. Disturbed, the President protested to Clarendon in a private letter that the new agreements were not "in the spirit of the Clayton-Bulwer treaty." He disliked especially a pledge given by England to "the great and mighty Republic of Nicaragua," assuring her of protection against filibusters. Buchanan felt that Nicaragua should have asked the United States to provide such protection. Soon afterward, the naval officer in command of America's Caribbean squadron informed Nicaragua, in a pride-swallowing note, that he would be glad to patrol her harbors to prevent filibusters from landing. The invitation was not forthcoming. A systematic patrol of Nicaragua's coasts by British warships went into effect, without American participation.

## V

Walker's hopes of landing another expedition in Nicaragua were gone. Commanders of American warships might be reluctant to fire on a ship of his on the high seas, and lacking authorization from Nicaragua, might find it difficult to prevent him from landing or to pursue him, once landed; but the British, it was safe to say, would not be so inhibited. In view of Buchanan's attitude, they would feel no qualms in destroying filibusters at sea or on land. If there was to be another Walker expedition, it would have to be based on a new strategy, and this he began to work out in the autumn of 1858. He would aim not immediately at Nicaragua, but at Honduras, where he would not be expected; and having made a landing there, would establish a strong base. A revolt by Honduran Liberals was then gathering force; he would collaborate with it, defeat the existing regime, establish the Liberals in power, and with a friendly government at his back, drive south into Nicaragua.

He still had enough funds at his disposal to charter a ship and take an expedition out of the country. The question now was, would he be able to clear a ship from a Southern port? Could Washington exert enough influence on port officials in Mobile and New Orleans to prevent his sailing? The answer came in the curious indirect way of politics.

At that moment all Latin America shared and enjoyed the feeling that the United States was, after all, a paper eagle. This feeling was intensified when British warships in the Gulf of Mexico began to stop American merchantmen suspected of being slavers, and even fired on one or two which disobeyed their orders. Not since 1812 had so much humiliation been heaped on vessels flying the flag of the United States. The British, who were apparently testing the extent of Buchanan's tolerance, this time touched its limit, for he found the courage to lodge a protest and to send naval vessels to protect the country's shipping. Thereupon England acknowledged that her navy had no right to search American vessels in time of peace, and discontinued the practice.

If England had deliberately tried to revive Buchanan's prestige in the United States, she could have found no better means. The American public was all at once delighted with him, for had he not compelled perfidious Albion to respect the American flag? Was this not proof, after all—especially when taken together with England's return of Mosquito to Nicaragua—of bold and forceful statecraft on the part of the administration? A number of senators who had been extremely annoyed with Buchanan once more veered to his side. Without opposition he was able to staff the Gulf ports with federal officers on whom he could rely not to connive with Walker at evasions of the Neutrality Laws.

The effect of this move by the President was fully felt by Walker late in 1858, when he assembled 300 men and a cargo of munitions at Mobile, and chartered a steamship to take them to Nicaragua as "peaceful emigrants." The new Collector of the Port, Thaddeus Sanford, flatly refused clearance, and the District Attorney summoned Walker before a Grand Jury, charged with conspiracy to violate the law. As usual, Walker spoke to the jurors in his own defense, and the old magic held. Gazing into the teeth of the evidence, the Grand Jury solemnly adjudged them false teeth, and exonerated him. But the expedition had been irretrievably damaged. His men, warned by United States marshals of their impending arrest, scattered to their homes, his ship was seized, and its cargo of munitions was confiscated.

Buchanan's campaign against Walker had turned out to be the single most successful effort of his administration.

# THE EASING OF PAIN

Close to the end of his resources, and with his chances of success steadily diminishing, Walker could not afford a long delay before trying again. Within a few days of his Grand Jury appearance, his veteran officers were scouting the Southern states to find yet more recruits and money for him. This time only about 100 men agreed to serve, and their quality, it was noted, was poorer than in the past. One of his chief aides, Doubleday, described them as "mostly of the class found about the wharves of Southern cities, with here and there a Northern bank cashier who had suddenly decided to change his vocation." Men of schooling or political conviction were few among them.

He had no money with which to charter a steamship, and this time his hope of taking an expedition out of Mobile centered on a sailing vessel, the schooner *Susan,* owned by one of his friends. On a December day the *Susan* put into harbor, and her owner asked for clearance, not to Central America, but merely to Key West. It was refused. Port Collector Sanford had no doubt of the true destination and purpose of the voyage, and he could not be budged. For a day or two it appeared that this expedition too would disintegrate before it could sail. One move alone was still open to Walker—defiance of the federal government—and he was desperate enough to try it. The *Susan* left Mobile without clearance papers. Walker's intention was to follow on another boat. But the *Susan* came to grief on a reef off British Honduras, and its company were brought back to Mobile by a British warship. Their return, on New Year's Day, 1859, struck a curious note of triumph. The people of Mobile were so pleased by the British action that the failure of the filibusters' mission was almost ignored. The city's leading men tendered a banquet to the officers of the warship and lauded them in warm speeches, with toast after toast to Anglo-American, or more correctly, Anglo-Southern friendship. Walker was not present. The changing mood of Mobile, the last stronghold of filibusterism, could not have been lost on him.

## II

There was no reason to believe that another effort to take an armed force to Central America would prove more successful than the last. On the contrary, the barriers against him were rising fast. Was he so committed to his dream as to rule out every other possibility of a career? If he had been willing to forego military adventures and enter politics, he might still have opened up new and impressive possibilities for himself. But to Walker the current excitements that were provoking the South to secession and war—the bloodshed in Kansas—John Brown's slave-liberating raids into Virginia—the agitation in the North for higher tariffs inimical to Southern interests —all this was the shadow of doom. As before, the one hope that he could see was the conquest of Central America in the face of European opposition, as a rallying point for the entire nation. All his efforts were still concentrated on this last declining chance, which was linked to his inner need to regain the power he had lost. For him the remaining alternatives were success or death.

A new strategy for outwitting the federal government occurred to him, and he and Henningsen obtained George Law's backing for it. A hundred men would be placed on board a schooner, the *Granada,* and cleared for Panama by way of Cuba with California as their eventual destination. The port authorities at New Orleans could not deny the right of American citizens to go from state to state. He himself meanwhile would travel to Cuba, wait for the *Granada* to put into Havana harbor, and board it. The expedition would proceed to Panama and cross the isthmus. A steamship would be waiting for them on the Pacific side. Since there were comparatively few British warships patrolling the west coast of Nicaragua, Walker had no doubt that he could effect a landing there, and maintain a strong position until reinforcements, to be recruited in California, could join him.

A single aide, Colonel Bruno von Natzmer, was with him when he embarked on one of Law's Panama Line steamships, for which

Havana was a port of call. His departure was observed, and a news-paper reporter, guessing part of the truth, concocted a story to the effect that Walker was going to Panama, and would proceed to California in order to recruit an army there. This report, published the very day of Walker's sailing, was a deadly misfortune for the plan. Federal authorities were alerted to the danger of permitting any vessel bound for Panama to carry what might be a filibustering expedition, and refused clearance to the *Granada*. Walker hastily tried to overcome the effect of the news story, by telling Havana correspondents that he was indeed going to Panama, but only "to take the English steamer for Southampton, intending to try what I can do in Europe." But it was too late to draw red herrings across his trail. On learning that his men had been taken off the *Granada* and dispersed, he returned to New Orleans.

If the piece of paper, a clearance certificate with an official sig-nature on it, that stood between him and his purpose could not be obtained in one way, then it would have to be got in another. Fays-soux concentrated on winning over key officials in the office of the port of New Orleans, and finally reported success. Elated, Walker took the next step, a journey to New York, where he and Henning-sen persuaded George Law to provide the funds needed for yet another expedition. By September 1859, all was ready. A hundred Southerners were again waiting for the word to take ship with him. A Panama Line steamer, the *Philadelphia,* left New York for New Orleans with cases of guns and ammunition in its hold, and in a secret compartment an even larger quantity of arms. A second ship, the *St. Louis,* was to follow with 200 recruits from New York in the familiar guise of "emigrants." The expedition, as planned, was the largest ever assembled for Walker.

As soon as the *Philadelphia* docked in New Orleans, requesting clearance for Panama, most of the New Orleans contingent left the city on a small boat, intending to board the steamer unnoticed, just before it entered the Gulf. At first, all went well; the port inspectors examined the *Philadelphia,* found no contraband, and approved the sailing. At the last moment, however, high federal officials, including Buchanan's Secretary of the Treasury, Howell Cobb, took a hand, and formal clearance was refused. A company of soldiers from the garrison at Baton Rouge were sent down river to arrest Walker's men; the *Philadelphia* was twice searched until all the arms aboard had been found and confiscated; the ship itself was seized; and its sister-vessel, the *St. Louis,* was not permitted to leave New York.

Cobb wrote to Buchanan: "You will be gratified to learn that the Walker expedition has in *all probability* been frustrated by the energy of our officers." It is some indication of the alarm still created by Walker's name in official quarters that even with the ships sequestered and the men under arrest, the Secretary was not quite sure that the expedition had been thwarted.

## I I I

The former sources of Walker's funds had dried up. George Law had concluded that the firmness of the federal government and the strength of British naval patrols in the Caribbean made the chance of taking another expedition to Central America too small to consider. To Southern magnates it also was evident that contributions to Walker's cause could no longer be regarded as a sound investment. He had, however, an invisible asset—his journalistic talent. In the autumn of 1859 a publisher offered him a contract for a book based on his experiences, and he spent the winter writing it. His hope for its success is suggested by a letter that he wrote to Fayssoux, reporting that the book was to be published in New York and Mobile simultaneously, and that the publisher expected to sell 20,000 copies in Alabama alone.

The haste of the writing shows repeatedly in the 430 pages of the volume, yet it is in many ways a remarkable production. Modeled in its third-person narrative after Caesar's *Commentaries*, it describes in clean and vigorous prose, with touches of classical scholarship, his adventures in conquest and the purposes that motivated him. Factually, the book is so accurate that even Central American historians to whom Walker was the great enemy accepted it as a reliable source of data. But Walker's passion for truth was at odds with the practical need to raise money for a new expedition, and much of the book was an effort to reaffirm his devotion to the South and to convince readers of the importance of Nicaragua to the future of Southern institutions.

The most remarkable feature of *The War in Nicaragua* is its impersonal restraint, which stands in sharp contrast to the highly emotional quality of his writing ten years earlier. It is as if Walker had deliberately censored every word that might reveal his feelings. The only expressions of pleasure come in his descriptions of landscape and of the bravery of his men in battle; the only regrets are for comrades lost; the only contempt is for the pusillanimity of American politicians. His attitude toward enemies is that of a gentleman whose hat has been accidentally knocked off by a passer-by—a slightly disdainful acceptance of an unpleasant fact. Probably his sharpest barb is a Dantesque reference to President Mora, who had just been banished from Costa Rica by a rival. "Let us pass Mora in exile, as Ugolino in hell, afar off and in silence."

# ALL OR NOTHING

❦

In April 1860, the last springtime of peace before the great holocaust, Walker went to Louisville to visit his sister Alice, the one living member of his family to whom he was close. On his return to New Orleans, he found the bearded Fayssoux waiting for him in a state of excitement, with hopeful news. An Englishman had come from the Caribbean to seek Walker out, and in his absence had confided his mission to Fayssoux. He spoke, he said, for most of the British community on the large island of Ruatan, in the Bay of Honduras, where he was a substantial merchant. Ruatan was one of those islands which England had arbitrarily appropriated years earlier, and which she now proposed to turn over to Honduras in return for commercial concessions on the mainland. The transfer was to be consummated late in July 1860; but many Englishmen on the island had agreed that, rather than submit to Honduran rule, they would seize the government office as soon as the British flag was lowered, set up an independent government, and defy Honduras. Would Walker assist them?

The prospect of action had a tonic effect on Walker. At once he began to conceive a grand scheme in which the liberation of Ruatan was only the first step. With the island at war with Honduras, he would be justified in attacking the mainland and allying himself with the country's Liberals, who were in revolt under the leadership of the former president, Trinidad Cabañas. To be sure, Cabañas had no reason to feel friendly toward Walker, who in his Nicaraguan days had refused to help him; but four years had elapsed since then, and the necessities of war could be counted on to bridge the rift between them. There would be no more talk of slavery. Together they would overthrow the Honduran dictatorship and establish Cabañas as president. Walker would then recruit an American army, descend on Nicaragua and Costa Rica, appeal to the democratic elements, call for aid from the United States, and make a last attempt to achieve the great goal, Central American federation.

Within a week a small party of chosen men were on the way to Ruatan, traveling as ordinary passengers on a cargo boat to study the situation. Walker himself, under the name of Williams, went to the island in June. After conferring with his Ruatanese allies, he established a secret supply depot on an uninhabited island not far away, with the fairy-tale name of Cozumel—this to avoid British interference with the landing of cargo on Ruatan. A message was sent to Cabañas, then said to be recruiting a rebel army of Hondurans in Salvador, to alert him to the new prospect, and to urge him to join forces with Walker in eastern Honduras in late August.

Returning to New Orleans, Walker took charge of the main body of the expedition, nearly a hundred men, who were to sail from Mobile in a schooner, the *Taylor,* with a port clearance arranged by Fayssoux. Another schooner, loaded with supplies, sailed from New Orleans with a party under the command of a noted Alabama soldier, Colonel A. F. Rudler. But the plan had a fatal flaw—it could not be kept secret. The British sponsors of the intended coup disclosed it to friends in the government, in the futile hope of enlisting their cooperation, and from that moment Walker's chances of taking Ruatan were negligible. England was intent on completing her deal with Honduras, in which the island was a minor item; and she did not intend to let Walker return to Central America if she could help it. To block him was an easy matter. All that was necessary was to postpone the transfer of Ruatan to Honduras. It was a safe assumption that so long as the Union Jack flew over the island, Walker would not attempt to land there. The strategy of delay was proposed to the Honduran government and eagerly accepted, as the best way to keep Walker out of their country.

Walker, as yet unaware that he had been outmaneuvered, ordered the *Taylor* to head for his supply base on Cozumel. The little island was by no means paradise, for the rainy season had begun early, but the men believed that they would have only a few days to wait before the British colors were struck on Ruatan. They would then take to their boat, make a landing, seize the government, and prepare for the invasion of Honduras. At Cozumel they were joined by a correspondent for the New York *Herald* who had got wind of the enterprise. He was greatly impressed; the expedition he described as "a fine-looking set of men," and Walker as "a silent, thoughtful man," "a wise leader"—"gentlemanly," with "cool determination."

A dull, wet week passed—and England still held Ruatan, with a warship in the harbor and a battalion of marines ashore. Walker's chief concern at this point was that Rudler's boat, which carried most of their ammunition, had failed to appear. Seeking to find Rudler and to maintain morale, Walker ordered the expedition onto the *Taylor* and sailed the surrounding seas. The blows of fate now became heavier. When finally Rudler and his men appeared off Ruatan, it was in a vessel other than the schooner in which they had set out. Their boat, together with its all-important cargo, had been seized by the British when necessity compelled a stop at a British port on the way to Ruatan.

With the entire expedition now aboard the *Taylor,* Walker continued to cruise off the Honduran coast. After a few more days, the painful truth became obvious: the British were determined to outwait him. Before Honduras took possession of Ruatan, his supplies would be gone.

He was trapped. The Ruatan project was finished. To return ingloriously to the United States would invite only mockery. What was left? Cabañas. True, without Ruatan Walker had little to offer the Honduran revolution—but that might be remedied. A wild scheme took shape in his mind—a way of making a grand gesture of defiance to the powers that were frustrating him, and at the same time, if he were lucky, of gaining enough military power to make an alliance with him worth Cabañas' while. He shared his idea with his men. The chance of success was slight, the risks were mortal; he would have no man follow him except by free choice. None refused. The extent to which his faith in his destiny and his urge to live had dwindled was known to no one but himself.

His proposal was nothing less than to storm and capture a great stone fortress, dating from the days of Cortez, that guarded the busy Honduran port of Truxillo. This done, they would take the town, join Cabañas, and win the country. Sailing in darkness, they made a landing three miles north of Truxillo and before daybreak were on the march. But some fishermen saw them, and before they reached the fort the alarm had been given. The fort's garrison was small, consisting only of some thirty Hondurans, but they had the advantage of artillery and walls, and once they were alerted, everything seemed to favor a successful defense.

## II

Walker's tactics at Fort Truxillo were based on his intuition of the Central American soldier, who usually shot at the nearest target and found it a strain to reserve his fire. Six men, willing to face the probability of death, volunteered to go forward to draw the first cannonade. If the Hondurans could be decoyed into firing their artillery prematurely, the main assault would be made from another direction before the guns could be reloaded and reaimed.

At dawn, the action began. It was one of those heavy, wet, dispirited tropical mornings in which even the birds and the monkeys are still. The hill leading to the fort was covered with slippery grass, and the grey stone walls above, with the mouths of the cannon visible in the embrasures, looked huge and formidable. Walker gave the signal. As the six volunteers broke from cover and ran forward, yelling and beckoning to an imaginary force behind them, every Honduran cannoneer discharged his load of grapeshot and canister at them. Three of the men were instantly killed, the other three badly wounded. Under the haze of smoke, the rest of Walker's force rushed the fort, ignoring a few panicky rifle shots. To hoist each other over the walls the Americans formed human pyramids, and as they jumped down on the other side the Hondurans took to their heels and fled.

Citizens of the town of Truxillo, who had climbed a hill nearby to view the battle, as at a spectator sport, saw with amazement the lowering of the Honduran colors hardly fifteen minutes after the first shots had been fired. Over the fort Walker raised the flag he had brought with him—the colors of the old Central American federation, symbolizing union and democracy. He was determined that the victory be recognized as the first battle in a democratic revolution, not as an act of piracy. Within an hour he was in Truxillo, reassuring the people that they would not be molested.

One of the first buildings in Truxillo occupied by Walker's men was the customhouse of the port, through which Honduras received most of its imports. Since the customs in most Central American countries were the main source of revenue for their governments, Walker believed that by cutting off the Truxillo duties he could inflict serious injury on the Honduran regime. With this end in view, he declared Truxillo a free port—an action also calculated to please local merchants. What he did not realize, however, was that England had an agreement with Honduras, under which all customs revenue from Truxillo was assigned to the British government for payment of an old debt.

When one of Walker's officers and a squad of men entered the building, the Honduran customs officials had already disappeared. There disappeared also, at this time, some $300 which had been kept in a locked box, awaiting transfer to the British inspector who periodically visited the port. Whether the Hondurans had taken this money with them when they fled, or whether it had been misappropriated by the Americans could never be ascertained. The one certainty was that its removal provided the British with a legitimate pretext for intervening with military force.

Unaware as yet of the trouble which the seizure of the customhouse invited, Walker set himself to win the confidence of the local population. A proclamation to the citizens of Truxillo told them that he had not come to make war on the people of their country, but only on their government, "which stands in the way of the interests, not only of Honduras, but of all Central America." The people could rely on him to protect their rights, "both of person and of property." The tone of his statement was mild and placatory.


## III


Walker knew that unless supplies came to him promptly he could easily be starved out. Already it was reported that a strong Honduran force was approaching Truxillo. Everything would depend, as it had depended from the beginning, on his success in joining Cabañas, and making the revolution their common enterprise. There were rumors in Truxillo that the old Liberal was not far away, but no one could say where.

To try to locate Cabañas' camp, Walker chose the most experienced jungle fighter on his force, Colonel Thomas Henry, who set out with a Honduran guide, and was gone for several days. On his return, before reporting to Walker he stopped at a Truxillo tavern for a few drinks to offset his fatigue. He was by nature a pugnacious man—the survivor of a dozen duels, twenty battles, and many wounds—and liquor invariably accented his belligerence. When he climbed the hill to the fort, his mood was dangerous. Unable to find Walker in his quarters, he waited briefly, smoking a cigar, and then began to search the fort. The door to one room—the powder magazine—was closed, and he pushed it open. Inside was a squad of men preparing charges for the fort's cannon, and loose gunpowder was scattered on the floor. The young lieutenant in charge pointed to Henry's cigar and ordered him out. Nothing more was needed to inflame the wrath of a man spoiling for a fight. Cursing, Henry struck the lieutenant and tried to grapple with him. In a panic, the young man leaped back and pulled a pistol from his belt, and when the colonel rushed him, fired blindly. The bullet struck Henry in the jaw, carrying away the lower part of his face, a wound so hideous that even the most hardened veterans of battle were shocked by the sight.

In great pain, Henry was taken to the hospital, where the surgeon gave him morphine, before sending for Walker. The message on which Walker's hopes rested now lay in the mind of a drugged man, whose wound made it certain that he would never be able to speak again. Walker waited at the bedside and himself performed such surgery as might help to save Henry's life; but the lack of needed antiseptics made for a dark prognosis.

While Walker was waiting for Henry to regain consciousness, he was faced by still worse trouble, with the arrival at Truxillo of the British warship *Icarus*, Captain Norvell Salmon. Within a few hours a sailor brought Walker a curt message: he was to surrender, lay down his arms, and restore the money which had been in the customhouse when his men took possession of it, and which was the property of the British crown. This was Walker's first intimation that the money had been stolen.

The problem now was to prevent Captain Salmon from shelling the fort and landing marines. Still hoping for news of Cabañas from Henry, Walker played for time. His hastily written reply to Salmon said, "I cannot, under the circumstances, regard it as dishonorable to lay down my arms to an officer of the British crown"; but he asked Salmon to particularize his terms for a surrender, and to investigate the facts surrounding the alleged theft.

Henry had meanwhile opened his eyes and recognized Walker. A slate was put to the hands of the voiceless man, and he managed to scrawl a few words, apparently enough to convey some faint notion of Cabañas' whereabouts. Walker's choice was painfully clear. On the one hand, there was the will-o'-the-wisp chance of finding the jungle encampment of the Liberal rebels, who might or might not be willing to accept him. On the other hand, there was the opportunity to surrender safely to the British. Salmon's second note, which arrived some days later, was specific, if supercilious: the Americans would have the protection of the British flag when they laid down their arms. They would then leave the country on a schooner; and Walker himself would have to make good on the money stolen from the customhouse by someone in his service. The note also pointedly remarked that 700 Honduran government soldiers had taken up a position just outside Truxillo.

Salmon's haughty tone may have influenced Walker's decision. Three times before in his life he had been compelled to surrender to officers of the American Army or Navy, and once he had wept at the necessity, but to bow to an Englishman was an even more crushing prospect. Consulting with his officers, he found them ready to follow him in a last desperate effort. Word went to Salmon, postponing until the next day a final reply to his demand for surrender.

While his men were spiking the guns of the fort and destroying all munitions they could not carry with them, Walker visited the hospital to say goodbye to the wounded and to leave a message for Salmon, asking that they be protected against Honduran vengeance. One of the filibusters later described Walker's farewell to the dying Colonel Henry. The gangrene in Henry's wound was spreading rapidly, maggots had appeared in the rotting flesh of his wound, and his voiceless suffering was agonizing for the men around him to see. There was a cup near him, and when Walker, after a few words, turned to go, he squeezed Henry's shoulder, and left alongside the cup a full bottle of morphine. The, turning abruptly, he strode away. The others watched as Henry painfully reached for the cup, emptied the bottle into it, and forced the drug down his gullet. Before dying, he pulled his blanket over his graveyard face.

# IV

Silently, before dawn, the men left the fort and, with a Honduran guide, followed a jungle track not far from the Atlantic coast, moving southeast toward the place in which Cabañas had last been seen. As soon as their flight became known in Truxillo, a strong force of Honduran soldiers set out after them. Twenty-four hours later, as the filibusters were about to ford a stream, the pursuers caught up with them and opened fire, wounding twenty men at the first volley.

Walker rallied the rest, and they managed to beat off the attack. In this engagement he sustained a flesh wound in his cheek, his first injury in all the battles in which he had fought in Central America. Carrying their wounded with them through narrow, twisting jungle trails they pushed on, until they came to the banks of a broad river, the Rio Negro, where a friendly tribe of Carib Indians provided shelter for them. Here their guide, after conferring with the Caribs, gave Walker an encouraging report. A day's journey toward the coast, on the banks of the Negro, they would find Cabañas and his men.

With Walker's long experience of treason in all forms, suspicion must have hammered at him and become near-certainty when the guide disappeared. Nevertheless, he decided to make the indicated move, for his men were subsisting entirely on bananas, the wounded men were in distress, and nothing was to be gained by tramping aimlessly through the jungle. He commandeered the Caribs' canoes, and they drifted downstream, until a few miles from the coast they saw signs of a deserted encampment. Whoever had been there, Cabañas or another, had long since gone.

As they got out of their canoes, they were attacked by waiting Honduran snipers. What saved them was the presence of some rotting barricades, from behind which they were able to defend themselves. A week of sleepless nights and hopeless days ensued. The camp was located in a swampy region, and the insects, the fetid odors, the drenching bursts of rain, the burning sun, and the incessant rifle fire reduced the hungry little band to a state of misery in which the only relief was an occasional successful shot at a Honduran. Several of the men were killed, others wounded. Walker himself came down with fever, which he tried to ignore. Moving from man to man behind their defenses, guiding their rifle fire, shifting their positions as necessity required, tending the wounded, he did what he could, until fatigue began to close down on them, like a fog. It was with a sense of mingled despair and relief that, nine days after the fighting began, he saw two British boats coming up the river, manned by British sailors, with Captain Salmon sitting stiffly in the bow of the lead boat. As the Hondurans ceased firing, a sailor got out of the boat, advanced to the camp, and gave Walker a message. The Captain wished him to come at once to his boat, prepared to surrender his force.

The last military decision of Walker's life was in some ways the easiest. His urge to resist was gone. The only gesture that he made to his reputation as he walked to the shore was a conscious straightening of his shoulders and lifting of his head.

Salmon was a big man, with a ruddy complexion and a booming voice—almost a caricature of his type. "Sir," he began, "I demand that you surrender to me immediately."

"To whom do I surrender?" asked Walker.

"To an officer of Her Majesty's Government. And you may thank me, too"—pointing at the Honduran soldiers in the distance—"that you have a whole bone in your body and that your men leave here alive."

Something in Salmon's manner must have aroused Walker's distrust, for he repeated his question in a slightly different form. "Do I understand you to say, sir, that my surrender would be to a representative of Her Majesty's Government?"

"Yes," said Salmon, "to me."

"Under these curcumstances," Walker replied, "I surrender to you, Captain." He handed his sword and pistol to Salmon, and turning, ordered his men to deliver their guns and knives to the British marines. That was all.*

He and Colonel Rudler were taken immediately to the *Icarus,* the rest of the men following in other boats. As soon as all were on board, Salmon ordered the ship to proceed at full steam to Truxillo. There, he announced, they would be handed over to the Honduran authorities. Walker's men would be protected by the British flag, but the fate of Walker himself, and Rudler, would be left to the Hondurans.

Walker was at first incredulous, then disdainful. The correspondent of the New York *Herald* boarded the *Icarus* at Truxillo, and before leaving the ship Walker dictated a short statement to him.

> On board the Steamer *Icarus*
> Sept. 5, 1860
>
> I hereby protest before the civilized world that when I surrendered to the captain of Her Majesty's Steamer *Icarus,* that officer expressly received my sword and pistol, as well as the arms of Colonel Rudler, and the surrender was expressly made in so many words to him, as the representative of Her Britannic Majesty.
> William Walker

When after a few days a Honduran officer came to him to say that he would be executed the next morning, he asked at once about

* New York *Herald,* Sept. 28, Oct. 4, 1860. *Harper's Weekly,* Vol. IV, p. 647.

Rudler, and was relieved to hear that the Colonel's sentence had been commuted to a limited imprisonment.

Many concocted versions of Walker's execution appeared in the American press, including "last words" which it is virtually certain that he never uttered. What is known is that at eight o'clock on September 12, 1860, flanked by two priests, he was led by a company of soldiers to a ruined wall, on the outskirts of Truxillo, followed by a large and jubilant crowd of Hondurans. He ignored the laughter and jests around him. His bearing was calm and resolute, and he seemed to give his attention wholly to the words of the priests. The soldiers formed a line around the square in front of the wall, as the last rites were administered. When the priests had concluded and withdrew, Walker stood erect, facing the soldiers impassively and without speaking. A squad of Hondurans stepped forward, aimed, and at an officer's command, fired. Walker was apparently dead when he fell. A second squad then advanced and fired another volley at the body, after which the officer walked forward, put his pistol to the head of the corpse, and pulled the trigger, mutilating the face beyond recognition. The crowd cheered, the troops marched off, and the priests removed the body, with the help of some Americans who had come off a ship in Truxillo, and who paid for a coffin. The interment was conducted with a Catholic service at an isolated spot. Afterward the Tennessee Historial Society, of which Walker was an honorary member, attempted to bring the remains to Nashville for burial, but the Honduran government refused permission. Captain Salmon, with a shrewd eye for British relations in Central America, gave Walker's sword to Nicaragua. There was considerable criticism of him in the United States for his mortal deception of Walker, but the British government winked at the episode and it did not interfere with his subsequent career.

## V

The speed with which Walker's fame evaporated had something of the same phenomenal quality that marked him all his life. The coming of the Civil War, with its new crop of heroes, was no doubt mainly responsible for the country's readiness to forget him, but there may have been also another, more subtle reason—the way of thinking and feeling for which he stood. Men of business had then begun to take possession of the United States; their special outlook and mentality was becoming dominant throughout the North and in parts of the South; and their standards of judgment were more and more regarded as identical with law, morality, and good government. Walker's entire career was a romantic challenge to economic man, his personality wholly antithetic to the great powers then about to reshape the American way of life. By his enemies is a man known, and Walker contended with the money-master, Cornelius Vanderbilt, was abandoned by the artful friend of wealth, Buchanan, and was castigated by the leading advocate of the economic virtues, Greeley.

A concerted and final attack on his reputation by the abolitionist press was in the making when he died. Its tone was set by Greeley in the New York *Tribune*. A long editorial, which appeared before news of the execution had reached the United States, called Walker "impudent"—"imbecilic"—"idiotic"—"insane"—"cowardly"—"contemptible"—"a vagabond"—"pestilent creature"—and found it "inexplicable that men should follow him." His death, the editorial plainly conveyed, would be a godsend. Even in that age of easy slander, this was remarkable. President Buchanan echoed Greeley's sentiments. In a message to Congress in December, 1860, when the nation was rocking toward civil war, he took time to express pious satisfaction in Walker's disappearance from the national scene. "I congratulate you on the public sentiment which now exists," he told Congress, "against the crime of setting on foot military expeditions within the limits of the United States, to proceed from thence and make war upon the people of unoffending states with whom we are at peace. In this respect a happy change has been effected since the commencement of my administration." Buchanan had chosen to forget that he himself had once advocated the forcible annexation of Cuba, that he had been elected on a Democratic platform which called on the administration to support Walker, and that he had received him at the White House with every civility and courtesy. His remarks were in fact an echo of statements made by the press of England, where Walker's death was regarded with unalloyed pleasure. On both sides of the Atlantic, official opinion took the stand that he had been simply a troublemaker; and the Northern interpretation of history which dominated American thought after the Civil War accepted this view.

The New York *Times* saw Walker otherwise. "Whatever hard things may have been said of General Walker—and much, we doubt not, would have been left unsaid had his fortune been more propitious—he was at least no vulgar adventurer, either by birth, habits, or education, or the honourable purpose with which he set out in life. His parentage was unsullied, his private walk and temperance unquestioned, his learning profound, and his original aims, however subsequently misdirected by an unchastened ambition, such as commended him to success, while enlisting the esteem of numerous friends. Even those who deny him all claim to military skill or political sagacity as a leader, pay the highest compliment to his moral force and personal integrity. Without these his first failure as an adventurer must inevitably have been his last."

Until the flame of his natural genius was quenched by despair, Walker had the glow of an idealist as well as the heat of a hero. *Harper's Weekly* observed that he failed because, instead of seeking to win support from the wealthy and influential, he relied only on himself. The real tragedy, *Harper's* commented, lay in the rejection of him by the American government. "Had William Walker been an Englishman or a Frenchman, he would never have become a 'filibuster,' but would have found ample scope for his extraordinary talents in the legitimate service of his country."* It was the kind of epitaph that Walker himself might have desired.

---

* It is impossible not to wonder what would have happened in Central America if President Pierce or Buchanan had chosen to support Walker in the first flush of his conquest, and before he made his fatal concession to the South. Would the flow of American capital and enterprise to the isthmian republics have enabled them to make more progress in the century that followed? It seems safe to say that they could hardly have made less. Would England have gone to war with the United States over Nicaragua in 1856? There is considerable reason to doubt it. Would American concentration on Central America and the construction of a canal there have eased the internal schism in the United States? Would Walker have been justified in his belief in the possibility of averting civil war by rallying the nation to an expansion of democratic institutions and productivity overseas? It may be noted that echoes of the idea persist in mid-twentieth-century politics. At a time when, as Adlai Stevenson has said, the world itself is threatened with civil war, there are not a few who feel that the most realistic hope of peace lies in the diversion of the energies of the great powers away from direct confrontation and to an effort to bring underprivileged peoples into "the column of Progress and Democracy" of which Walker wrote.

# The Klutz Yo-Yo Book

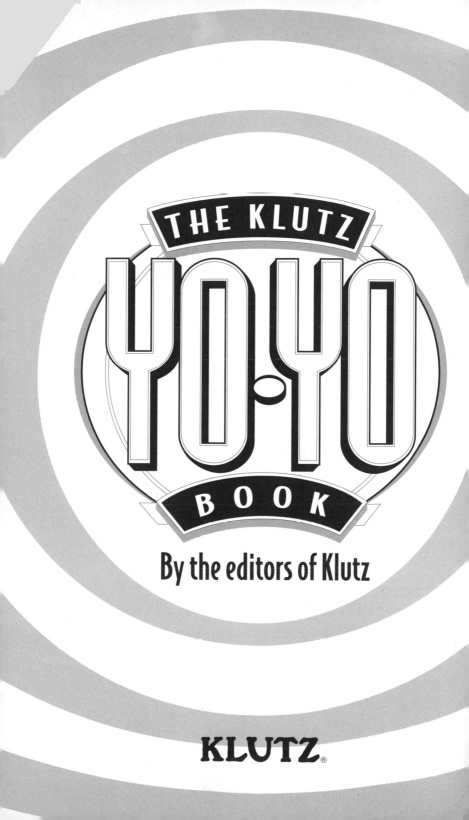

# THE KLUTZ

# YO·YO

# BOOK

## By the editors of Klutz

**KLUTZ**®

**KLUTZ.** is a kids' company staffed entirely by real human beings. We began our corporate life in 1977 in an office we shared with a Chevrolet Impala. Today we've outgrown our founding garage, but Palo Alto, California, remains Klutz galactic headquarters. For those of you who collect corporate mission statements, here's ours:

• Create wonderful things   • Be good   • Have fun

**Write Us**
We would love to hear your comments regarding this or any of our books. We have many!

**KLUTZ.** 455 Portage Avenue, Palo Alto, CA 94306

Manufactured in Taiwan

Published by Klutz, a subsidiary of Scholastic Inc. SCHOLASTIC and associated logos are trademarks and/or registered trademarks of Scholastic Inc. Klutz and associated logos are trademarks and/or registered trademarks of Klutz.

ISBN 1-57054-193-0            8 8 8 0 7

Distributed in the UK by
Scholastic UK Ltd.
Westfield Road, Southam
Warwickshire, England   CV47 0RA

**Visit Our Website**
You can check out all the stuff we make, find a nearby retailer, sign up for a newsletter, e-mail us, request a catalog or just goof off!

# Contents

# Yo-Yo Science 39

# Yo-Yo History 49

# Introduction

**L**et's say you took every yo-yo made and sold in the United States in the last 60 years and began piling them up, one on top of the other. At the bottom, you could start with the original Pedro Flores yo-yos that first appeared in Southern California in the early 1920s. On top of them, you could add the pre-war Duncans manufactured in Chicago, then would come a huge stack of Duncan 33s, 44s and 77s, carved in the Duncan factory at Luck, Wisconsin. Soon after that you'd have to add a pile of other brands—Goodies, Cheerios, and Royals at first, then the Festivals, followed by a huge mixed pile of premium yo-yos (a couple of million with the Coca-Cola logo alone). Add all the Duncan Imperials, Professionals, Butterflies, etc. and then top it off with a thick layer of velvet, chrome, electric and miscellaneous models.

Now stand back.

Even if you left off a couple of million yo-yos—say all those that rolled down the sewer, or were eaten by the dog—you'd still have an impressive pile. Figure an average of one-and-a-half inches each, you'd be looking at a yo-yo monument around 2,000 miles high, containing roughly half-a-billion "return top toys."

Afterwards, just for fun, you could take the strings off, tie them together, wrap them around the planet and take the loose end to the moon, where you could cut off the extra 40,000 miles or so and yo-yo-ize the Earth.

1

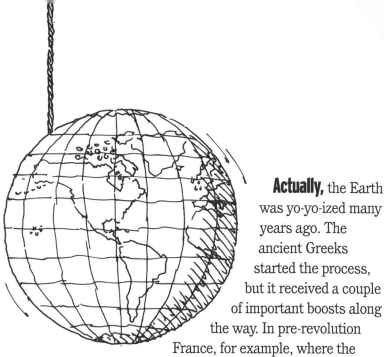

**Actually,** the Earth was yo-yo-ized many years ago. The ancient Greeks started the process, but it received a couple of important boosts along the way. In pre-revolution France, for example, where the emigrette was a favorite pastime amongst the (soon to be un-landed) gentry. Across the channel, it was called the quiz and like many French imports, it was particularly well-received by those who took their cultural cues from the continent.

Elsewhere, in places as distant as Persia, Malaysia and the Philippines, yo-yos had long been a part of the popular street culture. Yo-yos, after all, are cousin to the spinning top, a nearly universal toy with ancient and hopelessly tangled roots.

It was left to Donald F. Duncan, though, an American entrepreneur with a P.T. Barnum flair for promotion, to firmly establish the yo-yo forever in the constellation of immortal toys. Looking at the aforementioned 2,000-mile-high yo-yo monument, it would probably be safe to say that Mr. Duncan was directly or indirectly responsible for all but a mile or two of it.

# How to Yo

In the world of yo-yo-ing, the tricks are everything. Just going up and down does not measure on the scale. Sorry. You can't even show your face really until you can throw a decent sleeper, one that lasts 4 to 5 seconds.

To get you started, cut the string to the right length. With the yo-yo touching the ground, and the string on your finger, your hand should be at your belly-button. Tie a slip knot and put it over your middle finger, just past the *first* knuckle (not the second, like rank amateurs). See the illustration.

After a while, the slip knot will tighten to the point that it feels as if it's cutting off your circulation. The end of your middle finger will look blue. This is normal. If you pursue the yo-yo trade long enough, with enough purity of purpose, you will one day develop a callous here. More than anything else, a true yo-yo callous is the mark of a yo-yo pro.

## How Long Should the String Be?

*With the yo-yo touching the ground, and the string on your finger, your hand should be belly-button high.*

## Winding Up the Yo-Yo When It Wants to Be a Problem

When the string won't grab and you find yourself winding and winding and winding and getting nowhere, you've got the string-won't-start-winding problem. Solution? Look at the illustration. On the first wrap or two, pinch the string with the tip of your forefinger at the groove (this makes no sense unless you look at the illustration). On the third wrap, remove your forefinger and go back to normal.

Just catch the first wind with the tip of this forefinger

On the second winding, do the same thing

On the third winding, go back to normal, forefinger out of the way

Like this...

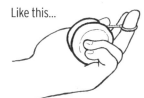

...not like this.

## Holding the Yo-Yo at the Ready

Hold the yo-yo in your hand palm-up with the string wrapped so it comes off your middle finger and goes over the top of the yo-yo as shown.

# The Power Throw and Sleeper

This is where it all starts. The Power Throw and Sleeper is the fundamental act of yo. Start with the yo-yo up by your ear, release it the instant you start your move and come down hard.

If your yo-yo refuses to sleep, try releasing a little earlier and "soften" the hit at the bottom. Still a problem? Let the yo-yo unwind. Worst case: Take it apart to get rid of any knots.

P.S. The most common problem is the first. Not releasing as soon as you start the move.

## If Your Yo-Yo Is Too Tight...

let it unwind at the end of its string. When it stops spinning, it's at neutral.

Put the yo-yo up by your ear. It should look like you're making a muscle. Let go of the yo-yo the instant you start to move your hand. If you wait too long to let go, the yo-yo will bounce, zip back, and hurt.

1.

The number two biggest problem that everyone has is the "leaning" yo-yo. When it hits the bottom of the string it leans and scrapes against the string slowing down all too fast. The solution? A careful, accurate release. It's not a power thing—a stronger throw won't fix it— what you need is an <u>accurate</u> throw.

A Leaner

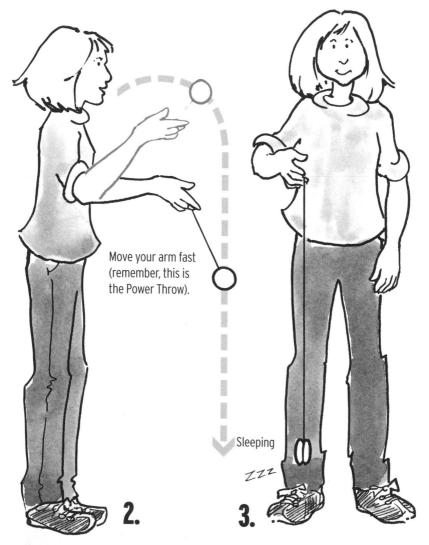

Move your arm fast (remember, this is the Power Throw).

Sleeping

zzz

**2.**

**3.**

# What If It Never Sleeps No Matter How Much You "Soften" the Jolt?

Then your string probably needs adjusting. No problem. Let your yo-yo hang until it stops spinning entirely. Then try again.

## Yo-Yo String X-Rays

Just right.

Tight. Won't sleep.

Too loose.

Still won't spin? Time to inspect for the dreaded axle knot.

## Axle Knots: The Bane of Yo-Yo

When in the course of yo-yo gyrations the string gets tangled to the point that it knots around the axle, then it becomes necessary to untie the knot.

**Step One:** Unscrew the yo-yo halves.

**Step Two:** Don't lose either half.

**Step Three:** Don't cut the string. Untie the knot. Straighten things out, put the yo-yo back together, you're done. **Warning:** Don't over-tighten the halves! Just snug. Too tight can ruin the threads.

# The Forward Pass

**S**tart with an extended arm held behind you as shown. The instant you start to come forward, release the yo-yo and swing the arm down and out. The yo-yo comes from your ankles up to chest height as shown.

**1.**

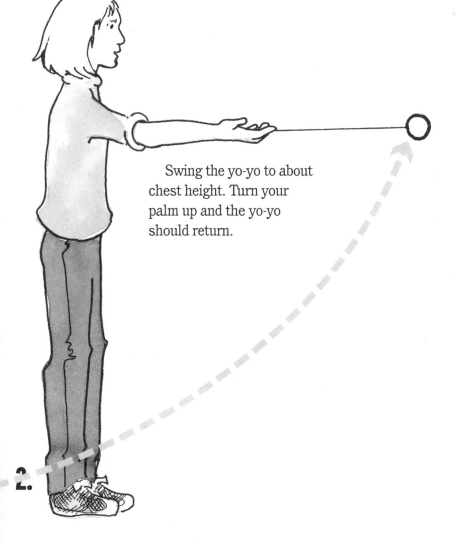

Swing the yo-yo to about chest height. Turn your palm up and the yo-yo should return.

**2.**

# Walk the Dog

This is, without doubt, the planet's most popular yo-yo trick. At first, you should be able to walk it a foot or two. Later, when you can throw a "power sleeper" you ought to be able to walk it 10 feet or more.

**HINT:**
If you throw a "leaner," don't even try to walk it. It won't spin long enough. Try again with a more accurate throw.

ZZZ

**1.**

Set the yo-yo on the floor gently when it's spinning full tilt. Keep its "leash" at full length. If you get any slack in it, your yo-yo will pop right back to you.

Keep the slack out of your leash.

zzz

2.

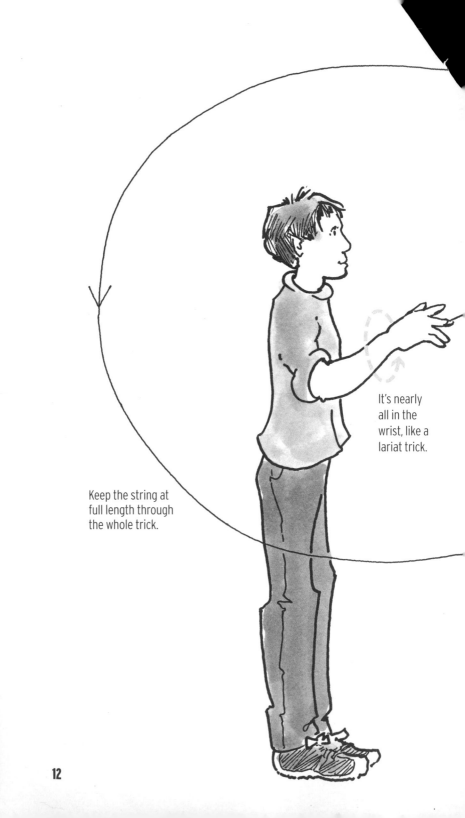

It's nearly all in the wrist, like a lariat trick.

Keep the string at full length through the whole trick.

# Around the World

**T**hrow a hard sleeper forward pass (page 8), then spin it around, sleeping all the way. Takes a loose wrist, since the wrist is about the only thing you need to move. At the completion of a full circle, a quick jerk should bring it back home. Make sure your string is loose enough around the axle. Not a good trick to do in a china shop.

Z ZZ

## The Automatic Rewind: The Best Trick in This Book

Hold like this.
Thumb in groove

After you've gotten tired of winding the yo-yo the 'round and 'round old-fashioned way, try this. Grab the yo-yo as shown with your thumb on the groove. String hand high above your head. Pull the yo-yo out of your hand so it spins off your thumb. It'll pop into the air, and hopefully wind itself back up.

# Hop the Fence

The hrow the yo-yo down (doesn't have to sleep), but instead of catching it on its way back up, let it flip over your wrist so it goes right back down. You can do this endlessly if you have a quick and flexible wrist.

If you're right-handed, this will gradually tighten the string. Lefties, just the opposite.

1.

When you can do five-in-a-row,
count yourself a pretty fair
Fence Hopper.

**2.**

# Loop-the-Loop

**Y**o-yo contests that end in a tie are often settled with a Loop-the-Loop sudden-death overtime. The contestants each begin a series of Loop-the-Loops. The winner is the one who can stay with it the longest.

Yo-yo pros will tell you that the Loop-the-Loop is the first trick you'll learn and the last trick you'll master.

**1.**

It starts with a Forward Pass (page 8). Note that the yo-yo's first move is straight down. Then swing it back out to chest height. As it returns let it come over your hand, inside your arm and back out again. Do all of this by rotating your wrist in a little circle. If you're right-handed, a lot of Loop-the-Loops will loosen the string.

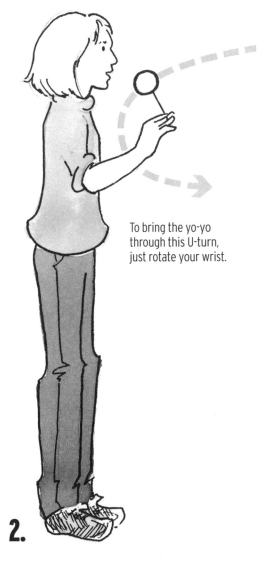

To bring the yo-yo through this U-turn, just rotate your wrist.

**2.**

# Breakaway

**M**ake a muscle with the yo-yo up by your ear. Throw a hard spinner directly out to that side. Swing the yo-yo down by your ankles out to your other side. Then a quick pop brings it back. Since this whole trick goes from side to side, you could actually practice it standing almost nose to a wall.

The Breakaway is a fundamental trick, the starting move to a lot of advanced stuff. As always, if it refuses to sleep, check the loop tightness.

This is a hard, fast, outward throw. Swing down by your ankles...

**1.**

**2.**

zzz

**HINT:** Try practicing this trick with your nose a foot or so from a wall. If you can do it then, you're doing it right.

...once it reaches chest height, pop it back in.

**3.**

# Around the  Corner

**T**hrow a hard sleeper, then raise your hand to about your ear (the "I swear" position) and put your elbow in <u>front</u> of the string. Then drop your hand down and tweak the string so that the yo-yo "wakes up" and flings itself over your shoulder.

Incidentally, the illustrations are about a thousand times clearer than these instructions.

**1.**

Tweak
the string by
jerking it up.

**2.**

**3.**

# Pinwheel

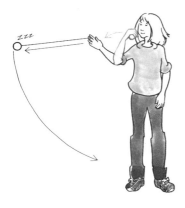

**S**tart with a Breakaway (check your loop tightness if you're having a hard time making your yo-yo sleep). Swing it by in front of you and then as it comes up on your other side, stick your forefinger out and let the yo-yo spin around it once or twice. The trick is to do it gently enough so that the yo-yo doesn't wake up.

**1.**

Stick your forefinger out and catch the string just a few inches from the yo-yo.

**2.**

Let your yo-yo pivot around your forefinger once. Pull your forefinger out of the way and the resultant pop should send your yo-yo back to your hand.

**3.**

# Over the Falls

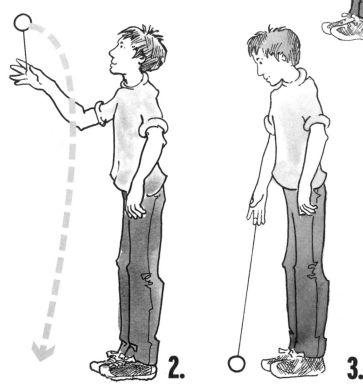

**S**tart with a Forward Pass, but as it's starting to come back, let it slow down. Then point your fingers straight down to direct the yo-yo inside your arm and straight down. One quick lift should bring it back up. End of trick.

**2.**

**3.**

# Three-Leaf Clover

This is a multiple Loop-the-Loop maneuver. Start with your arm pointed down, then bring it up hard, releasing the yo-yo the instant you start moving. Direct it into a skyward Loop-the-Loop, then use your wrist to re-direct the yo-yo back out in a regular straight-ahead Loop-the-Loop, then turn the next Loop-the-Loop down toward the ground and back to the hand.

Let go the instant you start to move your hand.

1.

# Flying Saucer

**1.** In order to TIGHTEN the string, start up here by your LEFT shoulder...

**2.** ...come down hard <u>across</u> your body to your opposite hip.

**3.** Grab the string in the middle...

The Flying Saucer isn't actually a
trick. It's a labor-saving device.
Use it to loosen or tighten the
string when you're too impatient
to just let the yo-yo sit there and
unwind at its own slow pace.

**4.** ...slide your
hand towards
the yo-yo.

## Big Important Point

If you start at your left
shoulder and throw to your
RIGHT hip, you'll tighten
the yo-yo. If you start at
your right shoulder and
throw to your LEFT hip,
you'll loosen the yo-yo.
Remember it this way:

RIGHTY = TIGHTY
LEFTY = LOOSEY

**5.**

If it's still
spinning hard
while you have
it here, you
could let go
and it should
pop back to
your hand. Not
easy but very
flashy.

# Sidewinder

**T**his is another way of doing the Flying Saucer. It's also designed to either loosen or tighten the string for those times when your yo-yo isn't sleeping right.

**1.** Get set. Make a muscle, hold the yo-yo up by your right shoulder...

**2.** ...and come down hard across your body to your left hip. When the yo-yo hits the bottom...

These illustrations show it going from right shoulder to LEFT hip so the string will loosen. If you go from left shoulder to RIGHT hip, the string will tighten.

**3.** …it should be off-center and out-of-kilter like this. It's not supposed to come back up. It's supposed to spin flat like a lariat.

**4.** Just as it's running out of steam, give it a pop, jerk it to…

**5.** …chest height. All the spinning it's doing is winding the string tighter. And if you're good, the yo-yo will now wind back.

# Rock the Cradle

This is the basic among the "string" tricks. String tricks are "cat's cradle" kind of maneuverings, but done under the time constraints of a sleeping yo-yo.

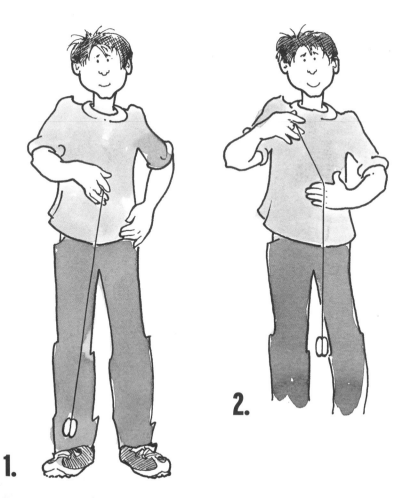

**1.**

**2.**

Throw a hard sleeper and then look at the illustrations. Anything we could say here would only confuse you. You may want to practice this a few times with a "dead" non-spinning yo-yo, so as to get a feel for the hand placement. It'll take about 4–5 seconds to do this, so your yo-yo will have to be pretty well asleep.

**3.**

**4.** After one or two rockings, drop everything so the yo-yo can pop back to your hand before it runs out of steam.

# Skin the Cat

**T**his is another "starting move" kind of trick, used at the beginning of some more advanced things.

Catch the string right about ← here with your forefinger, then slide your forefinger up to about...

**1.**

zzz

...here

as you simultaneously bring the yo-yo up about head height.

**2.**

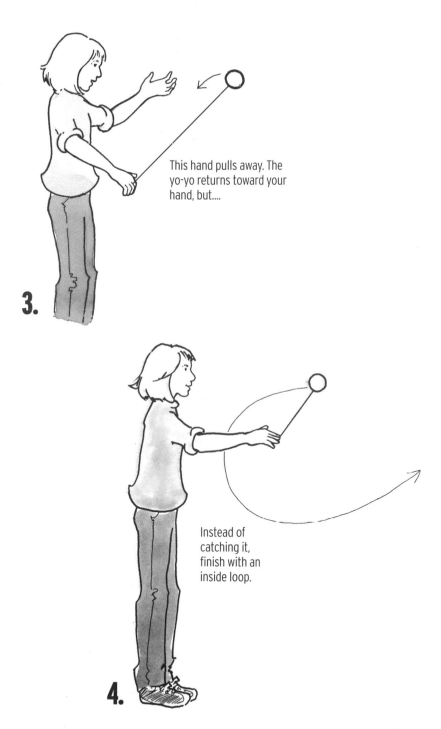

**3.**

This hand pulls away. The yo-yo returns toward your hand, but....

**4.**

Instead of catching it, finish with an inside loop.

# Trapeze

**Y**ou cannot be taken seriously amongst dedicated yo-yo-ers until you can execute the Trapeze effortlessly. This trick is the threshold to the State of Yo. It demands a high level of dedication and a loose loop around the axle.

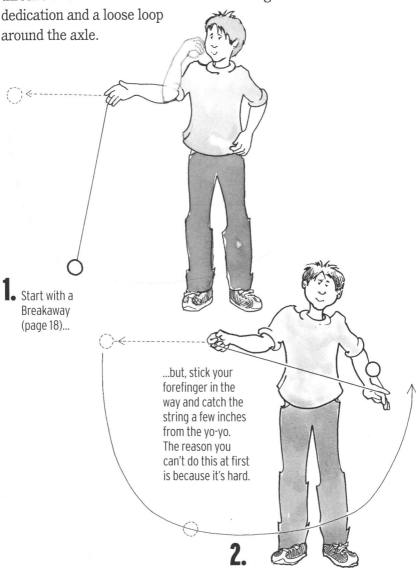

**1.** Start with a Breakaway (page 18)...

...but, stick your forefinger in the way and catch the string a few inches from the yo-yo. The reason you can't do this at first is because it's hard.

**2.**

Start with a Breakaway. Flex your muscle, throw a hard sleeper out to your side and as it swings up on your other side, intercept the string with your finger 3 or 4 inches from the yo-yo. As the yo-yo pivots around your finger, you have to catch it back on the string. This is hard. At first, it's impossible. But it can be done. Just takes a steady hand and dead aim.

## Two weeks later.

Now that you've finally managed to catch the yo-yo on its string, bring your hands together as per the illustration and then spread them apart quickly, popping the yo-yo off and completing the trick.

Take a bow.

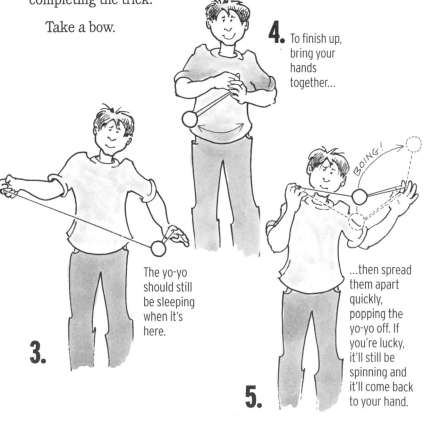

**4.** To finish up, bring your hands together...

**3.** The yo-yo should still be sleeping when it's here.

**5.** ...then spread them apart quickly, popping the yo-yo off. If you're lucky, it'll still be spinning and it'll come back to your hand.

# Double or Nothing

This is a trick well into the land of serious yo. You'll have to be quite reliable on the Trapeze before you can plunge ahead with this one. Nobody learns this in less than a month of trying.

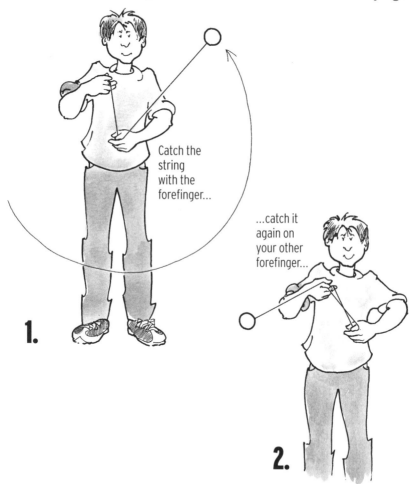

Catch the string with the forefinger...

...catch it again on your other forefinger...

**1.**

**2.**

The idea is to throw a hard Breakaway sleeper, then intercept the string THREE times, catching the yo-yo back on its string as per the Trapeze. If you miss catching it (see last illustration) you've fulfilled the "Nothing" part of the title.

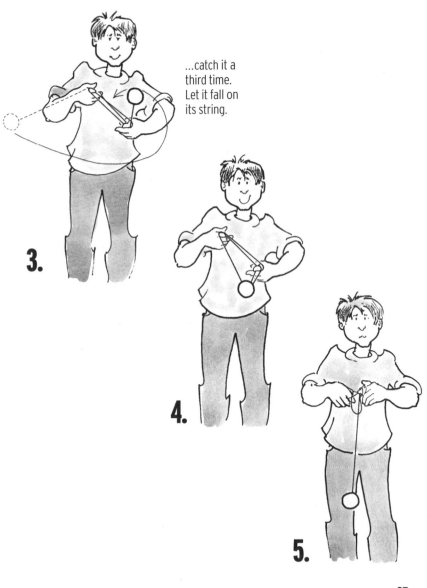

...catch it a third time. Let it fall on its string.

**3.**

**4.**

**5.**

# Yo-Yo
# Science

**Although the motion** and behavior of a yo-yo appears to be fairly
simple—up, down, round and round—it is actually quite
possible to turn it into a bewildering array of equations that
derive from thermodynamics and Newton's second law. Those
who choose to plow ahead with this section will never look at a
yo-yo in quite the same way again.

# But First, a Definition

Many of you, of course, have already been wondering: "Hey, what is a yo-yo, anyway?" Here, then, is your answer: "A yo-yo is a body of rotational symmetry with a slender axle, which is allowed to roll on a flexible string."

Any other questions?

**The second law of thermodynamics,** to which we must now regrettably turn, concerns the conservation of energy. Neglecting the special case of atomic yo-yos, the energy given to a yo-yo when it leaves your hand has to go somewhere: either into the up-and-down motion (translational), round-and-round (rotational), or it is lost to friction against the air (not much) or the string (quite a bit).

In addition, as Isaac Newton so ably pointed out, any object in motion will neither slow down, speed up, nor vary from its way unless it is influenced by another force.

**These are the constraints** that a yo-yo is up against as it performs its various tricks, and these are the constraints that enabled Dr. Burger to analyze a yo-yo's motion. He discovered, for example, that a yo-yo is at maximum speed about halfway down its string. For the rest of its trip to the bottom, it is slowing down.

*Wolfgang Burger is Germany's "Dr. Wizard." A distinguished professor of theoretical mechanics at the University of Karlsruhe, Germany, he has also been the host on a popular television science program for some years. Although Dr. Burger lists "nonlinear wave propagation" as his primary field of interest, he also confesses to a weakness for "physical toys." His analysis of yo-yo behavior has been published in both German and American scientific journals and represents the most in-depth treatment of the subject in print.*

This last observation enabled Dr. Burger to pass judgment on a story which has been repeated in countless newspaper articles, magazine features, and nearly every yo-yo book ever written, i.e., the myth of the deadly Filipino hunting yo-yo.

## Thinking About Going Hunting with a Yo-Yo?

**Some things to keep in mind before you head out.**

According to the story, the modern yo-yo is descended from a Filipino weapon. Hunters would perch in tree limbs, specially chipped flint yo-yos in hand, and wait for unsuspecting animals to pass below. If the first throw didn't work—no problem—it's a yo-yo! Just try again.

Unfortunately, as Dr. Burger's numbers point out, the unwinding string is actually a rather significant brake, acting to slow the yo-yo down and soften its impact at the bottom. From the prospective yo-yo hunter's point of view, this represents a serious shortcoming. (A second objection occurs to me. What if you miss? Then do you have a heavy, sharpened rock yo-yo hurtling up a string tied to your hand?)

# Why Does a Yo-Yo Sleep?

**A** good question, since the answer gets to the heart of the modern yo-yo and makes possible the elevated "State of Yo" discussed elsewhere.

A yo-yo doesn't really roll up and down a string, it actually rolls up and down the inside of a loop of string. Unless the loop is twisted very tightly, when the yo-yo reaches the bottom of a properly executed toss, it will simply spin inside the loop. A little jerk, and the axle will catch on the string, and begin winding it up.

◀ To be perfectly accurate, this is not a string, but a tightly twisted loop.

This yo-yo is sitting and spinning inside its loop.

This yo-yo has snagged its string loop and is now on its way back up.

# Can Modern Science Build a Better Yo-Yo?

This is the last question that Dr. Burger turned to, and armed with his calculations, he was able to isolate those factors that make the biggest performance difference.

**Number one** was weight distribution. A huge yo-yo with all its weight on the outside rim would spin for a much longer period. A couple of bicycle wheels, for example, make a fabulous yo-yo.

**Number two** was axle diameter. The skinnier the axle, the less friction it generates against the string (and, unfortunately, the quicker it breaks). A fat axle stores little of its energy in spin, falls very quickly, and hits with a great shock.

**Number three** was symmetry. When the yo-yo twists or wobbles it means that the weight is unevenly distributed, or that some twisting force (torque) is acting on it. Oftentimes this is the result of the string itself becoming too wound up.

# Kinematics and Rotational Flymass Behavior in BIG Yo-Yos

$A$s most students of yo-yo kinematics are aware, historical field work in the area has been exclusively conducted either on the surface of the Earth, or within 2 or 3 feet of it. In addition to which, experimenters have invariably utilized the so-called "classical" yo-yo size and shape, i.e., smallish and incorporating no bicycle parts.

$$t = \int_{o}^{t} dt = \int_{o}^{l} dx/v(x)$$

In an effort to break with these conventions, while at the same time advancing our understanding of some of the more extreme forms of yo-yo behavior, my colleagues and I have recently concluded a number of kinematic experiments outside the 11th-story window of our research facility. Inevitably, during the course of the experiments our apparatus traveled down to the 4th floor, back to the 11th, down to the 4th, up to the 11th, down to the 4th, up to the 11th, down to the 4th, up to the 11th...and so forth.

Nevertheless, we were able to record changes in yo-yo behavior at these higher elevations, freed from the distorting effects of ground-level gravity.

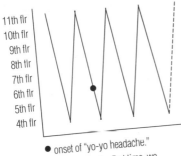

● onset of "yo-yo headache."

In addition, and for the first time, we incorporated a number of bicycle parts into our yo-yo apparatus. The photograph should be illustrative of both the apparatus and the experimental environment.

The results of the experiment confirmed a hypothesis first proposed nearly 2 weeks ago by ourselves as well as Frederick, Plotnick et al. in Geneva: Firstly, bicycle wheel yo-yos are possible, but awkward. They are difficult to handle, troublesome to wind up, and nearly impossible to use for certain tricks, notably Rock the Cradle. We were forced to conclude that their commercial possibilities are limited.

Secondly, and perhaps more surprisingly, we discovered a new phenomenon directly connected with our decision to utilize a 16 lb., 3-foot diameter yo-yo. We have dubbed this phenomenon "yo-yo headache" and Drs. Shelton and Wiener stumbled upon it while leaning out the 6th-floor window to record the yo-yo's behavior in its "going down" mode, as we called it.

The balance of our conclusions are best described in the language of analytical calculus and we turn with relish to that section now...

## Yo-Yos in Outer Space

Sooner or later, everyone comes around to the same question: "Sure they're fun here, but what could I do with a yo-yo if I lived in outer space?"

Fortunately, modern science has the answer to that one in the person of David Griggs, an astronaut who took a specially fire-proofed yo-yo with him on the shuttle in July of 1984. Mr. Griggs was participating in NASA's "Toys in Space" program.

Discouragingly enough, Mr. Griggs discovered that yo-yos don't sleep in outer space. Astronaut Griggs (who got his yo-yo training from Tom Kuhn a few months before lift-off) found that his yo-yo, when it came to the end of its string, would never stick. The reason has to do with outer space's weightless conditions. In the absence of any gravity, the jolt given to the yo-yo at the end of a throw was plenty to send it right back up the string.

On the plus side, Lunar Loops and Round the World turned out to be much simpler.

# Why Gyroscopic Stability Means So Much to Your Yo-Yo

(An Experiment You Can Do at Home)

**1.** Let your yo-yo simply hang on the end of its string.

**2.** Observe it begin to twist, or unwind. Make a note.

**3.** Now, with the same yo-yo, wind it back up and throw a sleeper. Why doesn't it continue to unwind, like it did before?

The answer, of course, is gyroscopic stability. A disc that is spinning (a yo-yo, a bicycle wheel...etc.) resists turning on any other axis but the one it's spinning on. The faster it spins, the more it resists. If you could mount a bicycle up in the air, spin the front wheel very fast, and then try the handlebars, you'd see what I'm talking about. Turning them would feel stiff. At some speed, they would nearly lock.

The scientific reasons are not very pretty, and I will leave them as an exercise. If it helps, nuclear submarines utilize the same principle (different equipment) as they navigate underwater.

Of course yo-yos generally don't spin fast enough to resist a serious degree of torque and many is the trick that has been foiled by a wobbling, tilted, or otherwise off-kilter yo-yo. Preventing this kind of wrong axis behavior is a large part of the yo-yo-er's trade.

*The first yo-yo fad was in France in the late 1700s. This is a woodcut from the period. An unflattering portrait of a Napoleonic soldier with his jou-jou in hand.*

# Yo-Yo History

**Trying to pin down** the owner and location of history's first yo-yo is a foredoomed exercise. D.W. Gould, author of the definitive history of the spinning top, after attempting to verify a number of competing theories, concluded that the top (and its more refined cousin, the yo-yo) were independently invented by many people, in many places. Our own theory is that the yo-yo was invented by the youngest kid of the guy that invented the wheel. We have evidence, too, although we are saving it for later publication.

**History's first** graphic evidence that the State of Yo existed in ancient times occurs on a Greek vase dating from 500 B.C. where a young Greek is depicted in full yo-yo stride. Subsequent mention of the yo-yo is spotty until it reappears in full cry in 18th-century France. Where and how it spent the intervening 2300 years seems to be an area ripe for speculation. The fabled Filipino hunting yo-yo may well offer a clue. Like most myths, it probably has a kernel of truth. Some writers have speculated that a retrievable (but non-yo-yo-ing)

rock-on-a-string weapon may have existed in the Philippines—alongside the more benign toy—for millenia.

If such were the case, it would support the theory that the yo-yo, like the top, boomerang, footbag and other pre-historic toys, simply became embedded in the street life of dozens of cultures. Whether as an import or an independently invented toy, it hardly matters.

**Its dramatic reappearance** in 18th-century France can be most directly traced to the Chinese version of the toy, probably imported, along with a number of other curiosities, by missionaries. A French minister of state at the time (Jean Baptiste-Berlin) was an amateur collector of things Chinese and his interest may well have given the new device an added boost.

The Paris Picayune

Sept. 14, 1789

# Europe Goes Yo-Yo

Versailles. Spokesman from the Royal Court today confirmed the rumors that have been circulating around the palace for a number of days: the future King Louis XVII has finally been able to "Rock the Cradle" with his yo-yo. "Of course, we're relieved," said one source who chose to remain anonymous, "the littly tyrant was becoming even more irritating than usual. Maybe now that he's finally got the thing, he'll cut us a little slack."

In any event, the jou-jou or emigrette, as it was sometimes called, soon needed no boost. It swept through French society with a Hula-Hoop's vengeance. The future King Louis XVII was painted (at the age of 4) in possession of one in the year 1789. Clubs were formed, competitions held. It was a National State of Yo.

**From France,** it soon took over England and the rest of Europe. The Prince of Wales (the future George IV) was portrayed with his "quiz" in hand. As in France, it seems to have been a fashionable diversion, particularly popular among the upper classes.

By 1824, however, it was a faded fad, described by one writer of the time as a "bygone toy."

**But** the little return top with the 2,000-year pedigree was not so easily dismissed. It may have dropped from fashion on the continent, but it was still destined for great things elsewhere.

**In the U.S.,** inventors spent the rest of the century busily adapting and improving the device, hoping to re-kindle the same kind of fever last seen in France and England. The patent files are filled with their efforts, but none of them appear to have gotten much further than the drawing board. In the Philippines, meanwhile, the yo-yo continued to be a common toy familiar to everyone, including a youngster named Pedro Flores, who emigrated as a young man to the United States in 1920 where he took a job at a hotel in Southern California.

**To his surprise,** Mr. Flores soon discovered that no one in his new home had ever seen a yo-yo before. Perhaps even more surprisingly, he found that a few impromptu demonstrations with his little return top could draw a crowd. Mr. Flores, showing no lack of entrepreneurial spirit, soon began manufacturing the tops. Not long afterwards he applied for, and registered, the trademark—"Flores Yo-Yo." According to reports of the time, the Flores Yo-Yo Company was doing a small, but profitable little business in Los Angeles, when its product was spotted by a mid-western American businessman in 1927 by the name of Donald F. Duncan.

And things were never the same again.

*Donald Duncan, an American salesman/entrepreneur who single-handedly turned the Filipino yo-yo into a marketing phenomenon.*

**In 1927** Donald Duncan was in California on business when his path crossed a yo-yo's for the first time. His initial impression, as he recollected later, was not overwhelming, but he did take one home with him.

The little top must have grown on him, because it wasn't too long before he was manufacturing his own in Chicago. A few years after that, he bought the Flores Yo-Yo Company, along with the "yo-yo" trademark, for a reported $25,000.

Thanks to a deal that Duncan struck with local newspapers, The Duncan Yo-Yo Company was soon advertising and running yo-yo contests that were drawing thousands of kids.

**In 1931,** success came in a huge way. The first full-blown American yo-yo fad was on. Duncan hired Filipino demonstrators who toured the country, like one-man carnivals, putting on demonstrations and contests wherever they went.

Although the fad died down after a few years, the yo-yo hung in there as a new American Classic.

**In 1962,** thirty years after the first fad, a second wave hit, even bigger than the first. Millions were sold, fueled by a new tool for selling toys—television advertising. Nineteen sixty-two was also the year in which an American court ruled that the word "yo-yo" was no longer a trademark of the Duncan Company. From now on, anybody could make a yo-yo and call it that.

# The Ups and Downs of the Yo-Yo Over 50 Years

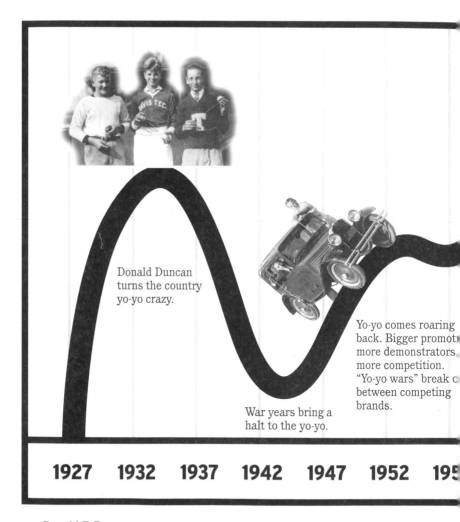

Donald Duncan turns the country yo-yo crazy.

War years bring a halt to the yo-yo.

Yo-yo comes roaring back. Bigger promot more demonstrators, more competition. "Yo-yo wars" break c between competing brands.

1927   1932   1937   1942   1947   1952   195

Donald F. Duncan sees his first yo-yo.

The peak year—1962. The Ultimate State of Yo arrives as 45 million yo-yos sold in one frantic season pushed by television advertising.

A mini-boom in the early '70s. Nashville, Tennessee (population: 320,000) reports 340,000 yo-yos sold in one season.

Duncan loses "yo-yo" trademark and soon thereafter declares bankruptcy. Flambeau Plastics buys rights to Duncan name.

*"If it isn't a DUNCAN...it isn't a YO-YO Top"*

'62    1967    1972    1977    1982    1987    1992    1997

# Bibliography

## Books

Crump, Stuart Jr. *It's Yo-Yo Time!* Creative Communications, Inc., P.O. Box 1519-KB, Herndon, VA 20171, A collection of stories and articles, plus more than 300 new yo-yo tricks from the pages of *Yo-Yo Times Newsletter*. $25.00 postpaid in North America; add $3.00 for other foreign orders.

Dickson, Paul. *The Mature Person's Guide to Kites, Yo-Yos, Frisbees, and other Childlike Diversions,* New American Library, 1977, New York. A compendium of facts and trivia about some of the toy immortals.

Flambeau Plastic Company. *The Original Duncan Yo-Yo & Spin Top Trick Book,* Flambeau Plastic Company, 1985, Baraboo, WI. This is the most recent edition of the little tricks booklet that Duncan has sold by the millions over the past 50 years.

Gould, D.W. *The Top: Universal Toy, Enduring Pastime.* Clarkson N. Potter, 1973, New York. Nothing more need ever be said about the top.

Malko, George. *The One and Only Yo-Yo Book.* Avon Books, 1978, New York. Easily the most complete treatment on the history of the yo-yo. Currently out of print, but check your library.

Olney, Russ. *The Amazing Yo-Yo.* Lothrop, Lee & Shepard Books, 1980, New York. Another in-depth volume of yo-yo tricks, basic to advanced.

Rule, Bob. *Yo-Yo Secrets.* Yo-Yo Promotions Inc., 1971, Atlanta, GA. Bob Rule is one of the best known of the Duncan touring pros. This is his tricks booklet.

Zeiger, Helane. *World on a String: The How-To Yo-Yo Book.* Contemporary Books, 1979, Chicago. A complete treatment on all the yo-yo's trickery, by one of the few female Duncan champions. Out of print—check your library.

## Newsletters

Crump, Stuart Jr., editor. *Yo-Yo Times Newsletter,* the first independent newsletter for yo-yo lovers of all ages. Published quarterly. $12/year. For a sample copy, send a self-addressed, stamped envelope to *Yo-Yo Times,* Creative Communications, Inc., P.O. Box 1519-KB, Herndon, VA 20171. Phone (703) 715-6187.

# Articles

Burger, Wolfgang. The Yo-Yo: A Toy Flywheel. *American Scientist*, March/April 1984. The most complete review of yo-yo science, by its foremost investigator.

Hoffman, Abbie. Yo-Yo Power. *Esquire*, October 1971. Abbie Hoffman, a former Worcester, Massachusetts yo-yo champ, talks about a youth spent on one end of a yo-yo string.

Zuckerman, Edward. Quest for the Perfect Yo-Yo. *Science Digest*, July 1985. A description of Tom Kuhn and his amazing yo-yos.

## Photo Credits

All photos by Peter Fox unless otherwise indicated.

pages 38 and 39, Donald F. Duncan, Jr.

page 40, The Bettmann Archive

page 41, Stormi Greener

page 43, Bob Weaver

page 45, AP/Wide World Photos

page 46, inset, NASA; starfield, Royal Observatory, Edinburough

page 48, Library of Congress

page 49, center and top, The Metropolitan Museum of Art, Fletcher Fund, 1928; bottom, Staatlichen Museen Preussischer Kulturbesitz, Antikenmuseum, Berlin

pages 52–55, Donald F. Duncan, Jr.

## Design and Model Credits

Cover design: Michael Sherman

Illustration: Sara Boore

Book layout and production: Nakamura Graphics

Loops and Tangles: John Cassidy

Yo-yo manufactured by Dale Oliver.

Models: Lincoln Atkinson, Braden Scott Cohen, Kendall Elise Cohen and Michelle

## Thanks

Grateful acknowledgments are hereby made to:
Dale Oliver
Anne Johnson
Dennis McBride
Donald F. Duncan Jr.
Barney Akers
Tom Parks
Steve Gelb (for the nudge)
Wilf Schlee
Tom Kuhn
The Flambeau Plastics Company
Lindsay Kefauver
Rebecca Hirsch

# More Great Books from Klutz

THE KLUTZ BOOK OF BALL GAMES

BATTERY SCIENCE • BUBBLE THING

THE BOOK OF CLASSIC BOARD GAMES

THE BEST CARD GAMES IN THE GALAXY

CAT'S CRADLE® • DOODLE FACES

THE ETCH A SKETCH® BOOK

THE FOOTBAG BOOK • THE FOXTAIL® BOOK

JUGGLING FOR THE COMPLETE KLUTZ®

THE KLUTZ BOOK OF PAPER AIRPLANES

ROAD TRIP TRIVIA • SLINGCHUTE®

THE SOLAR CAR BOOK

STOP THE WATCH®

TRICKY PIX: DO-IT-YOURSELF

TRICKY PHOTOGAPAPHY

And a whole lot more!

**Free KLUTZ Catalog!**

455 Portage Avenue
Palo Alto, CA 94306

## Want More?

Extra yo-yos and the entire line of 100% certified
Klutz products are available online at www.klutz.com.
While you're there, sign up for our free e-newsletter,
request a catalog, create a wish list or try out an
activity or two.